Tim Winton: Critical Essays

Tim Winton: Critical Essays

Edited by
Lyn McCredden &
Nathanael O'Reilly

UWA PUBLISHING

First published in 2014 by
UWA Publishing
Crawley, Western Australia 6009
www.uwap.uwa.edu.au

UWAP is an imprint of UWA Publishing
a division of The University of Western Australia

THE UNIVERSITY OF
WESTERN AUSTRALIA

National Library of Australia Cataloguing-in-Publication data:

Title: Tim Winton : critical essays / edited by Lyn McCredden and Nathanael O'Reilly.

ISBN: 9781742586069 (paperback)

Subjects: Winton, Tim, 1960—Criticism and interpretation. Australian literature—20th century—History and criticism. Australia—In literature.

Other Authors/Contributors: McCredden, Lyn, 1953-, editor. O'Reilly, Nathanael, editor.

Dewey Number: A823.3

Cover image by Marinelly Refuerzo
Typeset by J&M Typesetting
Printed by Lightning Source

This project has been assisted by the Australian Governmentthrough the Australia Council, its arts funding and advisory body.

CONTENTS

ACKNOWLEDGEMENTS

Nathanael O'Reilly

I extend my sincere thanks to all of the contributors for supporting this project and writing excellent chapters that are important additions to Winton scholarship. Massive thanks to my co-editor, Lyn McCredden – from the moment we conceived the project while riding a bus in Hyderabad in 2012 through to the completion of the book, working with Lyn has been a smooth, rewarding and enjoyable experience. University of Western Australia Publishing believed in this project from the outset; many thanks to all the staff at UWAP, but especially Terri-ann White. I would also like to thank my partner, Tricia Jenkins, for her support and patience while I worked on this project, and my daughter, Celeste, with whom I spent many wonderful hours reading Tim Winton's *The Deep* while she was learning to read and swim.

Lyn McCredden

Thanks, Nathanael, for your eagle eye and can-do attitude. It has been a pleasure working with you. Thank you also to our intrepid and very hardworking research assistant, Chloe Chandler. You have made this a better, richer book. Many, many thanks to our contributors from around the world for your scholarly and professional approach to your work. Literary criticism is certainly the better for your contributions. To Terri-ann White at UWAP, so many thanks for your enabling attitude to this book. And finally, thank you to my partner, Terry McCredden, for your unending patience while I have been swallowed up, day and night, in this wonderful project.

Introduction

TIM WINTON, LITERATURE AND THE FIELD OF LITERARY CRITICISM

Lyn McCredden and Nathanael O'Reilly

The title of this essay refers to three capacious, continuously evolving and contentious subjects. It also initiates an inquiry: why is it that Tim Winton, one of Australia's most popular *and* literary (let the debates begin) novelists, has received little sustained critical attention? We hope that the existence of this volume, the first collection of critical essays since *Reading Tim Winton* (1993),[1] will begin to redress the relative dearth of critical debate about the literature of Tim Winton. But this is to pre-empt the inquiry into what might be meant by 'the literary' and by 'literary criticism' (let alone 'Tim Winton'). The title and the subject of this introductory essay are, therefore, genuinely seeking debate.

Let's start with the question of literary critics and literary criticism. Literary critics – of whom thirteen diverse exemplars are collected in these pages – are not monsters, as is sometimes suggested by those who distrust or dislike or refuse to see the worth of literary criticism. Most literary critics do not set out simply to be 'critical' in the reductive sense of that word. At best, they are readers seeking to explore, question and debate texts, authors and contexts publicly – to understand more fully what is appealing, or unconsciously submerged, or worthy of celebration or interrogation in texts of all kinds. Critics are, like all other readers, affected by the works they read – 'loving' or 'detesting' or 'being intrigued by' them – but they take it further, and their professional training gives them the opportunity and frameworks within which to engage with literary creations in multiple ways.

Critics need to be alive to the richness, nuance and complexity of literary language. They examine *why* and *how* a work signifies – how it uses, and is used by, language; how literary texts seek to make meaning or to test the limits of meaning-making. They ask where a work comes from in the fullest sense. Should it be understood as arising from the author's individual genius? Or does the work bear the imprint of particular historical, political, geographical or ideological contexts? In what ways is the creative text a product of the author's psychological or ideological blindnesses? Critics often want to ask why audiences respond as they do to particular works. They ask this as part of the process of better understanding the cultures that have produced, and that in turn are influenced by, such creative works. In these ways, criticism at its best contributes to communal, ongoing and passionate cultural conversations. The community of readers is sometimes one of literary specialists; at other times it embraces the wider culture. These audiences intersect, and play a role in discerning and debating literary effect and worth.

While these kinds of critical questions are pressed upon a literary work by readers and professional critics alike, they can also be seen to emerge *from* that work as a critical reader enters into a dialogue with it. In literary criticism, additional players may then enter into this dialogue – other literary critics, reviewers, theorists, ideological critics – so that literary criticism often becomes more than dialogue, it becomes multi-vocal. This is the broader, fuller purpose of criticism: to contribute to cultural debates, to reflect on both the individual work and on the state of the culture in which that literary work participates. Students, different kinds of readers and fellow critics have to decide, then, what to 'make' of such criticism.

At one level, literary criticism today is a business: students are required to read and cite it in their school or university essays; teachers refer to it; fellow critics need to be aware of critical work and decide how to respond to it. But more than this, critical debates are an indication of the contested value of the literary. A literary text has the capacity to sustain vigorous and ongoing – sometimes combative – discussions, asking what matters about the text, and how the novel, poem or play under examination relates historically, aesthetically or ontologically to the larger culture. Attempting to explore and construct self-understandings (national, communal or private, authorial or readerly) can be a tumultuous process where difference jostles with unknowing, blindness and hope.

Winton's fiction is literary *and* popular, and therefore a remark-able barometer of Australian culture. His work is vernacular and lyrical, optimistic and dark, asking in nuanced ways what it means to be alive in contemporary Australia. In all of Winton's novels and short stories (and now increasingly in his dramatic pieces) there is contestation of what it is to be Australian, to be human and to make and question meaning.

While other kinds of discourse – political, historical or scientific – offer equally multi-vocal perspectives about how meaning is made, it is pre-eminently in literature that temporality, identity, relationships, language use, and the borders between the conscious and unconscious, are probed deeply and imaginatively. These, of course, are fighting words. More often in public discourse the literary or aesthetic is disparaged or occluded in favour of the eco-nomic or the political. But Winton's poetic and narrative language has impact, courageously taking on the weight of bringing to birth characters, voices and textual presences that come to matter to the reader. In the literary characters and narratives Winton writes there is often high anxiety or violence between people, and within individuals struggling against themselves. These texts hold up a strange, vernacular, peculiarly Wintonesque mirror through which Australians – and international readers, differently – can see themselves refracted.

This mirror does not create a straightforward, realist reflection. The contradictoriness of the human condition is everywhere in Winton's texts: tensions between the human ability to make meaning and the obliterating power of accident or temporality; between palpable, joyful intimacy and the ravages of violence in relationships; between the demands and pleasures of material existence and the intimations of a sacred, transcendent world sensed in the palpable and everyday. Literature is pre-eminently the form in which such contradictions can be evoked and explored. Literature (and its practitioners) is capable, as Keats wrote two centuries ago, 'of being in uncertainties, mysteries, doubts, without any irritable reaching after fact and reason'.[2] These, too, are fighting words. They stress the non-instrumental: literature doesn't simply get things done. So let's go deeper, asking in what ways literature – Tim Winton being our exemplar – is at the deepest levels valuable.

North American critic Michael Bérubé, writing in response to the supposedly ailing world of literature and literary critical work, asked in 1996:

[I]s there a deep connection between the category of civil society and the category of the aesthetic as it has been understood since Kant? Did the social forces of

the eighteenth century, which bequeathed us various
forms of nonauthoritarian government and plural public
spheres, also create the conditions for a noninstrumental
understanding...Are the autonomies of the aesthetic and
of civil society mutually defining and interdependent?[3]

Bérubé is writing from *within* the cabal of literary criticism, so
his questions regarding the relationship between the aesthetic and
the civil are rhetorical, the result of his desire to defend the value
of literature and literary criticism in the academy and in broader
culture. His defence of 'non-instrumental understanding' will be
dear to many writers, readers and literary critics, but his argument
goes further, not merely setting up the dichotomy 'instrumental–
non-instrumental'. It argues for the relationship between, even
the interdependence of 'civil society' and 'the aesthetic', and by
implication queries the harsh lines between use value and the
aesthetic. In order to test the implications of Bérubé's questions
we might ask if this set of relations applies to the work of Tim
Winton.

Winton's popularity nationally, and increasingly internationally, indicates that he strikes a chord of sympathy, or recognition, a
sense of the real for many readers. His work is realistic, but whose
'real' is it? Winton's novel *Cloudstreet* was described acerbically
in a 2005 *Westerly* essay by critic Robert Dixon as constructing
a nostalgic and conservative vision of an older, disappearing
Australia, not a real present. Dixon situated *Cloudstreet* in 'the field
of Australian literature', and in a

[N]ostalgia for lost places, for an Australian accent
and culture that are pre-American, pre-modern, pre-
1960s. These qualities find expression in the novel's

rich registration of Australian idioms of the 1940s and 1950s, and its superbly lyrical descriptions of places and landscapes in and around Perth. This goes a long way toward explaining the popularity of the novel, at least for a certain generation of readers, the baby boomers, who were the major cultural force in the 1990s, when the novel was published. But nostalgia is by its very nature conservative: it prefers the past to the future; it is at best ambivalent about modernity; it prefers the local and the traditional to the global.[4]

Dixon's essay captures, from global satellite height, 'the field of Australian literature' as a marketplace, as part of national and global patterns of readership and distribution. His essay praises the literary effects of Winton's texts but goes on to pit the seemingly tangential literary felicities of the writing ('rich registrations of Australian idioms', 'superbly lyrical descriptions of places and landscapes') against what the critic sees as *Cloudstreet*'s nostalgia and conservatism (not to mention the implied conservatism of the considerable number of baby boomers who read the work). This conservatism, so Dixon argues, 'prefers the past to the future', is 'ambivalent about modernity' and 'prefers the local and the traditional to the global'. Baby boomers join Winton as conservative in Dixon's argument, with their nostalgia for a dying Australia. But how reductive is it to see Australian baby boomers as the main readers of *Cloudstreet*, and of Winton's works more generally? Are school and university students who read and write on Winton only doing so at the behest of their teachers, teachers who are largely not baby boomers any more?

We might also ask how widely Dixon's argument about *Cloudstreet* can be applied in relation to Winton's oeuvre and his other representations of past and present. How, for example, does it sit with the popularity of Winton's writing for children, and about children, which both precedes and continues after *Cloudstreet*? The roles of children and their representation in Winton's writing are the focus of this current volume's essay by Tanya Dalziell, who is

> [I]nterested less in suggesting that Winton's works register some recognisable national or temporal 'trend' or 'taxonomy' of childhood, or applying categories of childhood a priori to Winton's fictions, than in taking seriously the ways childhood is debated and narrated within the worlds of these texts.

Dalziell finds a rich and complex set of approaches to childhood in Winton, approaches that can be nostalgic in the characters' responses but also restlessly pushing towards the future in Winton's narrative. Nathanael O'Reilly's individual essay in this volume, 'From father to son: fatherhood and father–son relationships in *Scission*', also complicates Dixon's description of Winton's purported conservatism or backward-looking fiction: 'Through his early works of short fiction, Winton challenges cultural norms, highlights dysfunction, celebrates intimacy and encourages new ways of being for both fathers and sons'.

Movement into the future is identifiable as both theme and source of poetic intensity in Winton. In her treatment of *The Turning* in this volume, Bridget Grogan concludes:

> Like the narrator of 'Big World', at their most complete and tender Winton's men embrace transience and the inevitable loss this entails while acknowledging the wide beauty of the temporal world and the love of and

for others that is both impermanent and yet eternal: 'I don't care what happens beyond this moment. In the hot northern dusk, the world suddenly gets big around us, so big we just give in and watch.'

Grogan's essay is alive to the poetic nuances of Winton's prose. Is such a turning to the bigness and beauty of the world, so different in its poetic expression from Dixon's big world, simply confirming a nostalgia in Winton, a poetic refusal or obfuscation of the real or material world? Is a focus on the contradictory and lyrically evoked 'impermanent and yet eternal' merely reducible to Dixon's claims that *Cloudstreet*'s 'twin themes of social consensus and spiritual transcendence are strongly supported by Winton's public references to his Christian, family-centred values'?[5]

This latter aspect, Winton's publicly declared religious values, has complicated critical debates. Brigid Rooney takes up questions of sublimity – and the literary limits of representing it – in her essay for this volume, 'From the sublime to the uncanny in Tim Winton's *Breath*'. She writes of the ending of that novel:

Returning Pike to the scene of white men dancing in the surf, the narrative seeks to retrieve for him, and for readers, that modicum of grace and equanimity won through hard work and humble service to what is left of family. Qualities of grace, endurance and survival are, in the end, what remain. These limited consolations express Winton's literary vision in its maturity. Even so, they cannot contain a troubling sense of fatalism...

Family – its material, moral and spiritual dimensions – does indeed loom large in Winton's oeuvre, but it is hardly summarised adequately by Dixon's description of Winton's 'Christian, family-centred values'. It becomes increasingly obvious that the charge of conservatism reaches its limits, and is indeed contested by, many essays in this current volume. In the decades since 1991, the year of *Cloudstreet*'s publication, relations between the local and the global, between family and nation, have continued to evolve, as indeed has Winton's oeuvre, and it may not be fair to extrapolate Dixon's placement of *Cloudstreet* to Winton's later works. Lyn McCredden's individual essay, '"Intolerable significance": Tim Winton's *Eyrie*', focuses on his most recent novel, charting a much darker, less redemptive narrative – the psychic disintegration of an individual and a family – than we have so far seen in Winton's work. The essay argues further that *Eyrie* is a novel about language and the limits of the linguistic to carry the full burden of meaning with which humans often seek to imbue it.

The tensions, blindnesses and contradictions in Winton's writing – conscious or unconscious – challenge readers and literary critics to think beyond such flat denominators as 'nostalgic' or 'conservative', 'religious' or 'masculinist', beyond the essentialising polarities of masculine–feminine, sacred–material, poetic–pragmatic. For example, Michael R. Griffiths' essay is concerned specifically with the ambivalently postcolonial implications of hauntedness in *Cloudstreet*. His essay, 'Winton's spectralities, or What haunts *Cloudstreet*?', raises some prickly questions about white and Indigenous Australia:

> We may gain much if Australians inherit Winton's novel
> as a 'modern Australian classic'. But we also lose much
> in not recognising that the novel is nonetheless marked
> by the effacement of indigeneity…

Like many of the writers in this volume, Griffiths has a keen eye for both the literal and the hidden or unconscious in Winton's writing. Indeed, Griffiths' own literary-critical even-handedness does not shy away from seeing that '[i]n this way, perhaps, the novel's greatest success – addressing Indigenous presence as constitutive of settler-colonial habitation – is also the source of its most profound failure: the reproduction of an ideology of settler-colonial innocence through the apparent naivety of the settler-inheritor'.

In another ideological reading, feminist critic Hannah Schürholz addresses a question to Winton's oeuvre, asking why 'Tim Winton's female characters show a strong affinity with self-threatening behaviour, transience and ferocity'. Around this question, Schürholz builds a critically suspicious reading of Winton's gender politics:

> The literal inscription or destruction of the female body functions as a form of *lieu de mémoire* in Tim Winton's work. It *speaks*. But this agency is a double-edged sword. It can be an objectification or an appropriation in disguise…

This legitimate argument rises from a deep vein of feminist questioning of Winton's work.

Fiona Morrison's essay, '"Bursting with voice and doubleness": vernacular presence and visions of inclusiveness in Tim Winton's *Cloudstreet*', is equally alive to both the ideological and poetic effects of the novel. While clear-sightedly discussing the limits of the pull to 'authenticity' in notions of presence and voice in Winton's writing, Morrison also perceives that '[i]t does seem impossible…to ignore the carnivalesque energies of *Cloudstreet*…

and the tendency of these unruly energies to both install and overthrow…neo-romantic investments'.

Concerns about Australia as nation, about belonging in place, and about gendered and racial identity inform Winton's works, and are sometimes partly occluded in them. But so, too, are concerns that resonate with wider global, and indeed more than global, sometimes sacred, expansiveness. There is no easy dismissal of 'Christian' or 'religious' motivations in the essay by North American critic Nicholas Birns. Rather, in 'A not completely pointless beauty: *Breath*, exceptionality and neoliberalism', Birns perceives the ways Winton's 2008 novel draws together Australian and American concerns, neoliberal economics and spiritual hunger:

> If one is to read the book under the aegis of neoliberalism, one can see the vulgarisation of the divine into a narcissistic market-god as no longer a national trait but an anthropology – what all men and women are like, are supposed to be like, under the mantle of neoliberal ideology: bearers of risk, liquid exceptions, self-motivated gods.

In this surprising and deft essay, Birns draws us back to why literature (and good literary criticism) is valuable. Literature refuses the linguistically flat, unresonant and purely categorising. It sees links – in the characters and the poetics of language – to what is lost, to what the divine in the human might be if only the 'narcissistic market-god' could be transcended. Birn's reading of *Breath*'s Australian and American characters and the increasingly shared modern, capitalist world they inhabit is written from the perspective of a North American critic. The essay by Chinese scholar

Hou Fei, entitled 'Extreme games, hegemony and narration: an interpretation of Tim Winton's *Breath*', forms an interesting juxtaposition to Birns' essay. This is not, of course, because Hou writes with a 'Chinese voice' (as if such a pure entity exists), but because her ideological and contextual reading of the novel is quite different from Birns' in distinctively ideological ways. Hou reads the retrospective time of the novel, which is set during the years of the Vietnam War and American and Australian involvement there, as a subtext crucial to understanding the dynamics between the main characters – the Americanised Australian Sando and the two young Australian boys:

> The relationship between Sando and the novel's two young protagonists is more like that of a guru/hegemon to disciple/follower. Analogously, it resembles the relationship between the United States and Australia during their involvement in the Vietnam War.

A distinctive ideological perspective certainly emerges from Hou's essay.

Per Henningsgaard, also based in North America, presents us with a detailed analysis of 'The editing and publishing of Tim Winton in the United States', and more broadly of the work of cultural translation. Henningsgaard's essay is a fascinating excursion for readers of Winton into the pragmatic details of difference and similarity in national vocabularies and in modes of perception between the purportedly symbiotic North America and Australia. We also gain an appreciation of what the material production of literature entails for authors, editors, publishers and readers globally. We are given the chance to contemplate how 'the literary' exists not *beyond* the marketplace, but certainly not simply as reducible to it.

Writing from within a German context, Sissy Helff also argues strongly that 'Winton's memory-work has a transnational or even transcultural quality'. Informed by Paul Ricoeur's important and influential critical work on memory, Helff reads Winton's *Shallows* and *The Turning* as creating 'rich mnemonic narrative landscapes...[that] imagine a multicultural Australia by applying diegetic modes of exchanging memories as well as using reciprocal interactions between the reader and the texts...' Memory can be double: it can be the net that draws us downwards, dangerous and suffocating; or it can release us across generations, calling us to forgiveness and rebirth.

It is with the first essay of this volume, Bill Ashcroft's 'Water', that this introductory essay concludes. More so than any essay in this volume, 'Water' is written in the spirit of Winton, energised by his lyricism, and in agreement with his major ideological effects. Ashcroft writes:

Water, death and renewal are tightly bound in Winton's novels. Whether launching off the water's edge, surfacing from dream or from the freedom of water, or emerging from the flirtation with death in free diving, water is the medium of rebirth.

While some Winton reviewers have simply pointed to the recurrent themes of surfing, water and the beach in Winton's work, they have missed the fact that the transformative power of the natural world drives so much of Winton's writing.

Ashcroft's essay takes the form of an empathetic meditation

but is also polemical and will not meet with universal agreement. For one thing, it writes in close accord with Winton, that

> Water is the medium of transformation, of rebirth to new life. For those who spend their lives in and on the water the experience is one of constant renewal, the renewal of beauty and grace, the renewal of the miracle of life. It is the continual renewal of the revelation that the world is holy.

Ashcroft's meditation on the holiness of the world finds in Winton's writings an active, earthed making of meaning, a convincing sense of belonging, what Ashcroft calls 'this vision of *Heimat*'. His essay sets up a strong and poetically persuasive first contribution to this volume, which might be read in dialogue with the more ideological or contestatory readings of Winton's work.

Wherever readers come to abide in their critical evaluation of Winton's writings, we as editors wish you an enjoyable and challenging journey. We are proud to be involved in the tumultuous and rewarding profession of literary criticism. Tim Winton remains for us one of Australia's most idiosyncratic, poetic and beguiling writers. While we do not always 'agree' with his political or aesthetic effects, we hail his courageous literary exploration of human, Australian, contemporary limitations and aspirations.

Notes

1   R. Rossiter and L. Jacobs, *Reading Tim Winton*, Angus & Robertson, Sydney, 1993.

2   J. Keats, *The Complete Poetical Works and Letters of John Keats, Cambridge Edition*, Houghton, Mifflin and Company, Boston and New York, 1899, p. 277.

3   M. Bérubé, 'Aesthetics and the literal imagination', *Clio*, vol. 25, no. 4, 1996, p. 446.

4   R. Dixon, 'Tim Winton, *Cloudstreet* and the field of Australian literature', *Westerly*, vol. 50, 2005, pp. 240–60. www.austlit.edu.au/common/fulltext-content/pdfs/brn686834/brn686834.pdf, accessed 8 December 2013.

5   Ibid.

Bibliography

Bérubé, M., 'Aesthetics and the literal imagination', *Clio*, vol. 25, no. 4, 1996, pp. 439–53.

Dixon, R., 'Tim Winton, *Cloudstreet* and the field of Australian literature', *Westerly*, vol. 50, 2005, pp. 240–60, www.austlit.edu.au/common/fulltext-content/pdfs/brn686834/brn686834.pdf, accessed 8 December 2013.

Keats, J., *The Complete Poetical Works and Letters of John Keats, Cambridge Edition*, Houghton, Mifflin and Company, Boston and New York, 1899.

Rossiter, R. and Jacobs, L., *Reading Tim Winton*, Angus & Robertson, Sydney, 1993.

1

WATER

Bill Ashcroft

In *Dirt Music*, remembering the time before a car crash took the lives of his brother Darkie, Darkie's wife Sal, and their two children, Bird and Bullet, Luther Fox recalls Bird's question: 'Lu, how come water lets you through it?'[1] Bird is the one who saw God, and 'if anyone saw God it would likely be her. Bird's the nearest thing to an angelic being'.[2] Bird's question suggests the function of water in Winton's novels. Water is everywhere in his writing, as people sail on it, dive into it, live on the edge of it. Clearly the sea and the river are vital aspects of the writer's own experience. But water is more than an omnipresent feature of his writing and his life, the oceanscape of his stories. It is something that 'lets you through'. It lets you through because it is the passage to a different state of being, sometimes in dream, sometimes in physical extremity, but it always offers itself as the medium of transformation. When it lets you through – whether to escape to a different life, as a rite of passage to adulthood, to see the world in a new way or to discover the holiness of the earth or the wonder of the world, whether it is the baptismal water of redemption or an opening to a world of silence – and it is all these things – you become different.

A common myth about Australia's coast-hugging habits is that since early settlement we have looked to the sea as we look to the signs of 'Home' 12,000 miles away, like the early colonists. Whether or not this has been true in the past for generations on the south-eastern seaboard, it is certainly not true of modern-day Western Australia. As Col says in *Rising Water*, 'some afternoons I can smell peri-peri blowin across the water from South Africa'.[3] The Indian Ocean is a very different proposition from the Pacific. Looking 2,000 miles across to Africa, this sea laps the edge of a continent the Dutch rejected because it looked so uninhabitable. But for Winton in *Land's Edge*,

> At first glimpse of the Indian Ocean I stop running and feel the relief unwinding in my chest, in my neck and shoulders. Dinghies twist against their moorings. Gulls scatter before the blur of my insane kelpie. Two days off the plane, I am finally home.[4]

In contrast to the towns on its edge, the sea in Winton's writing 'lets you through' to Home, but it is a home with far more resonance than our usual image of a place, a homestead set down in a more or less hospitable location. 'There is nowhere else I'd rather be', says Winton,

> [N]othing else I would prefer to be doing. I am at the beach looking west with the continent behind me as the sun tracks down to the sea. I have my bearings.[5]

The home offered by or through water is a version of that infinite vista of sea suggested by the Indian Ocean. It is a home that has form rather than location, more promise than foundation, it is the home Ernst Bloch calls *Heimat*[6] – the home we have all sensed but never experienced or known. Water is significant because as *Heimat* it cannot be tied to location, tied to our normal sense of home. Like Aboriginal country, it cannot be owned, divided or fenced, but instead is quite capable of possessing *you*. The oceanic vastness of *Heimat* in Winton offers a utopian sense of home in many ways: it is a medium of escape, of freedom and grace; it is the space of dream and the constant reality of the porous border between life and death. By 'letting you through it', water is the ultimate medium of change and transformation and, in Winton's imaginary, that transformation, that path to *Heimat*, is the path of rebirth.

But perhaps an even more powerfully utopian dimension of water is its timelessness, its capacity to fuse past and present. In 'Aquifer' the young narrator claims:

> I was right to doubt the 1194 man on the telephone. Time doesn't click on and on at the stroke. It comes and goes in waves and folds like water; it flutters and sifts like dust, rises, billows, falls back on itself. When a wave breaks, the water is not moving. The swell has travelled great distances but only the energy is moving, not the water. Perhaps time moves through us and not us through it [...] the past is in us, and not behind us. Things are never over.[7]

This disruption of the linear myth of time makes water the perfect location of the utopian. We think of time as either flowing or enduring, and the dismantling of this apparent dichotomy between succession and duration has profound consequences. Although the present may be seen as a continuous stream of prospections becoming retrospections, the sense that the past has gone and the future is coming separates what may be called the three phases of time. Friedrich Kummel proposes that the apparent conflict between time as succession and time as duration comes about because we forget that time has no reality apart from the medium of human experience and thought.[8] 'No single and final definition of time is possible…since such a concept is always conditioned by man's understanding of it.'[9]

Water is utopian because the energy of wave motion flowing through it perfectly corresponds to the cyclic continuity between the past and the future in the present. The polarity between past and future often seems insurmountable in European philosophy. Bloch asserts that for Plato 'Beingness' is 'Beenness',[10] and he admonishes Hegel 'who ventured out furthest', because 'What Has Been overwhelms what is approaching…the categories Future, Front, Novum'.[11] The problem with Being or the concept of Being in Hegel was that it overwhelmed *Becoming* – obstructing the category of the future. It is only when the static concept of being is dispensed with that the real dimension of hope opens.[12] The core of Bloch's ontology is that 'Beingness' is 'Not-Yet-Becomeness':

> Thus the Not-Yet-Conscious in man belongs completely to the Not-Yet-Become, Not-Yet-Brought-Out, Manifested-Out in the world…From the anticipatory, therefore, knowledge is to be gained on the basis of an ontology of the Not-Yet.[13]

We can see why Bloch is not interested in utopia as location. Utopianism is fundamental to human consciousness because humans are always striving forward, anticipating, desiring. While utopias exist in the future, utopianism, anticipatory consciousness, is heavily invested in the present. Water, a very present medium, becomes the promise of *Heimat* because it is the medium of physical and temporal movement, of weightlessness and timelessness. The fluidity of water denies location – the energy flowing through it is the opposite of location. Its flow is the movement of becoming, of 'fulfilling the wholeness of what we are capable of being'.[14] There is an unexpected connection between Luce Irigaray and Tim Winton in the sacred dimensions of becoming. Irigaray writes,

> Love of God has nothing moral in and of itself. It merely shows the way. It is the incentive for a more perfect becoming…God forces us to do nothing more except *become*. The only task, the only obligation laid upon us is to become divine men and women, to become perfectly, to refuse to allow parts of ourselves to shrivel and die that have the potential for growth and fulfilment.[15]

In Winton's work, water is the perfect medium of becoming, the continual promise of the Not-Yet.

For this reason, Winton's 'anticipatory illumination' is manifested principally through the medium of water in its many forms, and he shares with Bloch a sense of the transcendent, utopian possibilities of literature as avenues to the possible.[16] 'Literature' is not limited to fiction. In *Shallows*, Cleve Cookson is mesmerised by the journal of the region's first whaler Nathaniel Coupar:

> For Cleve, the realness and aliveness of the journal were precious […] He felt he was there, as though his eyes were Coupar's eyes. It was an almost supernatural feeling, as it had been in the dinghy on the estuary with

Queenie when he had been filled with wholeness and absence and an exceptional grace which let him feel what it was to be her and himself at once. These were the moments when he suspected there could be a meaning to his existence.[17]

This is imbued with hope not because it offers a vision of the future, but because it opens the door to a different way of seeing the world, a different way of being. Literature allows you to inhabit a different world. The supernatural feeling it gives – of being oneself and someone else at the same time – is one Cleve tellingly experiences on the water.

The link between reading and the experience of the sea can be found elsewhere in literature. In Michael Cunningham's *The Hours*, when Laura Brown delays the day to read Virginia Woolf's *Mrs Dalloway*, the experience is one best described in terms of the sea:

One more page, she decides; just one more [...] She is taken by a wave of feeling, a sea-swell, that rises from under her breast and buoys her, floats her gently, as if she were a sea creature thrown back from the sand where it had beached itself – as if she had been returned from a realm of crushing gravity to her true medium, the suck and swell of saltwater, that weightless brilliance.[18]

Water brings together Bloch's sense of the utopian potential of literature and Winton's perception of its capacity to detect the holiness of the world, best encountered in the weightless brilliance of the sea.

In *Dirt Music* Luther Fox has the wide reading of the autodidact but doesn't know what you're supposed to make of Wordsworth and Blake, how you might speak of them if you'd been taught by experts. But he knows he would have tried to explain this sense of the world alive, the way writers articulate their own instinctive feeling that there is indeed some kind of spirit that rolls through all things, some fearsome memory in stones, in wind, in the lives of birds.[19] But like our failure to apprehend the spirit that rolls through all things, our failure to capture in art and literature that instinctive recognition of the sacred, we tend to live on the edge of things, on the edge of water. The embodiment of that failure to apprehend the spirit that runs through all things is the failure represented by the littoral inhabitant.

Water's edge

The overwhelming sense we get of Winton's observation of humans and water is that they are very often stuck at the edge in a permanent state of moral numbness and unrealised potential. This is paradoxical because Winton regards himself as a 'littoralist':

> The littoral, that peculiar zone of overlap and influx, sustains my spirit and fuels my work. I'm still pulled between the sensual assault of the outdoors and the sedentary life of reflection. To go a day or two without seeing, feeling and smelling the ocean would be as disorientating as being without a book or an hour's privacy.[20]

But there are very different ways of inhabiting the littoral, a difference, perhaps, between 'water's edge' and 'land's edge'. For instance, the play *Rising Water* situates itself at a mooring at which three boats lie becalmed, not quite at sea, not quite on land, but in the moral space between the jingoistic revelry of Australia Day and the possibility of flight. None of the boats will make it out to sea, which represents some distant possibility of self-realisation or discovery. Col, Baxter and Jackie are all outsiders for one reason or another, but their mooring represents the border between a craven xenophobic nationalism playing itself out in Australia Day drunkenness on the land and the possibility of escape. The failure of spirit at the edge of the water takes on a sacramental dimension as Baxter assumes the role of a Christ figure, his boat sunk between the other two boats, called *Goodness* and *Mercy*. Baxter refuses to sink with his scuttled boat, but is resurrected by the 'Holy Spirit, symbolised by the "Freo Doctor" [and,] using his opened shirt, catches the famous south-westerly breeze to move on, raised up and renewed by the breath of the wind'.[21]

Whether or not the play is so overt a Christian allegory, such 'beached' characters carry a powerful allegorical weight wherever they appear. As Winton ponders in *Land's Edge*:

> Australians are surrounded by ocean and ambushed
> from behind by desert – a war of mystery on two fronts.
> What worries us about the sea and the desert? Is it scale
> or simple silence? Historically we see ourselves as out-
> back types, although we know we are suburbanites. Still,
> we do go to the desert more and more [...] Guiltily
> we spend the rest of our time living on the water or
> manoeuvring our way ruthlessly toward it. The desert is
> a spiritual place, we vaguely understand, and the sea the
> mere playground of our hedonism.[22]

Clearly, the opposite is the case for Winton. There is no guilt in his immersion, but an enthusiastic apprehension of the grace and beauty available to those who move in and on water. Yet the epitome of the society hovering, unsuspectingly, on the edge of the spiritual and imaginative possibilities of water is, ironically, the fishing village. Whether the whaling town Angelus in *Shallows* or the fishing town White Point in *Dirt Music*, the fishing village is 'wedged' between land and sea:

> White Point was then just a bunch of tin sheds in the lee of the foredune. A sandy point, a series of fringing reefs and an island a mile offshore created a broad lagoon in which the original jetty stood. The settlement lay wedged between the sea and the majestic white sandhills of the interior.[23]

'Wedged' is an apposite word. The town, although it lives off the sea, is a kind of no-place, a porous, changeable border between two fearsome possibilities. It was 'a personality junkyard [...] where people still washed up to hide or to lick their wounds'.[24] Nor will anything get the people of Angelus away from their houses around the harbour with its stinking flats. 'It's as though they believe the Second Coming or the Loch Ness Monster will erupt from the harbour itself and they daren't move an inch.'[25] The towns on the edge of the sea are a permanent location of a failure-to-escape, despite the various escapees who inhabit them. They stand as an admission of defeat, the habitation of the homeless.

Freedom

Water itself, then, is firstly a medium of escape and freedom, an avenue to the grace so lacking in those tawdry towns stuck on its edge. We sense the attraction of the boundlessness, the receptivity of water in the story 'Aquifer':

> I grew up in a boxy double brick house with roses and a letterbox, like anyone else. My parents were always struggling to get me inside something, into shirts and shoes, inside the fence, the neighbourhood, the house, out of the sun or the rain, out of the world itself it often seemed to me.[26]

In a more subtle way this sense of the confinement of boundaries articulates the difference between land and sea. The very solidity of land, its clear and coordinated landmarks, its sense of perspective, can appear as lack. In *Shallows*, Daniel Coupar, a man descended from the whaler Nathaniel Coupar, looks around him at his property:

> From here there had always been for Coupar a sense of perspective: there was order and sense, each landmark, each familiar plane of light or darkness consistent with memory and history, an immemorial constant around which, upon which, all else happened. To the north, the Ranges; to the east the white sides of Jimmy's Rock; to the west the cloudy tips of Fourpeaks; to the south-west only Bald Island hugging the thin shoulders of Stormy Beach. Ocean. Sky. Dead land.[27]

Despite its capacity to ground Coupar, the land is dead, or perhaps able to die, unlike the living, formless, fluid reality of the sea. This petrification of the land is not really Winton's attitude to place. He has an intuitive relationship with the landscape perhaps best indicated by Georgie Jutland's reaction in *Dirt Music*: 'Georgie couldn't understand this feeling of recognition. It was iconic

Australian landscape but not even twenty years of nationalist advertising could account for this sensation'.[28] Nevertheless, there is no question that sea and river are the avenues to fluid, joyous life.

Yet in its vastness the sea is also fearsome. 'I love the sea', says Winton, 'but it does not love me'.[29] Although brought up beside the sea,

> Queenie Cookson had never been in such an expanse
> of water before, and although she couldn't properly see
> it she sensed its vastness and felt the absence of land in
> every pore, and was afraid.[30]

But in its simple physical reality, its capacity to allow people to feel the lightness of their being, water is a medium of freedom. For Queenie, '[i]n the pool and in the surf she felt strong and quick and graceful, but in class she felt heavy, thought herself dull and plodding'.[31] In *Dirt Music*, Fox

> [B]egins to feel good. It's what he lives for, this feeling,
> knowing they're all still ashore in their beds sleeping off
> the Emu Export and the bedtime bong while he has the
> sea to himself.[32]

> As a boy he'd thought the place was alive somehow [...]
> Those days you could come down here and stand in the
> water on the shallow spit and clear your mind. Stare at
> the sun-torched surface and break it into disparate coins
> of light.[33]

For the young Pikelet in *Breath*, the sea brings forth an insouciant beauty and elegance:

[D]eath was hard to imagine when you had these blokes dancing themselves across the bay with smiles on their faces and sun in their hair.

I couldn't have put words to it as a boy, but later I understood what seized my imagination that day. How strange it was to see men do something beautiful. Something pointless and elegant, as though nobody saw or cared.[34]

Even in Winton's novels for children, such as *Blueback*, water is the medium of effortless suspension, of freedom and wonder:

Abel loved being underwater. He was ten years old and could never remember a time when he could not dive. His mother said he was a diver before he was born; he floated and swam in the warm ocean inside her for nine months, so maybe it came naturally. He liked to watch his mother cruise down into the deep in her patchy wetsuit. She looked like a scarred old seal in that thing. She was a beautiful swimmer, relaxed and strong.[35]

While Winton perfectly judges the tone of children's literature, the subtle power of this image is manifest. Water is an image not just of freedom but also of rebirth, an amniotic fluid in which can be found not just escape but the promise of birth and renewal. 'The ocean is the supreme metaphor for change', claims Winton. 'I expect the unexpected but am never fully prepared'.[36] The sea is never still. It is changeable and surprising, but as water it is also the medium of change, it 'lets you through it' – with the promise not just of life but of *Heimat*.

The freedom and grace people experience in water is a form of what Irigaray calls the 'sensible transcendental'; '[w]hy do we assume that God must always remain an inaccessible transcendence rather than a realisation – here and now – through the body?' she asks.[37] This experience of transcendence in the body is a vital aspect of Winton's conception of the sacred. The 'spirit that rolls through all things' runs through the body, and the freedom offered by water is a way to experience something of the holiness of the world. Luther Fox recalls his mother's conviction of the holiness of the earth:

> Holy? He always wanted to believe it, and felt it instinctively true from a thousand days spent dragging a stick through the dirt while crows cleared their throats benignly at him and those stones whined gently upon the hill.[38]

But it is in the water that Lu Fox feels the sacred in his own body, when he can float in the embracing oceanic experience of something eternal. For him the sea is life, and diving to the point of blackout leaves him tingling with vitality.

In *Cloudstreet* it is not the sea as in *Dirt Music* but the river that carries water's promise of life:

> The river. Remember, wherever the river goes every living creature which swarms will live, and there will be many fish, for this water goes there, that the waters of the sea will become fresh; so everything will live where the river goes.[39]

One of the most evocative visions of the freedom of water occurs on the river, when Lester Lamb buys a boat that is too large to truck home and asks Quick (with Fish as passenger) to row the many miles to Cloud Street's nearest jetty. The task is huge and, after nightfall, Quick just stops. He lies back to look at the stars and Fish, who has spent the journey listening to the long-desired water, is transformed:

> He lies back with his eyes closed. The whole boat is full
> of their songs – they shout them up at the sky until Fish
> begins to laugh. Quick stops singing. It's dead quiet and
> Fish is laughing like he's just found a mullet in his shorts.
> It's a crazy sound, a mad sound, and Quick opens his
> eyes to see Fish standing up in the middle of the boat
> with his arms out like he's gliding, like he's a bird sitting
> in an updraught. The sky, packed with stars, rests just
> above his head, and when Quick looks over the side he
> sees the river is full of sky as well […]
>> Are we in the sky, Fish?
>> Yes. It's the water.
>> What dyou mean?
>> The water. The water. I fly.[40]

It is not only for Fish that the water reflects the infinity of sky. When Luther Fox embarks on his odyssey,

> The sea is so flat and cerulean that clouds seem to
> founder in it. Planing through their reflections Fox feels
> more skybound than waterborne as he bears in toward
> the lagoon.[41]

The sea and sky reflect each other because they come together at the horizon, the permanent declaration of human possibility.

This feeling of something eternal can be called the 'oceanic'. In *Civilization and Its Discontents*, Sigmund Freud has some difficulty providing a psychoanalytic explanation for his friend Romain Rolland's description of a feeling of eternity:

> I had sent him my little book which treats of religion as an illusion and he answered that he agreed entirely with my views on religion, but that he was sorry I had not properly appreciated the ultimate source of religious sentiments. This consists in a peculiar feeling, which never leaves him personally, which he finds shared by many others, and which he may suppose millions more also experience. It is a feeling which he would like to call a sensation of eternity, a feeling as of something limitless, unbounded, something 'oceanic'.[42]

In his letter, Rolland describes it as '*the feeling of the "eternal"* (which can very well not be eternal, but simply without perceptible limits, and oceanic, as it were)'.[43] He goes on to explain that this sensation has never failed him: 'I have always found in it a source of vital renewal [and experience it] like a sheet of water which I feel flushing under the bark'.[44] Rolland adds that, for him, it has nothing to do with yearning, '[b]ut the sentiment I experience is imposed on me as a fact. It is a *contact*'.[45] This oceanic feeling connects the body to the eternal, which in Winton is both the sea itself and its merging with sky. Fish 'flies' because he is drawn to the water as to home, drawn to his cruelly denied death. But the water, while it lets you through it, is like the sky because it is the space in which past, present and future coincide. It is the intimation of the infinite, of timelessness. Water is the perfect medium in which to feel the 'oceanic' – the presence of the eternal – and it is the perfect medium of corporeal transcendence in which the eternal may be felt in the body.

Dream

But at the same time the feeling of the oceanic comes from the subconscious, and this is where the intimation of infinity re-emerges in dream. For Daniel and Maureen Coupar in *Shallows*,[46] and Pikelet in *Breath*,[47] the dream of water is often a dream of death. For Lu Fox in *Dirt Music*, the dream sea is filled with the dead:

> Swims in a winy sea. All around him, in a mist, the piping breaths of the dead; they surge and swirl and fin beneath, roundabout, alongside him […] The water grows thick with limbs, too tangled to swim through and streams of kelp-like hair snag in his teeth, catch in his throat.[48]

Coming up out of the dream is much like re-emerging from water, like being reborn.

Yet dream is also the apprehension of God, most noticeably in the sublime image of whales, as we find in the story of the final struggle against whaling in Albany, Western Australia, the last whaling station in the country. Canadian Greenpeace co-founder Bob Hunter led a direct action campaign in 1977 against the three whale-chaser ships operating from Albany. This was the first Greenpeace campaign in Australia, and the last whale, a sperm whale, was harpooned on 20 November 1978. The novel situates itself in the political landscape and includes this 1978 date, but despite Winton's own pronounced environmental activism,[49] the success of the anti-whaling expedition is secondary to the motivations of the people and the ways the sea becomes the backdrop for the petty venal corruption of the town, a confirmation of the freedom and vastness of water, the site of the powerfully theistic presence of whales in the consciousness of humans.

The whales are the epitome of the oceanic, and with strong links to both *Moby Dick* and the biblical story of Jonah, they become, in Queenie's dreams, the intimation of God. While the text is littered with biblical quotes, the water seems to offer a medium of the transcendent beyond narrative, beyond history, and this is particularly invested in the image of the whales in a way that lies at a tangent to the historical events. It emerges on the first page:

> I was only a little girl. I heard the voice of God calling from down in the bay. I got up to the window to look. He was calling Poppa. Quite a patient voice. Daniel… Daniel. Poppa didn't come out. After a while He stopped calling and from down in the bay came this thunderous splash and the whole farm shook and in the moonlight I saw this glistening black…whale inching up towards the house […] Poppa would be there by my bed with the lamp and a glass of milk. It was God, I'd say. And he'd smile and say, 'Yes, I know.'[50]

As well as the dream of God as a whale, Queenie has a dream of being inside the whale:

> Her body propelled itself, willed her on, informed itself, wanted, needed, burrowed onward to that space in the

light where she felt the beginnings of a vortex, farther, closer, then the long fence of ivory, and she tipped forward into the cavity, tumbling, then dark [...] The belly of a whale, she thought: this is the belly of the whale.[51]

Queenie on an impulse joins the anti-whaling protesters, pitting herself immediately against the town. But her investment in the whales goes much deeper than Georges Fleurier's desire to save them:

> She had listened to Fleurier with a forced scepticism, wanting to sneer, but remembering all the time those dreams of the whale lurching up across the paddocks, spiracle whistling like wind in the eaves, to take her Poppa from his bed, to bring a sign from God, to crush their fences and roll through the swamp.[52]

Whales are much more than threatened mammals to Queenie, they are the voice of God. While the novel does not draw back from the political events – the brazenness of the Greenpeace boats and the squalor of the town's resentment – the symbolism of the whales crowns the work, although in a deeply ambivalent way. At the end of the novel Cleve and Queenie rejoice at the return of the whales, which reappear at the same time Daniel Coupar dies. But this is no fairy-tale ending. The survival of the whales is paradoxically the reassertion of the rhythm of nature: the whales strand themselves on the beach,

> Queenie screamed. Surf thundered and the night was images in torch beams. Masses of flesh and barnacles covered the sand, creeping up, floundering, suffocating

33

under their own weight. A pink vapour from spiracles descended upon Cleve and Queenie Cookson as they moved between the heaving monuments.[53]

Death

While the beaching of the whales might seem to undermine the efforts of the activists to save them, death is part of the natural cycle and inhabits water as an ambivalent confirmation of the business of living. 'When I think of sleep or coma or fever or death', writes Winton, 'the ocean comes to mind'.[54] But death is not simply part of the natural cycle. It is a horizon rather than a boundary, something deeply embedded in the utopian vision of Winton's writing, the horizon one constantly approaches through water. Death cannot be separated from the oceanic. When Lu Fox finds himself trapped in a car with Bess and Horrie while travelling across the red vastness of the Western Australian landscape, Bess (who is dying) quotes from James Dickey's wrenching poem about a lifeguard at a children's camp who searches the depths for a drowned boy,

> *I wash the black mud from my hands.*
> *On a light given off by the grave*
> *I kneel in the quick of the moon*
> *At the heart of a distant forest*
> *And hold in my arms a child*
> *Of water, water, water.*[55]

The child of water is the image of one who failed to return. But one attraction of water in Winton's work is that it allows even the most foolhardy to return renewed, reinvigorated. One of the paradoxical features of Winton's characters is their desire to get to the very edge of life by holding their breath beyond the limits of their bodies' capacity. 'It's funny', thinks Pikelet in *Breath*, 'but you never really think much about breathing. Until it's all you ever think about'.[56] We do not need water to see how long we can hold our breath, but water seems to draw Winton's characters to the very edge. Although water 'lets us through' to a different state, free diving – diving without apparatus, holding one's breath to the very limit – takes us to the outer limit of water's acceptance. This is at one level a demonstration of control:

> [A]s a youth you do sense that life renders you powerless by dragging you back to it, breath upon breath upon breath in an endless capitulation to biological routine, and that the human will to control is as much about asserting power over your own body as exercising it on others.[57]

Breath is a story about asserting this power in various ways, of confirming existence itself by going to the edge of one's ability in what feels like a religious experience. 'For all the mess I made, I still judge every joyous moment, every victory and revelation against those few seconds of living',[58] says Pikelet as Sando enthuses about surfing impossible waves:

> When you make it, when you're still alive and standin at the end, you get this tingly-electric rush. You feel *alive*, completely awake and in your body. Man, it's like you've felt the hand of God.[59]

Although most of the story of *Breath* is a *Bildungsroman* taken up with Pikelet's experience of the increasingly awesome potency of the sea, the story hinges on the issue of breath and its boundaries. This focus begins with Pikelet's fascination with his father's sleep apnoea, but free diving stretches the flirtation with death to the limit. As Winton explains,

> Of all water occupations, freediving is the most forgetful. You turn your back to the land, to the sun, and slide down to where all sound is flattened to chirps and rumbles. The deeper you dive the heavier is the blanket that insulates you. You wilfully forget to breathe; you sidestep the impulse and your thinking thins out to the moment at hand. The poet John Blight had it clearly: 'All reason drowns: drowning in you.' It's a religious feeling. On the seabed, or gliding midwater with everything sharp in focus and my body aching with pleasant, urgent hunger, I understand the Christian mystics for moments at a time. I too feel swallowed, minuscule, ready. The diver, like the monk, however, contemplates on borrowed time. Sooner or later you have the surface to return to.[60]

This religious contemplation occurs at the very edge of life. Free diving has been described as a supreme illustration of the oceanic feeling. Free diver Tanya Streeter claims,

> I find it overwhelming and I don't think I've ever properly articulated it. I feel very much protected when I'm underwater...I feel as though the sea is on my side... I have an incredible sense of inner peace throughout

a dive. It's very introspective because you are forced to look within to understand how your body is responding to the experience, and to adjust accordingly. It's very quiet.[61]

Luther Fox feels this same transcendence:

There's a delirium in the water, something special in the way the reef morphs and throbs below [...] On a single breath you could live here on a God-given day like this when plankton spin before your eyes and fish leave their redoubts in phalanxes to swim to you.[62]

In *Syncope: The Philosophy of Rapture*, Catherine Clément describes oceanic feeling as 'a flood; a torrent of waves; a delicious immersion; a feeling of drowning; arriving in a liquid that rolls, shakes, exhausts, and draws one up'.[63] The term 'syncope' can be interpreted in various ways: 'a fainting or swooning and other kinds of loss or absence of consciousness; an irregularity in the heartbeat...a grammatical or other elision'.[64] But it captures very well that moment of rapture at the edge of death, the edge of *Heimat* in Winton's divers.

Just as water offers the kind of medium between reality and dream that can produce God as a whale, so water is the medium of the ultimately sublime, where death is ever present and the swimmers flirt with it in order to feel alive. This is the point at which the oceanic feeling resolves itself completely into corporeal transcendence, the realisation of the sacred in the body. Daniel Coupar dreams of his youth, camping at the old quarantine station with his friends:

They dared each other, dared themselves to dive deeper than they could bear, down into the greenish depths, further into the dark chill until the greyness of death reached out and brushed their skins. It was as if they willed themselves to death in order to feel alive; they toyed with life and did not understand it, felt no need to.[65]

It is as though the point of death is the edge of *Heimat* – a border that may be approached to feel the very edge of the future, of the possible. But this is the point: water takes you to the edge of death – it lets you through to that apparent boundary and you go there for the sole purpose of returning. The return is resurrection, rebirth: the return to life gives life meaning. And water, which draws you to the edge of death, allows you to return to the surface in joyous recognition of the vitality of life.

But this does not always happen. In *Breath*, when Eva Sanderson introduces Pikelet to auto-suffocation as a way of intensifying orgasm, it seems very much like free diving:

I suppose I knew well enough what it felt like. It was intense, consuming, and it could be beautiful. That far out at the edge of things you get to the point where all that stands between you and oblivion is the roulette of body-memory, the last desperate jerks of your system trying to restart itself. You feel exalted, invincible, angelic because you're totally fucking poisoned. Inside it's great, feels brilliant. But on the outside it's squalid beyond imagining.[66]

This has nothing to do with water or ultimately with discovery, but with what appears to be an increasingly grim self-gratification.

While it mimics the sense of rebirth offered by free diving, it fails to confirm life in Pikelet, instead seeming to render his existence an afterthought, an anticlimax. While water confirms the experience of life reinvigorated, the squalor of auto-suffocation denies it. Lu Fox experiences the opposite extreme to pull Georgie from the wrecked plane, where water releases them both back to life. Pikelet's experience with Eva appears to have stranded him, like Fish in *Cloudstreet*, half in and half out of life.

In *Cloudstreet*, when water releases Fish from death back into life it feels like tragedy:

> Fish feels death coming unstuck from him with a pain like his guts are being torn from him [...] he feels his fingers in the mesh, reaching up for anything, his... someone's...and then he's away [...] Hurrying toward a big friendly wound in the gloom...but then slowing, slowing. He comes to a stop. Worse, he's slipping back and that gash in the grey recedes and darkness returns and pain and the most awful sickfeeling is in him like his flesh has turned to pus and his heart to shit.
>
> Shame.
>
> Horror.
>
> Fish begins to scream [...]
>
> Never, never, was there a sadder, more disappointed noise.[67]

This is the scene of a drowning and a rescue. But the failure to drown, the failure of death, haunts the novel from then on. Fish the alert, the livewire, loved by everyone, becomes Fish the brain-damaged – a worse-than-dead – in a living body. The description of his death – the pus and shit that fills him – suggests the abjection that overtakes him. He becomes, in effect, the sublime abject. His reaction of horror – not at his death but at his return – is the reaction to the breakdown of the relationship between self and other. The consequent discarding of his subject as the alert, loved Fish, places him firmly at the interstices of living and dying, sanity and madness, time and space. He has entered the sublime reality of (no) place: 'It's like Fish is stuck somewhere. Not the way all the living are stuck in time and space; he's in another stuckness altogether. Like he's half in and half out'.[68]

Fish is half in and half out of life – or death – an ambivalence that gives him a form of prescience not unlike that of the divine fool. The doctor says there is nothing wrong with him but Fish is caught by life, withheld from the sublime moment of his death. But being stuck is a problem. It is a problem shared, although in a much more prosaic way, by all those timid souls who dwell on the edge of the water. Where Fish has been held back from death, they are afraid to realise their potential for living.

Rebirth

Water, death and renewal are tightly bound in Winton's novels. Whether launching off the water's edge, surfacing from dream or from the freedom of water, or emerging from the flirtation with death in free diving, water is the medium of rebirth. This is true even for Fish Lamb, who finally does not return. The process of going through water, coming to the point of death and emerging renewed is a clear metaphor for baptism. As Paul explains in Romans 6:4,

> We were therefore buried with him through baptism
> into death in order that, just as Christ was raised from

the dead through the glory of the Father, we too may live a new life.[69]

Water is the medium of transformation, of rebirth to new life. For those who spend their lives in and on the water the experience is one of constant renewal, the renewal of beauty and grace, the renewal of the miracle of life. It is the continual renewal of the revelation that the world is holy. Water is, then, also the medium of hope. In *Real Presences: Is There Anything in What We Say?*, George Steiner argues that,

> Above the minimal vegetative plane, our lives depend on our capacity to speak hope, to entrust to if-clauses and futures our active dreams of change, of progress, of deliverance. To such dreams, the concept of resurrection, as it is central to both myth and religion, is a natural grammatical augment.[70]

As baptism symbolises resurrection, so water exists as the constant medium of renewal in Winton's writing.

Daniel Coupar in *Shallows* knows the ecstasy of rebirth when he survives a near drowning:

> Oftentimes Daniel Coupar fished in the harbour from an old clinker-built punt. One morning he rowed out into the Sound, past the heads, to fish for sharks. He caught nothing and was capsized by a rogue swell. In a state akin to hysteria or religious ecstasy [sic] he swam the mile to shore – *I am the least and the most…they know it, I know it, and the Lord knows it, boy…I am the least and*

the most – and came floundering into the shallows of Middle Beach, full of seawater and a curious light.[71]

This is the very same ecstasy divers seek at the very end of their breath. The curious light on Fish is the one Quick sees emanating from him: 'The moon was all over his face, or it seemed to be until Quick saw that moony light was coming off Fish himself'.[72] Occasionally people emerge from water as true illuminati.

Water is, for Luther Fox, a passage, an escape route and a path to a different life. Since the death of Darkie, Sal, Bird and Bullet, Fox's life has been a 'project of forgetting':

> How might he have told her that the way he lives is a project of forgetting? All this time he's set out wilfully to disremember. And some days it really is possible [...] but it's not the same as forgetting. Forgetting is a mercy, an accident.[73]

The chance to forget, to be reborn, comes when White Point turns murderously against him. He swims out regularly to fish and raid other people's lobster traps, and when eventually his truck and his trespass are discovered, his dog shot and the truck disabled, Fox goes back out to sea to leave the boat and swim to shore. He leaves the boat a long way out to give the impression that he has drowned, and the swim of 'ten miles' is hellish. But this is a swim to leave the past behind. This swim is an attempt not just to disremember, but to forget: to forget the deaths of his family, to forget the music that now tortures him, and to forget the possibility of life briefly offered by Georgie. This swim is his last attempt to remake himself, and the water is a promise of the future. The swim brings him close to blackout, but when he finally staggers on shore his life will never be the same:

> He slips back in a swoon, could go down happy into sleep right now. But the water is all bellies and hips like a packed dancefloor. It holds him up. There are rolling white clouds ahead. The air is full of leaping bodies. Fox tumbles headlong into the clouds and surfs them onto the sand. He gets to his feet and hobbles up into the savoury smell of saltbush.[74]

This swim is one that comes in contact with death, as it does so often in Winton, but the water bears him up. Fox's rebirth is a long process. It will not progress until he rediscovers music, which has been a hellish reminder of Darkie and Sal. It will not be complete until Georgie has brought him back from death.

In a search for atonement, an attempt at his own rebirth, Jim Buckridge suggests they head north to look for Luther. Although they are unsuccessful, Lu watches them and is about to give himself up when the seaplane they have called in takes off, with him paddling his canoe after it. The seaplane banks and crashes back in the lagoon with Georgie trapped inside, and Lu risks his life to pull her free as she 'drank his hot shout and let him swim her up into the rest of her life'.[75] In the boat, at the edge of death, he turns blue:

> Georgie froze. She was as stuck as she'd ever been in her life. Luther Fox began to convulse.
>
> Well, said the guide. You're the nurse.
>
> Yes, she thought. This is what I do.

She fell on Luther Fox, pressed her mouth to his and blew.

She's real.[76]

This mutual salvation is a sign of ultimate renewal. The final phrase, '[s]he's real', indicates the corporeality into which both have been revived, to which both have been reborn.

One 'rebirth' in Winton's work is an exception that takes us deeper into the concept. Of all Winton's characters, Fish is the puzzle that holds the pieces together. His original rescue from water is felt as a rejection. Once saved, his whole life is directed towards the final baptism, the dying that leads to life, which he achieves finally, joyously:

His trousers rattle with knucklebones, pretty stones and pennies to make running music, going music, blood music in his temples and ears till right out at the end he finds the steps and the landing, the diving board in its sheath of guano. And the water.

The water.

And the mirror it makes.

Ah, the water, the water, the water [...]

Fish leans out and the water is beautiful. All that country below, the soft winy country with its shifts of colour, its dark, marvellous call. Ah, yes [...]

I feel my manhood, I recognize myself whole and human, know my story for just that long, long enough to see how we've come, how we've all battled in the same corridor that time makes for us, and I'm Fish Lamb for those seconds it takes to die, as long as it takes to drink the river, as long as it took to tell you all this, and then my walls are tipping and I burst into the moon, sun and stars of who I really am. Being Fish Lamb. Perfectly. Always. Everyplace. Me.[77]

Like Georgie's reality at the end of *Dirt Music*, Fish's epiphany suggests that for Winton the sacred is ultimately confirmed in the corporeal existence of human life. There is a stronger feeling in *Cloudstreet* than any other of Winton's novels that death itself is *Heimat*, the home we have sensed but never experienced or known. The beauty of water, of free diving, of going to the edge of life and flirting with death is the experience of utopia constantly deferred but constantly confirmed. The rapture, the 'syncope' of the oceanic, is ultimately realised in rebirth. The discovery of an edge to life is the flirtation with possibility, a possibility teetering between life and oblivion. In *Cloudstreet* the suspicion arises, through Fish's experience, that death is not a border but a horizon, one that confirms rather than shuts off the vision of a possible future. This possibility, this vision of *Heimat*, is the very essence of water.

Notes

1   T. Winton, *Dirt Music*, Picador, Sydney, 2001, p. 115.

2   Ibid., p. 110.

3   T. Winton, *Rising Water*, Currency Press, Sydney, 2012, p. 4.

4   T. Winton, *Land's Edge*, Pan Macmillan, Sydney, 1993, p. 4.

5   Ibid., p. 6.

6   J. Zipes, 'Introduction: toward a realization of anticipatory illumination', in E. Bloch, *The Utopian Function of Art and Literature: Selected Essays*, trans. J. Zipes and F. Mecklenburg, MIT, Cambridge, Massachusetts, 1988, p. xxxiii.

7   T. Winton, 'Aquifer', *The Turning*, Picador, Sydney, 2004, pp. 52–3.

8   T. Kummel, 'Time as succession and the problem of duration', in J. T. Fraser (ed.), *The Voices of Time*, Allen Lane, London, 1968, p. 31.

9   Ibid.

10 E. Bloch, *The Principle of Hope*, trans. N. Plaice, S. Plaice and P. Knight, University of Minnesota Press, Minneapolis, 1986, p. 8.

11 Ibid.

12 Ibid., p. 18.

13 Ibid., p. 13.

14 L. Irigaray, *Sexes and Genealogies*, trans. G. C. Gill, Columbia University Press, New York, 1993, p. 61.

15 Ibid., pp. 68–9.

16 Bloch, *The Utopian Function of Art and Literature*.

17 T. Winton, *Shallows*, George Allen & Unwin, Sydney, 1984, p. 114.

18 M. Cunningham, *The Hours*, Farrar, Straus and Giroux, New York, 1998, p. 40.

19 Winton, *Dirt Music*, p. 370.

20 T. Winton, 'A sea change', *New Statesman*, vol. 4, no. 10, January 2013, p. 14.

21 C. Beal, 'Sea, spirit, and salvation: a theological reflection on the writings of Tim Winton', *St Mark's Review*, no. 221, 2012, p. 47.

22 Winton, *Land's Edge*, pp. 16–17.

23 Winton, *Dirt Music*, p. 16.

24 Ibid., p. 17.

25 Winton, *Shallows*, p. 129.

26 Winton, 'Aquifer', *The Turning*, p. 39.

27 Winton, *Shallows*, p. 63.

28 Winton, *Dirt Music*, p. 208.

29 Winton, *Land's Edge*, p. 84.

30 Winton, *Shallows*, p. 179.

31 Ibid., p. 109.

32 Winton, *Dirt Music*, p. 60.

33 Ibid., p. 104.

34 T. Winton, *Breath*, Hamish Hamilton, Melbourne, 2008, p. 23.

35 T. Winton, *Blueback*, Pan, Sydney, 1997, p. 6.

36 Winton, *Land's Edge*, p. 85.

37 L. Irigaray, *An Ethics of Sexual Difference*, trans. C. Burke and G. C. Gill, Cornell University Press, New York, 1993, p. 148.

38 Winton, *Dirt Music*, p. 361.

39 T. Winton, *Cloudstreet*, McPhee Gribble, Melbourne, 1991, p. 178.

40 Ibid., p. 114.

41 Winton, *Dirt Music*, p. 130.

42 S. Freud, *Civilization and Its Discontents*, Chrysoma Associates, Aylesbury, 2000 (first published 1929), p. 2.

43 R. Rolland, with original italics, cited in W. B. Parsons, *The Enigma of the*

Oceanic Feeling: Revisioning the Psychoanalytic Theory of Mysticism, Oxford University Press, Oxford, 1999, p. 36.

44 Ibid., p. 37.

45 Ibid.

46 Winton, *Shallows*, pp. 214, 64.

47 Winton, *Breath*, p. 155.

48 Winton, *Dirt Music*, p. 159.

49 Winton's activism includes the 2002 fight against the Ningaloo development. He is the WA vice-president of the Australian Marine Conservation Society, the winner of the Wilderness Society Environment Award for Literature and was declared a Living Treasure by the National Trust.

50 Winton, *Shallows*, p. 1.

51 Ibid., p. 109.

52 Ibid., p. 128.

53 Ibid., p. 234.

54 Winton, *Land's Edge*, p. 85.

55 Winton, *Dirt Music*, p. 252.

56 Winton, *Breath*, p. 40.

57 Ibid., p. 41.

58 Ibid., p. 33.

59 Ibid., p. 76.

60 Winton, *Land's Edge*, p. 6.

61 A. Bosanquet, 'Luce Irigaray's *Sensible Transcendental*: becoming divine in the body', *Transformations*, no. 11, 2005, p. 4, www.transformationsjournal.org/journal/issue_11/article_01.shtml.

62 Winton, *Dirt Music*, pp. 126–7.

63 C. Clément, *Syncope: The Philosophy of Rapture*, trans. S. O'Driscoll and D. M. Mahoney, University of Minnesota Press, Minneapolis, 1994, p. 201.

64 Ibid., p. xix.

65 Winton, *Shallows*, p. 214.

66 Winton, *Breath*, p. 190.

67 Winton, *Cloudstreet*, pp. 30–1.

68 Ibid., p. 69.

69 Romans 6:4, *New International Version*, International Bible Society, Zondervan, Grand Rapids, Michigan, 1985.

70 G. Steiner, *Real Presences: Is There Anything in What We Say?* Faber & Faber, London, 2010, p. 63.

71 Winton, *Shallows*, p. 74.

72 Winton, *Cloudstreet*, p. 419.

73 Winton, *Dirt Music*, pp. 103–4.

74   Ibid., pp. 142–3.
75   Ibid., p. 459.
76   Ibid., p. 461.
77   Winton, *Cloudstreet*, pp. 423–4.

Bibliography

Beal, C., 'Sea, spirit, and salvation: a theological reflection on the writings of Tim Winton', *St Mark's Review*, no. 221, 2012, pp. 47–54.

Bloch, E., *The Utopian Function of Art and Literature: Selected Essays*, trans. J. Zipes and F. Mecklenburg, MIT, Cambridge, Massachusetts, 1988.

—— *The Principle of Hope*, trans. N. Plaice, S. Plaice and P. Knight, University of Minnesota Press, Minneapolis, 1986.

Bosanquet, A., 'Luce Irigaray's *Sensible Transcendental*: becoming divine in the body', *Transformations*, no. 11, 2005, pp. 1–12, www.transformationsjournal. org/journal/issue_11/article_01.shtml.

Clément, C., *Syncope: The Philosophy of Rapture*, trans. S. O'Driscoll and D. M. Mahoney, University of Minnesota Press, Minneapolis, 1994.

Cunningham, M., *The Hours*, Farrar, Straus and Giroux, New York, 1998.

Freud, S., *Civilization and Its Discontents*, Chrysoma Associates, Aylesbury, 2000 (first published 1929), see www2.winchester.ac.uk/edstudies/courses/level two sem two/Freud-Civil-Disc.pdf.

Irigaray, L., *An Ethics of Sexual Difference*, trans. C. Burke and G. C. Gill, Cornell University Press, New York, 1993.

—— *Sexes and Genealogies*, trans. G. C. Gill, Columbia University Press, New York, 1993.

Kummel, T., 'Time as succession and the problem of duration', in J. T. Fraser (ed.), *The Voices of Time*, Allen Lane, London, 1968.

Parsons, W. B., *The Enigma of the Oceanic Feeling: Revisioning the Psychoanalytic Theory of Mysticism*, Oxford University Press, Oxford, 1999.

Steiner, G., *Real Presences: Is There Anything in What We Say?* Faber & Faber, London, 2010.

Winton, T., 'A sea change', *New Statesman*, vol. 4, no. 10, 2013, pp. 42–3.

—— *Rising Water*, Currency Press, Sydney, 2012.

—— *Breath*, Hamish Hamilton, Melbourne, 2008.

—— *The Turning*, Picador, Sydney, 2004.

—— *Dirt Music*, Picador, Sydney, 2001.

—— *Blueback*, Pan, Sydney, 1997.

—— *Land's Edge*, Pan Macmillan, Sydney, 1993.

—— *Cloudstreet*, McPhee Gribble, Melbourne, 1991.

—— *Shallows*, George Allen & Unwin, Sydney, 1984.

2

'BURSTING WITH VOICE AND DOUBLENESS': VERNACULAR PRESENCE AND VISIONS OF INCLUSIVENESS IN TIM WINTON'S *CLOUDSTREET*

Fiona Morrison

Cloudstreet, Tim Winton's domestic–comic saga of Western Australian urban life in the mid-twentieth century (1943–63), has recently been published as a boutique hardcover by the Folio Society. It is interesting to note that these quintessentially English publishers of hardcover editions of world literature have added *Cloudstreet* to their list and that the Australian–English novelist, Alex Miller, is the author of the introduction to this new edition.[1] The Folio Society's online catalogue devotes a page to the new edition of *Cloudstreet*, and it quickly becomes apparent that it is Winton's command of voice in the novel that is at the heart of its selection as an Australian national classic to be published so sumptuously at the heart of the old imperial centre. Alex Miller's commentary on Winton's fidelity to the voice of 'uneducated, native-born, working-class Australians'[2] is foregrounded, and an excerpt from a review in London's *Sunday Telegraph* highlighting the richness of Winton's Australian idiom is included among other glowing testaments to the book's vitality and imaginative scope.

This essay proposes to investigate in some detail the matter of voice and the related intensity of *presence* in Tim Winton's critically successful and now securely canonised novel of mid-twentieth-century Australian regional life. Winton's use of the vocative and the vernacular is of specific interest to this investigation. This essay will argue that in the process of bringing literary language closer to a lived and spoken language from a particular time and place, Winton infuses a continuum of narrative modes (omniscient narration, free indirect discourse and free direct speech) with the vitality of Australian idiomatic language in striking ways. As Kobena Mercer suggests, the vernacular offers not only access to contested ideas of authenticity, materiality and the democratic ethos, it also represents 'a heterogeneous site of aesthetic invention'.[3] In line with Mercer, I will argue that the vernacular voice of *Cloudstreet*, which seems anachronistic in light of Australian literary history, is in fact decidedly experimental and, I would suggest, works to unsettle longstanding claims about Winton's essentialism and nostalgia. The various kinds of voices of *Cloudstreet* and the novel's evocative intensity relate closely to the overarching genre of comedy and associated narrative drives to reconciliation and unity, as well as a cognate commemorative urge to make the past palpably present.

Cloudstreet offers a story of something like that of Winton's own family, and in this sense it works as an origin story that unites two very interesting strands. One of these is a broadly comic vision committed to carnivalesque rambunctiousness, bodily presence and versions of reconciliation, which are, at the same time, plucked from countervailing instances of fragmentation, division and alienated absence. Winton was born in 1960 at about the same time as Wax Harry, the son who unites the Lamb and Pickles families, and *Cloudstreet* is therefore a story set in the recent past of Winton's parents and grandparents. The intensity of the reincarnated speech community is memorial in its scope and certainly equals the intensity with which Winton records the *inner* lives and visionary experiences of the stereotypically less articulate working-class people, particularly the men. Of course, the speaking body cannot be constituted through writing, but the celebratory and memorial trace of this body and its powerfully local speech community provides the engine of this novel. The vision of the whole that opens the novel is a driving force: whole community, whole being and whole masculinity are visionary possibilities that underlie the desire for both demotic and sacred unities. This desire for an inclusive unity built on a material sense of the social and physical world is a memorial desire in this work and drives Winton's elegy to the lost world of the working-class regional Australian community.

The question of voice in Winton's fifth novel takes us to the strange and ambiguous continuum of speech and writing. In *Of Grammatology*, Derrida describes logocentrism (via Ludwig Klages) as Western culture's systematic preference for speech over writing because speech indicates the authentic presence of the speaking body whereas writing is only ever the trace or ghost of this original speech.[4] Derrida argues that this preference amounts to a metaphysics of presence in Western culture that is ultimately motivated by a belief in or a desire for a transcendental signified, a meaning that transcends all signs – a kind of final destination or guarantee of meaning.

Winton's *Cloudstreet* deploys a range of narrative means to evoke a metaphysics of presence, grounded in a belief in the possibility of wholeness – of past and present, self and other, community and individual – and secured by a sense of the possibility of final transcendent or sacred meaning (in the water/in the sky/ beyond the narrative). The *word* in *Cloudstreet*, however, is not necessarily the external word of direct speech, directly and faithfully reported. For a work so associated with *voice*, direct speech (the kind we would commonly associate with earlier vernacular tales and local-colour yarns) is comparatively rare, but the texture of the speaking community is nevertheless everywhere to be found, and this is the powerful and ambiguous point of collision between speech, writing and a mediating consciousness.

Winton presents us with a vernacular range, to use a musical metaphor, where the vernacular voice operates in interesting and mobile ways in the form of the narrator and in the *thinking* of the characters, conveyed through flexible and sophisticated free indirect speech. Direct speech is certainly the most obvious rendition of the vernacular in the novel, but this is not in any obvious way *reported* – no speech marks and often no reporting clause – so it also blends in interesting ways with the hybrid narrator–character orchestrations of free indirect speech to deliver an immediacy, intimacy and inclusiveness of vision that is both celebratory and commemorative.

The men and women that form the historical community of *Cloudstreet* are not especially big talkers, but their speech community saturates every page, even the moments when speech itself recedes, and visionary sight and poetic apprehension take over. Winton's sustained dramatisation of the way vernacular orality interpenetrates consciousness and subjectivity connects *Cloudstreet* to Joyce's oracular rendition of Dublin in 1904 in *Ulysses*, or even Faulkner's American South of 1910–28 in *The Sound and the Fury*. Winton's literary ambitions are less elevated than Joyce's and less tragic than Faulkner's; he works more closely with the American nineteenth-century traditions of vernacular realism associated with humour and the rural or regional scene. Nevertheless, Winton's desire to invoke presence (as well as the populist and democratic tradition) through the vernacular has an equally interesting and far-reaching impact on the novel's realism.

The *Oxford English Dictionary* tells us that 'vernacular' means the native or indigenous language of a country or district, which is how mainstream linguists would use the word. Sociolinguists, on the other hand, would emphasise the way vernacular indicates the speaker's use of a variety that stands in opposition to *standard* use (i.e. non-standard or 'substandard' use). This second definition is much more useful for the purposes of this essay, most particularly because Winton's language is quite clearly neither native nor indigenous; indeed, *Cloudstreet* makes a quite emphatic point about indigeneity and settler-colonial oppression by leaving key Indigenous figures in the novel silent, except for dissident laughter. In line with this, as Jonathan Arac reminds us, issues of domestication and political domination are at the heart of the etymology of vernacular[5] – from the Latin, *verna*, a slave born in a master's house – but as Benedict Anderson also notes, the vernacular is a powerful indicator of 'particular solidarities'.[6] For an Australian readership, *Cloudstreet* has had a strong impact on the sense of a possible 'imagined community' (following Anderson), both because of its ties to a tradition of cultural nationalism invested in local realism, but also because it acknowledges the constitutive and violent dislocation of indigenous people that makes this kind of settler-colonial inhabitation possible. As Ashcroft, Griffiths and Tiffin suggest, the vernacular comprises 'the complex of speech habits which characterize the local tongue, or even the evolving and distinguishing local english [sic] of a monolingual society trying to establish its link with place',[7] and we must add to this formulation the centrality of class to Winton's work. The working-class men and women of *Cloudstreet* spend the twenty-year span of the novel uneasily settling the divided house to which they are neither native nor indigenous. The vernacular recreation of a life lived in a working-class speech community is one very powerful way this family is positioned *between* the silent and dispossessed Aboriginal community on the one hand and the white ruling class of Perth represented by Tony Raven and his university crowd on the other.

American literary studies and postcolonial literary studies provide two productive lines of thinking about the vernacular that apply to *Cloudstreet*. The American studies work on the vernacular emphasises the centrality of dialect, idiom and vernacular writing to the construction of national identity. The importance of the vernacular, observed Ralph Ellison more than half a century ago, 'lies in the ongoing task of naming, defining and creating a consciousness of who and what we have come to be'.[8] Standing behind Ellison's commentary is Kenneth Burke's work on the American vernacular, but the role of the vernacular in the making of the American nation was also argued, to great effect, by Leo Marx, who contended that Mark Twain's use of the vernacular in *Huckleberry Finn* was central to the making of the American nation.[9] Jonathan Arac later claimed that Marx's elevation of *Huckleberry Finn* to a kind of hyper-canonical status in American studies has been centrally founded on what Marx suggested was Twain's greatest invention, the 'distinctive, supple, evocative prose style of *Huckleberry Finn*'.[10] Marx argued that Twain and Whitman between them 'establish once and for all the literary usefulness of the native idiom' and 'they fashioned a vernacular mode' which made possible a 'national style'.[11] The vernacular tradition, for Marx, was a matter of language and the egalitarian social values it carried: 'the core of the American vernacular...is not simply a style, but a style with a politics in view'.[12]

For postcolonial literary critics, the use of vernacular language also represented a particular and politically inflected set of choices about the construction of literary time and place. Postcolonial use of the vernacular particularly serves as a way of marking differential relationships with dominant or hegemonic uses of language and modes of writing. This marking-off has been a feature of the settler-colonial use of the vernacular in Australia since Lawson and Baynton's work participated in, or was pulled into, nationalist traditions of authentic Australian writing in the late nineteenth century. *The Bulletin*'s promulgations of the *bush* tradition were various, but easily the most significant forebear of Winton's historical novel is the Queenslander Steele Rudd and his enormously popular and long-running Dad and Dave stories of life *On Our Selection* (print, radio, television, film): regional, rural humorist stories that grew out of the American examples of local-colour humour.[13] Joseph Furphy's *Such Is Life* is also an important forebear of *Cloudstreet*, perhaps most significantly because of the idea that vernacular humour can also allow for (or even *create* space for) moments of Romantic (masculine) insight. The combination of the Furphy and Rudd traditions in *Cloudstreet* (and, I would argue, strong influences from regional American writing) produces an intriguing blend of the demotic and the insightful that is registered by the characters themselves:

> Quick thought about it. They lived like some news-paper cartoon – yokels, bumpkins, fruitcakes in their passed down mended up clothes, ordered like an army floorshow. They worked their bums off and took life seriously: there was good and bad, punishment and reward and the isolation of queerness. But there was love, too, and always there was music and dancing and jokes, even in the miserable times after Fish drowned.[14]

Of course, Winton's domestic epic set in and around a divided house in the regional *city* of Perth in the mid-twentieth century draws on these particular lines of Australian literary tradition with a slightly different emphasis in its representations of the working-class man and his position in street, city, region and nation.

Cloudstreet is a work that demonstrates a genius for various forms of comic plenitude and eventual reconciliation: idiom with moments of heightened lyricism, colonial yarn with postcolonial neo-Romanticism, natural with supernatural, past with present. *Cloudstreet* opens and closes with a picnic on the banks of the Swan River – the moment in the early 1960s when Fish Lamb achieves his final transformation. Here, Fish is reunited with the part of himself that became separated and lost in a drowning accident in the early 1940s. Fish's union of his separated halves (one in a developmentally delayed body and the other mysteriously beyond and above the narrative action) is the primary union/division of the book, and this divided-narrator structure powers or indeed accommodates the pervasive thematic interest in reconciliation and inclusion.

In this sense, despite the comic mode (and the vernacular realism and regional detail that superficially suggest quite an anachronistic work), *Cloudstreet* actually presents the reader with uncompromisingly experimental narration. It is driven by a complicated kind of omniscient narration, which seems to emanate from the transcendent half of the transfigured Fish Lamb who failed to return to his earthly body during a drowning incident. The reader and the characters are sometimes explicitly addressed by this Fish from 'the other side of the mirror',[15] sometimes the aerial Fish addresses himself from beyond/above/below the water and at other moments the omniscient narrator seems much less palpable and much more formal. Winton's wide-ranging experiment with narration includes the related use of the spectrum of first- (singular and plural), second- and third-person voices.

The novel opens in medias res – a 'whole restless mob of us on spread blankets […] in a good world in the midst of our living'[16] – but the heroic dimensions of this are undercut by the carnivalesque tableau of the Aussie picnic. Winton's seemingly effortless combination of the lyrical declamation of plenteous vision and the rambunctious picnic relies on the unembarrassed vocative address, the sweeping declamatory sentences and the inclusion of both idiom and figuration: the 'mob', 'skylarking' and 'chiacking' combine with the 'clear, clean, sweet day' and the 'blocks and points of mirror light down to the water's edge'.[17] The narrator's imperative address to the reader commands attention: 'Will you look at us by the river!'[18] is a direction to the reader to engage with this earthly vision, which the narrator himself is both inside and out. The opening image of the 'earthly vision' of the 'whole group'[19] near the transcendent water is therefore structured by the explicitly inside/outside narrator and, in a further gesture to unities, the pastoral idyll itself is inevitably surrounded by an elegiac inclusion of the dead and departing: 'the gone and taken are with them in the shade pools of the peppermints'.[20]

Compound neologisms ('bagnecked', 'chickenlegs' and 'treethick') give way to a comic–heroic blazon of picnic food and, significantly, speech falls away and purer sounds take over: 'belch', 'applause', 'blurts on a baby's belly' and then 'a song strikes up'.[21] The refrain associated with Fish is heard in the context of this song: 'the beautiful, the beautiful the river'.[22] 'The river' and 'the water' are the Fish-as-character incantations throughout the novel, and this is his vision of wholeness and proliferation, the source of all desire and the goal of the faith with which the Lambs struggle. The river, for Fish Lamb, is always 'calling, softbottomed and the colour of food'; it has 'the rich saucy look of a meal you'll feast on forever'.[23] The food metaphor here is intensely material ('softbottomed', 'saucy', 'meal', 'feast') but Fish's attempt to convey the whole vision of the water also flows inevitably into registers of the sublime and associated pressure on representation – seen later as a pressure on syntax (parataxis) and diction (repetition):

> Remember, wherever the river goes every living creature which swarms will live, and there will be many fish, for this water goes there, that the waters of the sea will become fresh; so everything will live where the river goes.[24]

This vital imagery of proliferation and plenty resonates with the opening picnic as well as the more magisterial invocations of a sublime and undivided space and time: '[f]rom the broad vaults and spaces you can see it all again because it never ceases to be'.[25] It is important to note that the singular moment of sublime union for Fish is that 'for a few seconds he'll truly be a man'[26] and this reveals not only the masculinity that grounds Winton's version of the sublime, but also the fact that the masculine quest for wholeness and proper place (Quick Lamb's quest to find a place where he fits in) is at the heart of Winton's fifth novel.

The narrator of *Cloudstreet* works with both visionary and idiomatic material. The capacity for sublime experience is unapologetically woven together with the regional and working-class experience, and the narrative instantiates this combination repeatedly. In conveying the texture of the lives of the Lambs and the Pickles, Winton works with both direct and indirect speech. The passage summarised in the following excerpts seems to move into a general sense of the way the Lamb family as a speech community uses language, before including some actual direct speech. In the escape from the failed miracle of Fish's half-resurrection in the Margaret River, the Lambs flee to Perth in 'the old flatbed Chev', which 'gives up the fight' on the crest of a hill, just as the sun is 'ducking down'.[27] The shortened name of the car, the idiomatic usage and the idiosyncratic verbs ('ducking', later the onomatopoeic 'scuffle')[28] inducts the reader into the social and comic world of the eccentric Lambs on the move. The kids 'groan like an opera' out on the tray of the truck, and '[a]ll around, the bush has gone the colour of a cold roast'.[29] The specificity of 'the colour of a cold roast' underpins the whole comic–epic experience, as does 'the Chev gives out a steamy fart'.[30] Oriel says to Lester, her slightly hopeless husband, '[y]ou'll have to back her up, Lest', indicating that he should reverse the benighted truck and 'someone' from the back – with a rambunctious mob it is hard to tell – calls, '[c]arn Dad!'[31]

The actual utterances in the above example and throughout *Cloudstreet* are not marked off by speech marks. The absence of quotation marks to indicate reported speech means that direct speech does not seem at all *reported*, rather it seems immediately interwoven or simply *there*. This approximates the sense of a character talking in our presence, another way Winton moves towards the effect of dramatic immediacy and inclusion in *Cloudstreet*. The intervention by author–narrator around speech is very minimal, and the delineation between speech and thought is also minimised, which constructs a kind of storytelling seemingly without an intermediary or 'interference' in report, 'as if [the] author has vacated the stage and left it to the characters'.[32] Geoffrey Leech argues that *free direct speech* of this kind suggests that speech and narrative are 'inseparable and relatively indistinguishable aspects of one state'.[33]

The earliest free direct speech in *Cloudstreet* belongs to the Pickles family. Spoken interactions in this family are relatively uncommon and always quite short compared to the lengthier dramatisation of the internal life of Dolly, Sam and Rose. The inaugural occasion of Sam's accident is surrounded by wonderfully flexible free indirect discourse, but the external reaction of Dolly, Sam, Ted and Chub to the event is characteristically underplayed and phlegmatic. Winton works with the non-standard orthography of vernacular speech to capture the lack of expressiveness in this family – both emotional and linguistic. In the following extract, the sentence length and idiom are notable – Winton is also adept at the orthography required for the transcription of speech from the social world of the Pickles: 'bin', 'nup', 'gunna', 's'posed', 'youse', 'dreckly', 'ya mays well'.[34] Rose's sarcastic comment to her mother is wonderfully finished off by 'cryin':

> He bin awake?
>
> Nup.
>
> The boys, Ted and Chub, scratched themselves and pulled at their shorts.
>
> We go down the jetty? He's not gunna wake up.
>
> S'posed to be in school, youse.
>
> We'll be back dreckly. Dad might be awake, eh.
>
> Oh, ya mays well.
>
> Don't drown from cryin, Rose said, from the bedside.[35]

Later in *Cloudstreet,* some of the most sustained examples of free direct speech occur in the description of Rose Pickles working on the switchboard at Bairds, the Perth department store. Here, free direct speech takes over and becomes a source of intensely immediate comedy as well as finely observed registrations of historical speech in the context of department store commodification and the striking strangeness of working life: 'Rose Pickles discovered that she really could talk [...] The talk that came out of her mouth was like a spiritual inspiration'.[36] For a girl who struggles with orality in the shape of speech and food, it is a lovely irony that, when she is paid, speaking is likened to 'a spiritual inspiration'.

The larger, more rambunctious Lamb family speaks at only slightly greater length than the Pickles, although more often (there are key dialogue scenes between Oriel, Lester and Quick that only a few exchanges between Rose and Sam might rival). Their sentences are not lengthy either (except parts of Lester's unusual monologue to Quick about looking after Fish; Quick had 'never heard his father say words like that'),[37] although they have more lyricism. Quick is generally inarticulate, which is related to his sense of feeling guilty and unsettled or out of place, but direct speech is only the tip of his particular iceberg, since Winton's narrative also provides a sustaining and substantial sense of his inner life through colloquially inflected free indirect speech. The carnivalesque family scenes of knife-twirling and plate-rumbling involve free direct speech, but the sentences still attend to the palpable sense of the wonderfully material and rich social world of a working-class family struggling hard with larger questions of faith and belief:

> Garn, Dad, yer all bluff.
> Did I tell you about me and Roy Rene?
> Arr!
> Did he Mum?
> Oriel finished a sock and threw it at Lon whose foot belonged to it. Yes, Yes. The Les and Mo Show.

At the Tivoli, said Lester, and then The Blue Room. Ooh, I was a lair then. All the best people'd sing me songs. I wrote for the best of em.

He was good, said Oriel, not dirtymouthed like Roy Rene.[38]

Again, Winton's commemorative record of Australian usage in this family world relies on non-standard grammar and inventive orthography ('garn', 'arr', 'dirtymouthed') and period idiom ('bluff', 'lair') as well as period references (Roy Rene, the vaudeville acts at the Tivoli in Perth, The Blue Room). The importance of music in Lester's early life, and the way song features in the Lambs' life, is part of the inclusive and immediate sense of the texture of their whole lives. In some senses music is often more directly expressive than many of the Lambs' spoken interactions with one another or with outsiders, and this is familiar from vernacular use in regional literatures and twentieth-century literature recording African American experience as well.

The relative brevity of the Lambs' and Pickles' free direct speech is nevertheless given an expansive backdrop of extensive and superbly flexible free indirect speech, in which the narrator takes on vernacular inflections of certain characters. Where the direct speech is wonderfully evocative of time, place and class, the use of free indirect speech (combining features of the characters' *direct speech* with features of the narrator's *indirect* report) constructs a ballooning world of thought (quotidian and sublime), and Winton's vernacular inflections here are really where the sense of *voice* emerges in the novel. Winton's capacity to have the rather complicated narrator (inside/outside Fish) move into the characters' points of view without relinquishing oversight of the narrative is one of the most powerful and effective aspects of *Cloudstreet*, and a strong basis for the intimate, inclusive and evocative hold of the novel. The *blurring* effect of free direct speech is compounded here because the distinction between narrator and characters becomes less distinct in free indirect discourse.

These characters, whose social world is so strongly intimated by a continuum of vernacular use inside and out (thinking and speaking), are social agents whose speech is usually a mere glimpse of, if not an actual mask for, a rich internal life. This internal life seems most intense in the case of Sam and Quick, who are in many ways the wounded and stranded men on either side of the *Cloudstreet* domestic (and national) divide between luck and labour in working-class communities. Sam's inner life is introduced at satisfying length, after a short opening with Rose Pickles' younger and more disoriented meditations in Chapter 1:

> Sam knew, as anybody will know, that when you wake up on a summer morning fifty miles out to sea on an island made entirely of birdshit and fag-ends, where only yesterday the rubbershod foot of a Japanese soldier was washed up, and you turn in your bed and smell your dead father right beside you, then you know the shifty shadow of God is lurking. And Sam knew damnwell that when the shifty shadow is about, you roll yourself a smoke and stay under the sheet and don't move till you see what happens.[39]

Sam's internal world is actually virtuosic. None of the above is spoken out loud, although the reader supposes that if it were, then this is exactly what Sam would sound like. In fact, Sam generally speaks very little, but our very full sense of Sam, as well as of Dolly and Rose, relies on the kind of free indirect narrative exemplified in this passage. The use of the second-person *you* meaning *one* mimics a kind of didactic genre of process analysis, which provides a comic gap between what is being analysed step by step (avoiding the shifty shadow of fate), the way it is expressed (vernacular tour de force) and the mode of process analysis.

Oriel, a much more practical and hard-nosed character, is also granted substantial moments of internal reflection. The following gives an example of the way her thinking is practically vocative, especially through the use of italics and curse words. Oriel is furious with Lester because he has let Quick row back with Fish from Fremantle in the new dory:

> Oriel Lamb shoved her hands into the dishwater and didn't utter a sound. It was hot enough to cook in but she went ahead scouring and scrubbing, letting herself absorb its heat into her own until she felt fire behind her eyes. It was even making *him* sweat, she knew, *him* standing there dumb against the kitchenette, waiting for her to say something. She slapped dishes onto the draining board. Her hands were the colour of crayfish. He can wait, she thought; he can jolly-well, flaminwell, he can *damn*well wait [...] She thought: people murder each other.[40]

As Rose and Quick mature, the novel's malleable free indirect discourse swings around to them more frequently and they acquire moments of the sustained seemingly first-person point of view that circulates strongly with the other adults. Quick's anti-pastoral quest into roo-shooting and Rose's excursions into dating Toby Raven and dances at the Embassy in the second half of the novel provide good examples of this. Their rite-of-passage moments are differently experienced: Rose's concern the practical world of work and the gendered arena of dealing with her mother and her boyfriends, while Quick's relate to more visionary experience with Fish, the water and fishing. When they eventually find their way to one another, it is after Rose's disastrous and humiliating experience with Toby Raven. She finds Fish and Quick fishing on the Swan River.

The strength of voice in *Cloudstreet* is often identified by reviewers and readers as the reason for the critical and commercial popularity of the novel. The translation of this novel into a very successful theatre production in Australia and overseas attests to the vigour and dramatic impact of voice, among other factors, in this work. I have argued that the vernacular voice is a central commitment of this novel, a voice that works in both direct and indirect modes and is choreographed by a complex narrator. In line with Bakhtin's work on speech genres and the importance of the utterance in social life, I also think the continuum of the vernacular in this novel performs a version of inclusiveness and immediacy that is sourced in folk culture and stabilised by the genre of comedy. This follows Bakhtin's notion in *Speech Genres and Other Late Essays* that utterances find their most significant 'home' in the overall genre in which they are generated,[41] and comedy is the generic home of *Cloudstreet*, despite the notes of pastoral elegy that persist throughout. Winton's heteroglossic and carnivalesque comedy is sourced in his flexible use of vernacular speech in a range of narrative modes, but this speech also relates to a commemorative desire to recreate a lost past through the ambiguous materiality of written speech and thinking.

I want to turn finally to the moments of sublime vision in the novel and examine how voice works in these passages. Sublime insight within literary works is typically the preserve of men but not of working-class provincials, or what Northrop Frye might call the low mimetic character of comedy.[42] Winton's effort is to secure a sense that the Australian working-class man is not merely the subject and spokesperson of ethnographic 'local-colour' humour or even bleak colonial realism but the locus of full poetic apprehension. The question of transcendent experience and meaning is at constant dialectical play in *Cloudstreet* because of the presence of the halved/doubled Fish as narrator–character. Fish as narrator speaks from the space beyond the mirror/water/ sky, and as character performs a constant desire for the fullness and wholeness of transcendent and transfigured experience.

Quick Lamb, the slow-moving comic hero and inarticulate survivor of family tragedy, is on a demotic quest through his adolescence and early adulthood to find a place to fit in. He feels lost between city and country, between the time before Fish's accident and after, between the inside of the Cloud Street house and the river, and between faith and its loss. He is at home on the water, rather like Huck Finn, but this is shadowed by guilt about the damage done to his brother on the water. He is a sensitive tuning fork for the suffering of others and a crack shot, and in some senses he must be read as the most important focaliser of action in *Cloudstreet*, because his visionary sensitivity both here and later as a policeman indicates that, even though he has never felt he really fitted in anywhere, he is both of the clouds and of the street.

In Quick's roo-culling interlude in the wheatfields, he comes to a nadir of long-standing disorientation and alienation, and experiences what seems to be a waking dream. This vision in the enormous wheat lands of southern Western Australia creates a parallel between the vastness of ocean and vastness of wheat:

Out of the slumber of giants he comes, and there in the waking world with the Southern Cross hanging over him is his brother Fish rowing a box across the top of the wheat.

Quick pushes the sound against his teeth. Fish?

HARVEY ORANGES says the box. The oars are tomato stakes. Fish's body is silver with flight.

Fish?

Carn.[43]

This waking dream crosses elements of strong lyricism and every-day life. The box in which Fish is flying is a 'Harvey Oranges' box, tying the dream to a specific time and place, and his oars are tomato stakes, tying the dream to a quotidian pastoral mode. The Southern Cross is only 'hanging' over him and in the vision Fish says 'Carn'. Nevertheless, Fish's body is 'silver with flight', and Quick, ironically or not, comes out of 'the slumber of giants'. This eruption of dream or vision into the fabric of *Cloudstreet*, especially in a section devoted to graphic accounts of roo-culling, repre-sents a significant shift in the kind of possibilities of Australian working-class masculinity in the context of vernacular use in Australian literary history.

Late in the novel, Quick, Rose, Fish and Wax Harry witness a supernatural passing of a multitude of children through the wheatfields while they are on a camping trip. Of all the visionary moments in *Cloudstreet*, this is perhaps the most interesting – since it is an interaction with a vision of plenitude experienced by the small Lamb–Pickles family of the next generation. This vision of benediction and farewell is not a solitary or masculine preserve, and there is a new tone here, modulated from Fish's incantations about the water and from Quick's sometimes quixotic, sometimes intensely lyrical visions of plentiful fish. There is a modicum of figurative language here, but what is really noticeable is the long drawn-through sentences and the quiet lack of idiom; even 'the great adventure of sleep'[44] appears un-ironic. The final line, 'the children parted the wheat like the wind itself and took all night to pass to pass',[45] is visionary in tone, and also has the final downward inflection of the end of a parable or Bible story:

> In the night Quick woke with the moon white on his face, and Fish was awake beside him, kissing him on the cheek [...]
>
> There was a long, steady rustling in the wheat, rhythmic as the sound of sleep. Quick thought of a herd of roos grazing, but it came closer and was too musical to ignore. He propped himself on an elbow and saw a line of figures moving between the trees. Fish sat up beside him and let out a gasp of delight. Quick shook Rose awake and saw the black widening of her eyes. They were children, naked children. Placid faced, mildly curious, silent but for their footfalls rising from the ground like a mineral spring, following the faint defile of the land to a gravity beyond them, faces and arms, eyes and legs travelling in eddies, some familiar somehow in the multitude that grew to a vast winding expanse, passing them with a lapping sound of feet. Rose sniffed, awake, but none of them spoke anymore not even Wax Harry, who watched curious as the tide of naked children swirled around them, dizzying, heady, making a vortex, an indrawing whirl deeper than exhaustion, until the stars were low enough to touch their eyes heavy, and

the great adventure of sleep took them back. The children parted the wheat like the wind itself and took all night to pass.[46]

This vision elicits no speech at all. It is worth noting that the defeat of speech (including a generalised sense of the oral or the vocative), in a work so saturated by 'voice', is quite singular and otherwise only reserved for the Indigenous characters in the novel. Rose is the only woman in the novel to participate in a visionary experience; even though she 'sniffed' she does not speak. The 'tide of naked children' is like a watery vortex in the wheat-sea with their 'lapping sound of feet' and the 'indrawing whirl' of their passing. This passing reads as both a benediction and a proleptic registration of Fish's final reunification with himself – the long-interrupted passing at the picnic that marks the beginning and the end of the work. This last supper/picnic that provides the structure for the book as a whole demonstrates some of what Ato Quayson has argued is the role of the disabled character in certain contemporary texts as the generator of epiphany or ritual insight.[47] Quayson argues that this positioning is a sign of 'aesthetic nervousness'[48] in the face of disability, but beyond the reification of the disabled as equipped with particular insight, there is also a sense in which the disabled disrupt social codes and indeed import an ethical sense of the experience of Others in new and vigorous ways.

Kenneth Burke, in *Attitudes Toward History*, in which his dialogue with Ralph Ellison about the form and function of the American vernacular is continued, argued that vernacular discourse has the capacity to 'contain both transcendental and material ingredients'.[49] Winton's *Cloudstreet*, perhaps following the poetic labours of Les Murray in the 1970s and 1980s, takes the historical novel and sets out on an ambitious project of comic reconciliation, but with a greater focus on class and region, and tests the capacity of the contemporary Australian novel to wield both transcendental and material ingredients.

In postcolonial terms, the vernacular has been synonymous with the idea of the subaltern and on other occasions allied to the idea of the popular – a mode with marked distance from high culture and cultural prestige. *Cloudstreet*, given its wide publication, many prizes and presence on the secondary curriculum, has clearly never lacked cultural capital, even though part of its impetus is surely a carnivalesque desire to disrupt just these kinds of aspects of the literary and academic marketplace. In Winton's work, and *Cloudstreet* in particular, the vernacular is a marker of class and the life lived in a certain class position in a certain region. Working-class vernacular delineates the middle ground between Indigenous and hegemonic; the in-between position, with which Fish and Quick both struggle in quite different ways, is the self-conscious position. Winton's novel proves, as Murray's poetry had done a decade before, that the non-standard, the local and the homegrown languages, have more than enough capacity to hold the potentially lyrical subjectivity of Australian men. Winton's work points to the way even this recuperation of subaltern experience was itself a marginalisation of Indigenous experience, although it is worth noting that neither Murray nor Winton have much to add to Australian formulations of femininity and the sublime.

The greatest commitment of Winton's fifth book is to make the relatively recent past a living entity – to construct an 'earthly vision' even if only fleeting and flawed, as the origin moment of epic and the community of this combined family. In this sense, it does very much resemble what Scott Hames argues is one of the three registers of Scottish vernacularity, where language is about heritage and authentic roots, and where there is a prevailing rhetoric of revival of cultural self-presence rooted in claims about authenticity and obsessed with an aesthetics of embodiment.[50] Hames's claims are very persuasive, as is his overall critique of the vernacular as it is deployed in the service of representations of region and nation. It does seem impossible, however, to ignore the carnivalesque energies of *Cloudstreet*, sourced in a virtuosic control of the vernacular and the vocative, and the tendency of these unruly energies to complicate such potentially neo-Romantic investments in identity and place.

Notes

1   The other Australian classic on the Folio books list is Frederic Manning's First World War novel published by Peter Davies in London in 1929, *The Middle Parts of Fortune*, also recently republished as a tastefully designed hardcover bound in buckram, with colour plates and a new introduction, this one by David Malouf.

2   A. Miller, 'Introduction', *Cloudstreet*, T. Winton, The Folio Society, London, 2013, pp. ix–x.

3   K. Mercer (ed.), *Pop Art and Vernacular Cultures*, Iniva and the MIT Press, London, 2007, p. 7.

4   J. Derrida, *Of Grammatology*, trans. G. C. Spivak, Johns Hopkins University Press, Baltimore, Maryland, 1974.

5   J. Arac, *Huckleberry Finn as 'Idol' or Target: The Function of Criticism in Our Time*, University of Wisconsin Press, Madison, 1997, p. 160.

6   B. Anderson, *Imagined Communities*, Verso, London and New York, 1983, p. 133.

7   B. Ashcroft, G. Griffiths and H. Tiffin, *The Empire Writes Back: Theory and Practice in Post-colonial Literatures*, Routledge, London, 1989, p. 38.

8   R. Ellison, *Going to the Territory*, Vintage, New York, 1987, p. 143.

9   L. Marx, 'Introduction', *The Pilot and the Passenger*, Oxford University Press, New York, 1988, pp. xviii ff.

10   Ibid., p. xiv.

11   Marx, 'The vernacular tradition in American literature', *The Pilot and the Passenger*, p. 4.

12   Ibid., p. 8.

13   As Julianne Lamond wrote recently (in J. Lamond, 'Unfounded attack on Dad and Dave comedies!', *Inside Story: Current Affairs and Culture from Australia and Beyond*, 9 October 2013, inside.org.au/unfounded-attack-on-dad-and-dave-comedies, accessed 20 October 2013):

> [F]irst appearing in a series of episodic stories of a family on a struggling bush property by 'Steele Rudd' (Arthur Hoey Davis) in 1895, the Rudd family went on to feature in no less than nine short story collections (1899 onwards); one of the most popular stage plays in Australian theatre history (1912); seven films (1920–95); a long-running radio serial (1937–52); and a television series (1972). The Rudds haunt the history of Australian popular culture like a family culture that refuses to die, the ubiquity cause for both celebration and handwringing.

14   T. Winton, *Cloudstreet*, McPhee Gribble, Melbourne, 1991, p. 304.

15   Ibid., p. 219.

16   Ibid., p. 1.

17   Ibid.

18   Ibid.

19   Ibid., p. 2.

20   Ibid.

21   Ibid., pp. 1–23.

22   Ibid., p. 2.

23   Ibid., p. 120.

24   Ibid., p. 178.

25   Ibid., p. 3.

26   Ibid., p. 2.

27   Ibid., p. 25.

28   Ibid.

29   Ibid.

30   Ibid.

31   Ibid.

32   G. Leech and M. Short, *Style in Fiction: A Linguistic Introduction to English Fictional Prose*, Pearson Education, Harlow, 1981, p. 323.

33   Ibid., p. 259.

34   Winton, *Cloudstreet*, pp. 15–16.

35   Ibid.

36   Ibid., p. 179.

37   Ibid., p. 94.

38   Ibid., p. 72.

39 Ibid., p. 9.
40 Ibid., p. 111.
41 M. Bakhtin, *Speech Genres and Other Late Essays*, trans. C. Emerson and
    M. Holquist, University of Texas Press, Austin, 1986.
42 In his first essay in *The Anatomy of Criticism*, 'Historical criticism: theory of
    modes' (N. Frye, *The Anatomy of Criticism: Four Essays*, Princeton University
    Press, Princeton, New Jersey, 1957, p. 33), Frye offers the following rubric
    about the hero of comedy:

> If superior neither to other men nor to his environment, the hero is
> one of us: we respond to a sense of his common humanity, and demand
> from the poet the same canons of probability that we find in our own
> experience. This gives us the hero of *the low mimetic mode*, of most
> comedy and of realistic fiction. [my emphasis]

43 Winton, *Cloudstreet*, p. 200.
44 Ibid., p. 419.
45 Ibid., p. 420.
46 Ibid., pp. 419–20.
47 A. Quayson, *Aesthetic Nervousness: Disability and the Crisis of Representation*,
    Columbia University Press, New York, 2007.
48 Ibid.
49 K. Burke, *Attitudes Toward History*, University of California Press, Berkeley
    and Los Angeles, 1961, p. 166.
50 S. Hames, 'On vernacular Scottishness and its limits: devolution and the
    spectacle of "voice"', *Studies in Scottish Literature*, vol. 39, no. 1, 2013, p. 220.

Bibliography

Anderson, B., *Imagined Communities*, Verso, London and New York, 1983.
Arac, J., *Huckleberry Finn as 'Idol' or Target: The Function of Criticism in Our Time*,
    University of Wisconsin Press, Madison, 1997.
Ashcroft, B., Griffiths, G. and Tiffin, H., *The Empire Writes Back: Theory and
    Practice in Post-colonial Literatures*, Routledge, London, 1989.
Bakhtin, M., *Speech Genres and Other Late Essays*, trans. C. Emerson and
    M. Holquist, University of Texas Press, Austin, 1986.
Burke, K., *Attitudes Toward History*, University of California Press, Berkeley and
    Los Angeles, 1961.
Derrida, J., *Of Grammatology*, trans. G. C. Spivak, Johns Hopkins University
    Press, Baltimore, 1974.
Ellison, R., *Going to the Territory*, Vintage, New York, 1987.

Frye, N., *The Anatomy of Criticism: Four Essays*, Princeton University Press, Princeton, New Jersey, 1957.

Hames, S., 'On vernacular Scottishness and its limits: devolution and the spectacle of "voice" ', *Studies in Scottish Literature*, vol. 39, no. 1, 2013, pp. 203–24.

Lamond, J., 'Unfounded attack on Dad and Dave comedies!', *Inside Story: Current Affairs and Culture from Australia and Beyond*, 9 October 2013, inside. org.au/unfounded-attack-on-dad-and-dave-comedies, accessed 20 October 2013.

Leech, G. and Short, M., *Style in Fiction: A Linguistic Introduction to English Fictional Prose*, Pearson Education, Harlow, 1981.

Manning, F., *The Middle Parts of Fortune*, The Folio Society, London, 2012.

Marx, L., *The Pilot and the Passenger*, Oxford University Press, New York, 1988.

Mercer, K. (ed.), *Pop Art and Vernacular Cultures*, Iniva and the MIT Press, London, 2007.

Quayson, A., *Aesthetic Nervousness: Disability and the Crisis of Representation*, Columbia University Press, New York, 2007.

Winton, T., *Cloudstreet*, The Folio Society, London, 2013.

—— *Cloudstreet*, McPhee Gribble, Melbourne, 1991.

3

WINTON'S SPECTRALITIES OR WHAT HAUNTS *CLOUDSTREET*?

Michael R. Griffiths

Quick leans around from the back. Looks flamin haunted.

Well, Oriel says without a smile, we'll be hauntin it from now on.[1]

First published in 1991, Tim Winton's *Cloudstreet* is now presented in one of its several Penguin editions as a 'Modern Australian Classic'. Might this detail of the book's marketing reveal something about the novel's metatextual status? It might be seen to imply that *Cloudstreet* figures a certain Australian modernity. Indeed, this modernity would have to be commensurable with something classic, standard, which is also to say formative. And insofar as it is formative of the present, a classic is also implicitly, at least in part, of the past. *Cloudstreet*'s metatextual status, then, implies that the novel figures Australia's modernity even as it relies on a classicism that is spectral: haunting the present in all its modernity. If the paradoxical canonical status claimed by the novel implies a certain spectrality, in this way then it is perhaps not surprising that in fleeting but essential moments the novel functions not only as a family epic, but also as a ghost story.

Classically modern: formed in the past but central to the present of an imagined community, that which is present at the precise moment that it is past: is this not also precisely the definition of a ghost? To ask, then, what haunts the house at Number One Cloud Street, West Leederville, is also a way to stage a question about what haunts the wider political community of which it is (arguably) a synecdoche: Australia, in all its spectral classicism and unstable modernity.

Cloudstreet narrates the intersecting stories of two working-class families in Second World War and postwar suburban Perth, conjoined in a family epic – and a hybrid one at that. A ghost story and a family epic together ground this 'modern Australian classic': what are we to make of the politics of this generic choice? The family is very often a metonym of political community. If there is always something haunting about the foundation of the modern, then what are we to make of the hauntedness of the two families at the centre of *Cloudstreet*? Further, if nations have often been imagined as bound together on the model of the family, grounded in paternal power (take Locke's *Two Treatises of Government*),[2] then Winton's concern with family might be understood not only as a reflection on family as such, but also on the degree to which the centrality of the familial inscribes a wider politics of belonging and nationhood.[3] And if we accept these premises, then what haunts the Lambs and the Pickles also, in some way, reflects the hauntedness of Australia as a settler-colonial nation-state.

If *Cloudstreet* is about the gradual hybridisation of two clans – culminating as it does in the marriage of Rose Pickles and Quick Lamb and the birth of Wax Harry – then it can also be read as a meditation on the unwieldy and complex intersections of families and backgrounds that mark Australia as a (post-)settler-colonial political community. Certain questions are, then, raised by the novel, which might include the relationship between kinship and imagined community per se; kinship and class (since Rose and Quick's engagement is precipitated by the untenability of the former's cross-class courtship with Toby Raven); the legitimacy of property and habitation (which, in the settler-colonial context, cannot *not* be haunted by the spectre of indigeneity and colonisation); and indeed community and catastrophe (from the woundedness of the Pickles patriarch to the parallel fate of Fish Lamb – and it should not go unremarked that the woundedness that marks this catastrophic dimension of community is aligned with a certain tragicomic masculinity). I want, however, to narrate the politics of the family in *Cloudstreet* by beginning hermeneutically with a topos that touches all of these (from politics to the family, and the politics of the familiar per se): that topos is inheritance.

Inheritance is what narrates Cloudstreet the house (and *Cloudstreet*, the 'modern Australian classic' novel) from the outset. The convergence of the Pickles and Lamb families is made possible by Sam Pickles' literal inheritance of the Cloud Street house when Uncle Joel, the novel's Geraldton publican, dies, leaving Sam the house. As 'men were reading his Last Will and Testament to a small gathering of sunburnt people in the Ladies' Lounge of the Eurythmic Hotel',[4] Sam finds his luck changing. Typically broke due to his gambling habit, Sam unexpectedly stumbles upon a basis by which his family can survive: 'Two thousand pounds [...a]nd there was a house, a large house down in the city, left to the same Samuel Manifold Pickles with the proviso that it not be resold for the next twenty years'.[5]

As a result the Pickles are able to survive, despite their lack of income, by renting half the house for twenty years to the Lamb family, who – despite their status as tenants and not owners – find themselves similarly provided for by the relationship as they open a successful shop in one of the front rooms of the house. Inheritance, then, is the foundational political economic structure that allows the narrative to unfold as the two families' tragedies and triumphs are limned in Winton's distinct vernacular. Of course, the house is haunted.

So what haunts the house? In order to answer this question, we need to first ask what it means to haunt, or be haunted, more generally. Jacques Derrida has suggested that inheritance might be a constitutive concern in the political thought of what he calls 'spectrality'[6] – a concept he locates as foundational to logics of political economy. In a conversation with Bernard Stiegler, Derrida poses a '[h]ypothesis: there is always more than one spirit. Whenever one speaks of spirit one immediately evokes spirits, specters, and whoever inherits chooses one spirit over another'.[7] What one inherits is not only what one owns but also a sense of being bound to a particular political and economic order, entailing not only rights but responsibilities and even prohibitions (such as the publican's twenty-year prohibition on selling Cloudstreet). As Derrida notes,

> If to inherit is to reaffirm an injunction, not simply a possession, but an assignation to be deciphered, then we are only what we inherit. Our being is inheritance, the language we speak is inheritance.[8]

One's inheritance, then, is haunted by the injunctions of the spectre of the bequeather who is both absent from the home and present within it – in the mode of injunction and prohibition.

As David Crouch has suggested, with a mind to the specific Australian context, such 'haunted houses provide a precise figure for an unsettled country'.[9] In Cloudstreet, the situation of

inheritance and habitation is indeed haunted by the inheritors
who enable it, and those whose legitimate possession they have
usurped – a parallel haunting. It is the apparently peripheral ghosts
haunting Cloudstreet who figure a spectral possession of the titular
house, just as the relationship of various characters to these figures (notably Quick and Fish, but also Sam Pickles, as proprietor
and awkward patriarch) structures a spectral logic of ownership
and habitation synecdochic of settler-colonial nationhood per
se. This is the case in no small part because the ghosts that haunt
Cloudstreet figure a history of Indigenous prior occupation, as
well as colonial dispossession and its form as assimilation. There
is 'the shadow girl', also referred to as 'the dark girl', who, despite
Fish Lamb's entreaties, will not come out but instead hides away,
'always either crying or angry and nothing else'.[10] Later in the
novel, by contrast, Sam encounters the other spectral figure who
haunts the house's library:

> He stepped into the room whose atmosphere made his
> stomach twist, and when he turned he saw the most
> vicious-looking old bitch he'd ever seen in his life. She
> was white and dressed in some outfit from another time.
> There were lacy gloves in her hand that were beautiful,
> delicate as he'd ever seen. She seemed to be smiling;
> a sweet frightening smile [...Sam was] certain at that
> moment that he'd finally laid eyes on Lady Luck herself.[11]

A 'dark' ghost and a 'white' ghost, then, haunt the house. While
these ghosts appear relatively late in the text and recur infre-
quently, the novel nonetheless opens by inaugurating a structure
of foreshadowing that allows the reader to identify them in a move
that is almost proleptic. This knowledge is, in turn, constitutive

of the narrative as a whole and the central question: who owns Cloudstreet and who lives there (and will continue to live there)?

This moment of foreshadowing comes at the beginning of the book's Part II.[12] Part I introduces the two families in their respective rural sites of Geraldton and Margaret River. Part II establishes how the Lambs and the Pickles come to converge in the house at Number One Cloud Street. But before doing so, the first chapter describes the backstory of the house: a story of the history of Australia's Aboriginal assimilation policy. In this chapter, titled 'Back in Time',[13] we learn that the Cloud Street house was established as a home for Aboriginal girls removed from their families. The proprietor is revealed to have been a wealthy widow: '[b]ack in time there was a big empty house. It was owned by a very respectable woman who had cheated several people in order to get it'.[14] The respectable woman is, of course, to become the same 'vicious-looking' spectre Sam Pickles will encounter much later in the novel. Beyond the individual psychology of this vicious and cheating upper-class Australian widow, the unnamed character allegorises a critique of class in the supposedly classless Australian society, implying that Australian class respectability is premised on the project of the colonisation and assimilation of Indigenous people. As 'Back in Time' further reveals, an Anglican priest convinces the widow to 'open her house [...t]o native women, perhaps'.[15] The priest woos her with the prospect of her becoming the 'Daisy Bates of the city'.[16] This line will be particularly telling to students of Australia's twentieth-century history of assimilation, and will immediately resonate in its polysemy, as I shall shortly detail. Yet the girls' home scheme ends in tragedy, as the 'mission girls [who] had been taken from their families and were not happy'[17] understandably resent the putative philanthropy to which they are subjected, and eventually, we are told, one girl commits suicide, drinking ant poison in the library. '[A] few weeks after'[18] the widow herself dies sitting at the piano in the library, and it is in this way that the novel anticipates for the reader the identification of the ghosts that will later appear to Fish Lamb and Sam Pickles. Cloudstreet/*Cloudstreet*, both the house and its narrative, are then constitutively haunted by the dispossession of Indigenous peoples in Australia and the history of child removal more particularly. And if what the Pickles inherit and the Lambs find themselves occupying is a house inscribed irreparably in this history – as a synecdoche of family as nation – *Cloudstreet*'s spectrality inscribes the political community it allegorises, rendering it inseparable from this history of dispossession.

'Back in Time' both refers to historical correlates and succinctly mythologises Australian history, condensing and displacing historical details into a mythic basis for a family epic and the wider allegory of the settler nation-state this epic narrates in turn. Under assimilation, Indigenous girls – particularly those whose mixed descent had led to fairer skin, read as implying their assimilability – were taken from missions such as Moore River Native Settlement in Mogumber and brought down to a house in Perth. Unlike the fictive Cloudstreet, the East Perth Girls' Home in Bennett Street (established in 1931) was not located in West Leederville, and was administered by the Native Affairs Department under A. O. Neville (in other words, was not a private or Church-administered operation). There are resonances, however, between Winton's fictive account of Cloudstreet and the history it draws upon. Grace Campbell, the East Perth Girls' Home's first matron, was indeed a widow – the wife of a former Moore River superintendent, Thomas Campbell.[19] Nonetheless, recalling the history of the Bennett Street Girls' Home, Winton's mythic account of assimilation condenses this traumatic kernel at the heart of twentieth-century Australian history as the basis for the inheritance by Sam Pickles of the titular house (and the dysfunctional, though not dystopian political community it figures).

Another invocation of Australian history (and its relation to Indigenous people in particular), the novel's reference to Daisy Bates, is telling within a narrative so constitutively haunted by the ghosts of Indigenous people and those who have wronged them.[20] On the one hand, Bates – a real-life lay ethnographer who worked with Western Australian Indigenous people (particularly the Noongar, or Bibbulmun people, as she called them, employing one of the fourteen clans within the Noongar nation as her name for the people as a whole) – was known in the non-Indigenous community as a respected advocate of Aboriginal social-justice issues. On the other hand, she was also one of the most prominent advocates of the 'smoothing the pillow of a dying race' premise: the idea that Indigenous people were inevitably doomed to extinction and that all that could be accomplished philanthropically was to ease this passing, while recording the details of Indigenous culture and language.[21] Daisy Bates functions as *Cloudstreet*'s signifier of the ambivalence of such putative philanthropy.

It is also telling that Sam Pickles perceives the widow's ghost as 'Lady Luck herself'. If the house is haunted by Sam's inheritance of an already appropriated space, it is also haunted by the idea of the luck that so vexes Pickles from the outset, and that the novel names 'the shifty shadow'[22] from the beginning. The figuration of the ghost of the Aboriginal girl as 'the shadow girl' seals this association. Where Pickles' luck is his 'shifty shadow', the misfortune of this young girl, wronged by colonisation, renders her a shadow. Indeed, Pickles' inability to recognise consciously that his own inheritance of fortune (Cloudstreet itself) is predicated on the history of dispossession instantiated in the house is a point to which I will return.

Scott L. Morgensen has importantly argued that '[s]ettler colonialism has conditioned not only Indigenous peoples and their lands and the settler societies that occupy them, but all political, economic and cultural processes that those societies touch'.[23] If *Cloudstreet* is a 'modern Australian classic', it may be this haunted inheritance that makes it so, a point that connects it to the Derridean logic of inheritance and spectrality and, as Morgensen suggests, globally so. Derrida's meditation on politics and its constitutively spectral dimension is negotiated, in part, through an exploration of Marx and of Shakespeare. 'Who's there?' cries out Barnardo to a presence that will turn out to be the ghost of the dead King Hamlet.[24] This first line in Shakespeare's *Hamlet*, then, inscribes the play in a meditation on ghosts, inheritance and the legitimacy of political sovereignty.[25] To risk being grandiose, I would suggest that if *Cloudstreet* is indeed a 'modern Australian classic', then in being so it reveals a logic of state, family and legitimacy in Australia as a settler-colonial space analogous to that Derrida assigns to *Hamlet*. Australia is a settler-colonial space in so far as it is foundationally rooted in the appropriation of Indigenous land. Yet it is, in many ways, also a proxy Europe, deriving many of its legal and political norms from the Westminster and Westphalia orders (respectively and in convergence). If *Hamlet* asks 'Who's there?' in relation to Elsinore, it also asks about the status of land for the whole of Europe, and Elsinore becomes a synecdoche of Europe in toto (even as Denmark is a slippage of Tudor England). Could *Cloudstreet* as a 'modern Australian classic' be a site to ask who belongs in Australia within the structure of its (post-) settler colonialism?[26] Who goes there? Who owns Cloudstreet?

As Derrida has argued, this rational and material basis for property, commonwealth and political community is also haunted by its externalities. What haunts the settler-colonial nation-state called Australia also touches the putatively exceptional history of Europe it structures and in relation to which it is structured.[27]

This is the nature of the Derridean logic of spectrality: the haunting of the present by the injunctions of a past sovereignty. Yet this is complicated in the settler colony for two reasons, because (as Derrida himself intuits) there is never one but in fact a plurality of ghosts. Consider, for example, that Cloudstreet is haunted by both the widow and the shadow girl, coloniser and colonised: what haunts and is therefore politically constitutive is not only the claim of Indigenous political priority, but its thwarting, disruption and colonisation. Secondly, as is attested in the recurring figure the novel merely names, at turns, 'the blackfella' and 'the black man',[28] not only are there multiple figures haunting *Cloudstreet/* Cloudstreet, but it is also unclear whether they are all necessarily ghosts at all. If the presence (in all its senses) of 'the blackfella' challenges the figuration of Indigenous people as 'passing' (in Bates's terms),[29] then *Cloudstreet* might allow us to rethink spectrality in a settler-colonial context.

Winton's spectral and otherworldly figurations are as often as not fleshy, corporeal and therefore indeterminate: as in *Cloudstreet*, it is rarely clear whether the many ghosts that populate Winton's oeuvre are ever simply dead, buried and absent. Take, for instance, 'the riders' whose strange presence opens and closes Fred and Billie Scully's journey around Europe in the novel of that name.[30] While these ephemeral ancestral figures are clearly otherworldly, Winton's prose also renders them highly corporeal.[31] Indeed, when Scully first perceives them, it is as bodies: 'the glistening, steaming bodies of horses [...] the bearded faces of men'.[32] And Fish Lamb is another living character who could also be read as exposed to a certain spectrality, since after his near drowning 'not all of Fish Lamb had come back'.[33] In other words, there are multiple topoi at which one might begin to examine the question of Winton's spectralities. For present purposes, I want to contrast the ghosts of Number One Cloud Street with the corporeal and yet prophetic figure of the 'black man' who appears at various times in the novel – first to Quick Lamb, and then to both Fish Lamb and Sam Pickles. Like the riders, the status of 'the blackfella' who appears in *Cloudstreet* is both ghostly and present.

In Part VI, while Quick is in self-imposed exile from Number One Cloud Street, he encounters 'a blackfella standing with his thumb out and a gladstone bag at his feet',[34] who mysteriously leads Quick back to Cloudstreet. The novel's 'black man' drinks wine and smokes, locating him as corporeal. Yet he also functions as a prophetic figure – not only is he represented as Christ-like, but also almost a Tiresius or even Hamlet père archetype – knowledgeable about the nature of Cloudstreet the house: its history and, most strikingly, the necessity that Quick should return to it – or, at least, return somewhere. The spectral or otherworldly sense of this presence is most emphasised when the two meet again late in the novel, prompting Quick to ask: '"Are you real?" The blackfella laughed. "Are you?"'[35] Ken Gelder and Paul Salzman have suggested that the novel's use of the 'black man' as a figure of, in my terms, inheritance, normalises Indigenous dispossession. As they put it, he hands over property to the inhabitants of Cloudstreet, 'giving them his blessing into the bargain',[36] with no consideration of native title. I agree with Gelder and Salzman that this ventriloquised figure of Aboriginality does indeed normalise the dispossession of Indigenous peoples by settler colonials. My only caveat would be to suggest that we can learn much about the chronotope of such settler-colonial presumption by examining how the novel works to authorise this ventriloquism as well as by highlighting the particular mode of haunting it engages. As Nathanael O'Reilly proposes, the novel's engagement with representation is nothing if not complex, even as he must ultimately accept that the novel cannot be exonerated of its conservative and reactionary elements.[37]

If questioning Indigenous presence is constitutive of settler-colonial ignorance, it also precipitates an encounter with the reality of a settler colonialism that relies, at least in part, on an appropriation of the Indigenous status of Aboriginal others – as I have argued elsewhere in relation to twentieth-century settler-Australian writing about indigeneity.[38] It is perhaps no accident that *Cloudstreet* foregrounds Sam's sense that 'the black man' resembles his father: 'Jesus, thought Sam, paint him white and he might be me old man'.[39] This curious moment marks 'the black man' almost as the symbolic original owner of Cloudstreet in his symbolic status as father and, therefore, bequeather.[40] As Elizabeth Povinelli has noted, even where indigenous rights are thwarted or disrupted, the nation-state nonetheless demands that they 'ghost [indigenous] being for the nation'.[41] The play between presence and absence that marks the novel through this recurrent figure of indigeneity is metonymic of a wider tension that settler-colonial spectrality imposes on indigenous people more generally.

Is this more corporeal spectrality of 'the blackfella' a redemption of white-settler colonisation or a challenge to it? The two are perhaps not mutually exclusive but rather constitutive of an ongoing logic of dispossession, normalised and even (more problematically) exonerated as a naive – if haunted – inheritance of stolen land. Quick's second meeting with 'the blackfella' takes place by the suburban house he and Rose have been struggling to pay for:

> It's the blackfella wearing nothing but a beach towel and a pair of rubber thongs.
>
> 'Go home,' says the black man. 'This isn't your home. Go home to your home, mate.'
>
> Quick fronts him, emboldened by his [police] uniform. This is a black man he's talking to. But the man lays five fingers spread on Quick's chest. 'Go home.' Quick turns. Already he's alone.[42]

One way to read this scene is as indicative of a sense of displacement that haunts settler Australia: one is always already not at home in the place one calls home, since (like Cloudstreet itself) this home has been appropriated.[43]

Sam, too, encounters 'the black man' in a scene in which he is warned off selling Cloudstreet. What haunts this appropriated space Sam has inherited? It is 'the black man', which is also to say the authorising presence of indigeneity. For 'the black man' to insist that Quick 'go home' to a place that is already (and in multiple senses) not *his* – Oriel's remark in the quote with which I opened this essay emphasises that the Lambs (and Pickles) haunt as much as they are haunted – then going and remaining 'home' is constitutively unsettling. What Sam Pickles has inherited, and what the 'whole restless mob'[44] of Lambs and Pickles come to haunt, is most theirs in being haunted in turn by the colonising nature of their claim to proprietorship.[45]

In a similar vein to Gelder and Salzman, Crouch suggests 'there is no real negotiation between indigenous and

non-indigenous characters' in *Cloudstreet* since Indigenous characters 'are either spectres, watchers from the distance, or helpful
prophets'.[46] Crouch is, I think, substantially correct on this point.
But I want to tarry momentarily with his supporting claim that
while not all the Indigenous characters in the book are literally
spectres, they are not 'given fleshy reality'.[47] One might suggest
that by refusing to simply render 'the blackfella' a literal ghost,
this unreal yet insurmountably corporeal and revelatory figure
of indigeneity operates to challenge the political status of the
settler-colonial family. *Cloudstreet* refuses at first to succumb to
the trap of rendering indigeneity as simply passed: a spectral
presence haunting (but never quite thwarting) settler-colonial
sovereignty. 'The blackfella', as much as he metaphorically 'haunts'
Quick, is distinct from the definitively spectral ghosts of the
widow and the shadow girl, since he must be acknowledged in his
living presence with all the claims he makes on the family and on
Sam and Quick in particular. Crouch, and Gelder and Salzman
respectively have rightfully critiqued the overly spectral dimension of the novel's engagement with Indigenous presence and
the consequent justification of dispossession it entails.[48] I would
suggest that while Winton's novel is not ultimately redeemable on
this front, its ambivalences (such as that between 'the black man's'
spectrality and his corporeality, which distinguishes him from the
ghosts of the house) explore the psychological nature of hauntedness and its limits as a condition of settler-colonial guilt and
self-justification. What haunts Quick – and indeed the original
inheritor of the house on the part of the Pickles and Lamb clans,
Sam himself – is ironically not the hauntedness of their house but
the imperative given by 'the black man' that they not sell it: that
they feel and remain at home with(in) the uneasy and haunted
space of which they are the inheritors. In this way, *Cloudstreet*

insists on the hauntedness of settler-colonial space: in order to inhabit a settler colony such as Australia, one cannot disavow the sense that one inhabits a land inherited from appropriators of the land of Indigenous peoples.

Yet on the other hand, for all Winton's efforts to insist upon an unstable and precarious settler coloniality, it may be precisely the success of his sense of spectrality that ultimately fails. This unease culminates in the scene on Election Day, 1964, when Sam is warned by 'the blackfella' from selling Cloudstreet:

> 'You live there,' said the black man.
>
> 'Yeah, I own it. Don't tell anyone, but in the new year I'm gonna sell it [...]'
>
> The black man's stare put a foul sweat on him [...]
>
> 'You shouldn't break a place. Places are strong, important.'[49]

This scene is highly ambiguous. One could argue that Sam, like Quick, comes to recognise the presence of indigeneity through this scene. He obeys 'the black man', and it is on this basis that the Lambs and Pickles remain in the house, preserving it as the place they at once call home and feel connected to, and as the place haunted by the widow and the shadow girl, and thereby marked by an ethics not of forgetting, but of continuing to be haunted. Yet one could also argue, and I think more appropriately, that the close of the novel figures a self-perpetuating settler colonisation, authorised by a ventriloquised 'black man'. Acknowledging 'the blackfella' seems to mean accepting Cloudstreet as one's home (Quick), or accepting that the settler-colonial nation-state has refused accommodation (civil rights) to Aboriginal subjects, but there does not seem any room to imagine Aboriginal land rights beyond this framework – perhaps an understandable dimension of a text that appeared after the bicentennial of European arrival in 1988 but before the Mabo decision in 1992.[50] Later, when Sam is puzzled by the question of whether 'the black man' voted, Rose informs him that 'Blacks haven't got the vote'[51] – and they, indeed, would not gain it until the famous constitutional referendum of 1967.[52] In a perverse multicultural acknowledgement of the Indigenous idea of belonging that stipulates one should 'not break a place', the characters ironically undertake not only a colonisation of Indigenous land but also an appropriation of this very idea of belonging; Indigenous ideas of belonging are themselves stolen by settler-colonial logic as self-authorising. This tells us something about the logic of multiculturalism in settler-colonial space, for which the very toleration of Indigenous alterity ironically becomes a further means for dispossession; Indigenous difference is tolerated, even admired, but not to the point of acknowledging Indigenous presence with its robust claims to land rights.

It is naivety in relation to these tensions that troubles *Cloudstreet* in all its efforts to acknowledge Indigenous presence. Sam, the inheritor, stands for the central instance of this innocence in his inability to comprehend 'the blackfella's' plight. If Sam has inherited a history whose relation to dispossession he does not comprehend, then, the novel almost suggests, perhaps settler colonials not directly implicated in the dispossession of Indigenous people are similarly innocent: naivety becomes the alibi for an exculpation of Australia as a settler colony. Sam's naivety (for instance about the fact that 'Blacks haven't got the vote' in 1964), the novel seems quite problematically to suggest, is a synecdoche for the naive innocence of Australians generally.

As such, Cloudstreet haunts and is haunted, and what haunts *Cloudstreet* is what is classically constitutive of modern Australian engagements with indigeneity: the recognition of dispossession as exculpation from a more radical political addressing of, and to, settler-colonial history and Indigenous possession. In this way, perhaps, the novel's greatest success – addressing Indigenous presence as constitutive of settler-colonial habitation – is also the source of its most profound failure: the reproduction of an ideology of settler–colonial innocence through the apparent naivety of the settler–inheritor. No 'modern Australian classic' can be understood without reference to the paradigm of settler colonialism as constitutive of the nation-state it seeks to allegorise. This is particularly so in a novel that seeks to allegorise possession, dispossession, haunting and such themes. We may gain much given that Australians now inherit Winton's novel as a 'modern Australian classic'. But we also lose much in not recognising that the novel is nonetheless marked by the effacement of indigeneity that the very status of an 'Australian classic' entails.

Notes

1   T. Winton, *Cloudstreet*, Simon & Schuster, New York, 2002, p. 48.

2   J. Locke, *Two Treatises of Government*, ed. P. Laslett, Cambridge University Press, Cambridge, 2003 (first published 1689).

3   Indeed, though it is not my primary concern here, the recurrent theme at the centre of Winton's various families is one of masculinity, and its instability – most notably in *The Riders* (Picador, London, 1995), but also in *Dirt Music* (Scribner, New York, 2003), and, indeed, as early as such short stories as 'A Blow, a Kiss' (*Blood and Water: Stories*, Picador, London, 1993, pp. 12–18) – represents a related topos worthy of further critical reflection.

4   Winton, *Cloudstreet*, p. 37.

5   Ibid.

6   J. Derrida, *Spectres of Marx: The State of Debt, the Work of Mourning and the New International*, trans. P. Kamuf, Routledge, London, 1994, p. 45.

7   J. Derrida and B. Stiegler, *Echographies of Television*, Polity, Cambridge, 2002, pp. 25–6.

8   Ibid., p. 26.

9   D. Crouch, 'National hauntings: the architecture of Australian ghost stories',

JASAL Special Issue: Spectres, Screens, Shadows, Mirrors, 2007, p. 94.

10   Winton, *Cloudstreet*, p. 273.

11   Ibid., pp. 343–4.

12   In the Australian edition this is Part III.

13   Winton, *Cloudstreet*, pp. 35–7.

14   Ibid., p. 35.

15   Ibid., pp. 35–6.

16   Ibid., p. 36.

17   Ibid.

18   Ibid.

19   A. Haebich, *For Their Own Good: Aborigines and Government in the South West of Western Australia 1900–40*, University of Western Australia Publishing, Perth, 1992, p. 252.

20   Daisy Bates is mentioned in the text on one further occasion, when Lester Lamb refers to his wife Oriel's crusading local fame as though she believes she might be 'Daisy-flamin-Bates' (p. 230). That Oriel's fame in the community and busybody-ish philanthropy might be a misguided metonym of Australia's 'well-intentioned' (to cite the problematic phrase of stolen generations deniers) policies of Aboriginal assimilation suggests that this connection could represent the possible beginning point of a reading of one of the most baffling details of the text: if Fish Lamb can see the ghosts of the widow and the 'shadow girl', why can't he see the living presence of his own mother? That is, after his near-death experience in the novel's Part I, Fish's partial status in the world of the living seems to give him access to the constitutive hauntedness of Cloudstreet, and yet severs his connection with his ultimate bequeather: his mother. If Oriel is, in some sense, Daisy Bates, then Fish's inability to perceive her aligns him with a privileged relation to such hauntedness.

21   Bates held to this view until her death. See, for instance, her *The Passing of the Aborigines: A Lifetime Spent Among the Natives of Australia*, John Murray, London, 1944, as well as A. Haebich, *Broken Circles: Fragmenting Indigenous Families 1800–2000*, Fremantle Press, Fremantle, 2002, pp. 141–2. As I have written elsewhere, the motif of Indigenous death has remained a pervasive aspect of the representation of Indigenous Australians in Australian literature and film. See M. Griffiths, 'Biopolitical correspondences: settler nationalism, thanatopolitics, and the perils of hybridity', *Australian Literary Studies*, vol. 26, no. 2, June 2011, pp. 20–42.

22   Winton, *Cloudstreet*, p. 7.

23   S. L. Morgensen, 'The biopolitics of settler colonialism: right here, right now', *Settler Colonial Studies*, vol. 1, no. 1, 2011, p. 53.

24 W. Shakespeare, *Hamlet*, 3rd series, Arden Shakespeare, London, 2007, p. 140.

25 M. de Grazia, Hamlet *without Hamlet*, Cambridge University Press, Cambridge, 2007, pp. 1–22.

26 Of course, Europe is not extraneous to Australia. As Bruno Cornellier, a theorist of settler colonialism in Canada, has recently insisted, the European-ness of Europe often defines itself in relation to a colonial space that is consequently doubled: '[European] selfhood is all the more difficult to plot out and maintain as settler colonialism incessantly extends the geopolitical and metaphysical body that is Europe over territories that have been defined as Europe's otherness' (A. Cornellier, 'The "Indian thing": on representation and reality in the liberal settler colony', *Settler Colonial Studies*, vol. 3, no. 1, 2013, p. 57).

27 Western political economy and political theory more generally are supposed to be premised on the notion of social contract and not inheritance: on the legitimacy of the state as mechanism of war and not on the more property-oriented question of who owns what and by what legitimate right. This tradition of thinking about sovereignty, commonwealth and property that begins with Hobbes, runs through Locke and leaves its mark on the present in the distinct forms of property that define Australia's relationship with its (post)colonial status. Even native title, for instance, is premised on the notion of the Crown's radical title and ultimate sovereignty over land alienated by settler and Indigenous occupants (and this is so even after the overturning of terra nullius with the 1992 Mabo decision, given that the notion of radical title cedes to the Crown ultimate sovereignty over lands granted under native title).

28 Winton, *Cloudstreet*, p. 209.

29 Bates, *The Passing of the Aborigines*.

30 T. Winton, *The Riders*, Picador, London, 1995.

31 The word 'ghost' appears several times in *The Riders*, but never in relation to 'the riders' themselves. Rather, it is used as a simile to describe Jennifer and Billie – particularly after the latter is attacked by a dog in Greece. Spectrality, at least in this novel, then, is not necessarily connected to the signifier ghost. Luther Fox in *Dirt Music* similarly describes his reclusiveness and desire to disappear from the world as motivated by a sense of 'already [feeling] like a ghost' (p. 92).

32 Winton, *The Riders*, p. 79.

33 Winton, *Cloudstreet*, p. 32. Indeed, *Cloudstreet*'s ending arguably culminates in Fish's oddly triumphant suicide, as he returns to 'the water' that has so obsessed him, a full person 'whole and human' (p. 424), before (again arguably) drowning in the Swan River.

34 Ibid., p. 208.

35 Ibid., p. 368.

36 K. Gelder, K. and P. Salzman, *After the Celebration: Australian Fiction 1989–2007*, Melbourne University Press, Melbourne, 2009, p. 31.

37 N. O'Reilly, *Exploring Suburbia: The Suburbs in the Contemporary Australian Novel*, Teneo Press, Amherst, New York, 2012, p. 133.

38 Griffiths, 'Biopolitical correspondences'.

39 Winton, *Cloudstreet*, pp. 405–6.

40 'Original owner' is an appropriate, if ironic, rhetorical turn on my part, since 'original' or 'traditional' ownership often marks the precarious state of Indigenous ownership within the discourse of land rights and native title by which settler-colonial Australia recognises Indigenous ownership in the mode of a rearticulated settler sovereignty – what was called in the Mabo decision 'radical title'. This concept means that Indigenous land granted through native title can always be re-appropriated by the settler state (as was the case in the 2007 Northern Territory Emergency Response Act).

41 E.A. Povinelli, *The Cunning of Recognition: Indigenous Alterities and the Making of Australian Multiculturalism*, Duke University Press, Durham, North Carolina, 2002, p. 8.

42 Winton, *Cloudstreet*, p. 362.

43 On this topic, see K. Gelder and J. Jacobs, *Uncanny Australia: Sacredness and Identity in a Postcolonial Nation*, Melbourne University Press, Melbourne, 1998, pp. 23–42.

44 Winton, *Cloudstreet*, p. 1.

45 Ibid.

46 Crouch, 'National hauntings', p. 100.

47 Ibid.

48 Gelder and Salzman, *After the Celebration*, p. 31.

49 Winton, *Cloudstreet*, pp. 405–6.

50 This double bind nonetheless resonates in the present. Is this not, indeed, precisely the logic of the post-2008 practice of 'welcome to country', whereby acknowledging 'traditional owners' at public events functions precisely to negate the more radical claims to sovereignty and title that Indigenous agents might otherwise demand of the Australian nation-state?

51 Winton, *Cloudstreet*, p. 411.

52 Though while 1967 is functionally the date when Aboriginal people began to vote in Australia, as Marcia Langton has recently noted there is much misinterpretation of what the referendum did, in law, actually change (M. Langton, 'Reading the constitution out loud', *Meanjin* (blog), 2013, meanjin.com.au/articles/post/reading-the-constitution-out-loud).

Bibliography

Bates, D., *The Passing of the Aborigines: A Lifetime Spent Among the Natives of Australia*, John Murray, London, 1944.

Cornellier, B., 'The "Indian thing": on representation and reality in the liberal settler colony', *Settler Colonial Studies*, vol. 3, no. 1, 2013, pp. 49–64.

Crouch, D., 'National hauntings: the architecture of Australian ghost stories', *JASAL Special Issue: Spectres, Screens, Shadows, Mirrors*, 2007, pp. 94–105.

Derrida, J., *Spectres of Marx: The State of Debt, the Work of Mourning and the New International*, trans. P. Kamuf, Routledge, London, 1994.

—— and Stiegler, B., *Echographies of Television*, trans. J. Bajorek, Polity, Cambridge, 2002.

Gelder, K. and Jacobs J., *Uncanny Australia: Sacredness and Identity in a Postcolonial Nation*, Melbourne University Press, Melbourne, 1998.

Gelder, K. and Salzman, P., *After the Celebration: Australian Fiction 1989–2007*, Melbourne University Press, Melbourne, 2009.

de Grazia, M., Hamlet *Without Hamlet*, Cambridge University Press, Cambridge, 2007.

Griffiths, M., 'Biopolitical correspondences: settler nationalism, thanatopolitics, and the perils of hybridity', *Australian Literary Studies*, vol. 26, no. 2, 2011, pp. 20–42.

Haebich, A., *Broken Circles: Fragmenting Indigenous Families 1800–2000*, Fremantle Press, Fremantle, 2002.

—— *For Their Own Good: Aborigines and Government in the South West of Western Australia 1900–40*, University of Western Australia Publishing, Perth, 1992.

Langton, M., 'Reading the constitution out loud', *Meanjin* (blog), 2013, meanjin.com.au/articles/post/reading-the-constitution-out-loud.

Morgensen, S. L., 'The biopolitics of settler colonialism: right here, right now', *Settler Colonial Studies*, vol. 1, no. 1, 2011, pp. 52–76.

O'Reilly, N., *Exploring Suburbia: The Suburbs in the Contemporary Australian Novel*, Teneo Press, Amherst, New York, 2012.

Povinelli, E. A., *The Cunning of Recognition: Indigenous Alterities and the Making of Australian Multiculturalism*, Duke University Press, Durham, North Carolina, 2002.

Winton, T., *Dirt Music*, Scribner, New York, 2003.

—— *Cloudstreet*, Simon & Schuster, New York, 2002

—— *The Riders*, Picador, London, 1995.

—— *Blood and Water: Stories*, Picador, London, 1993.

4

'OVER THE CLIFF AND INTO THE WATER': LOVE, DEATH AND CONFESSION IN TIM WINTON'S FICTION

Hannah Schürholz

Up in the mud and the furrows of light, my Ida drowned. She felt the heat and the wind in her throat. Blood was her only voice. For perhaps a second she had hold of a thought, a memory.[1]

Tim Winton's female characters show a strong tendency towards self-threatening behaviour, transience and ferocity. This is evident in the violent deaths of Jewel in *An Open Swimmer*,[2] Maureen in *Shallows*,[3] Ida's murder in *In the Winter Dark* (see above), Tegwyn's self-harm in *That Eye, the Sky*,[4] Dolly's alcoholism in *Cloudstreet*,[5] Eva Sanderson's Hutchence-lookalike death in *Breath*[6] and, obviously, the ephemerality of mothers in *Dirt Music*.[7] Equally, Rose in *Cloudstreet* suffers from anorexia, while Georgie in *Dirt Music* shares Dolly's addiction and her depressed sister, Jude, ends up in hospital after a suicide attempt. In all these novels, female death and self-harm are constantly present, either as an explicit experience, a haunting memory or an inescapable consequence of the character's present life circumstances. Such motifs are reflected in Bruce Pike's narration in *Breath*: 'Death was everywhere – waiting, welling, undiminished. It would always be coming for me and for mine'.[8] Winton's narratives enact stories of

love and pain that can be effectively used for 're-stor(y)ing'[9] (dis)
empowered gender identities in Winton's fiction.

In this chapter the female body as text is considered as a
site of ambiguity manifested within the uneasy relationship
between control, re-inscription and resistance. Elizabeth Grosz[10]
highlights in her essay 'Feminist theory and the politics of art'
that the body and the text are still seen as crucial in cultural
discourses, re-alerting 'feminists to the investments power has in
the inscription of the body, with the human body as the terrain
and object of various struggles and points of resistance'.[11] Bodies
are not pre-given natural objects; they are the product of cultural
representations and inscriptions, which transform them into both
object and subject simultaneously.[12]

More specifically, the body can be perceived as a form of *lieu
de mémoire*,[13] to borrow Pierre Nora's term. It is a memory site or a
'traumascape'.[14] It provides mnemonic cues, exceeding the purely
personal by entering the domain of the collective and the cultural.[15] In Nora's influential study *Les Lieux de Mémoire*,[16] memory
is defined as an active and living phenomenon that is affective,
magical, selective and symbolic. It is subject to 'permanent
evolution, open to the dialectic of remembering and forgetting,
unconscious of its successive deformations, vulnerable to manipu-
lation and appropriation, susceptible to being long dormant and
periodically revived'.[17] *Lieux de mémoire* are over-determined in the
gap between memory and history, private and public, individual
and collective, which Nora compares metaphorically to shells on
the shore in times when the sea of living memory has receded.[18]

This chapter illuminates the interaction between self-harm
and death as self-conscious acts of emotional survival for both
men and women. The literal inscription or destruction of the
female body functions as a form of *lieu de mémoire* in Tim Winton's

work. It *speaks*. But this agency is a double-edged sword. It can be an objectification or an appropriation in disguise, affirming Kay Schaffer's point that women are both '*telos* and origin of man's desire and of his drive to represent it, at once object and sign of [his] culture and creativity'.[19] I argue that female transience in Winton's fiction functions as a signifier of knowledge that is controversially destructive for the woman. In contrast, the painful insecurities and problems of self-definition experienced by Winton's male characters are inscribed upon the bodies of their female counterparts. Here, death as a gendered sphere initiates a rite of passage for the male characters, allowing them to seek redemption through the telling of their story.

Pain and death of the maiden/mother

Death as a gendered metaphor in literature and the visual arts is a Western tradition. The portrayal of women as closely related to death and dying in canonical narratives has been a source of considerable critical interest.[20] Death is often mythologised as the Other, the constant representation of the unknown.[21] Life, on the other hand, is afforded an immediacy and practicality that, for Jean Baudrillard, transforms death into an evasive 'form in which the determinacy of the subject and of value is lost'.[22] In the context of the close alliance between femininity and death in prominent cultural representations, Elisabeth Bronfen remarks that the woman is a 'symptom of death's presence, precisely because she is the site where the repressed anxiety about death re-emerges in a displaced, disfigured form'.[23]

The academic discourse surrounding female death in contemporary literature, especially when it comes to death and dying as a gendered sphere, is small in comparison with the extensive scholarly attention paid to death and the female in nineteenth- to early twentieth-century literature. In the Australian postcolonial context, Allan Kellehear and Ian Anderson argue that the way death is represented in literature and the arts is revealing when it comes to existing dominant values and norms in the broader context of history, society and identity itself:

> There has been, and there continues to be, a masculin-
> ist, European tradition of death in Australia but it has
> dominated the Australian imagination at a cost. That
> cost can be seen in the way broader experiences of death
> are hidden away from popular view. The hidden nature
> of that broader cultural experience of death serves to
> remind us, yet again, that dominating images of death
> reflect dominating influences in life itself. For national
> history and identity, the politics of death reflect the
> politics of everyday life.[24]

Death is not hidden in Winton's work. It is a major theme he regularly explores. But what interests me is the consistency with which transience is practised as a transgressive act by female characters in Winton's narratives. Their bodies become the site where death and pain become visible, turning the woman into a medium that speaks with many voices but not necessarily her own. Female trauma becomes mediated, submerged or, as Bronfen has it, 'displaced'. The collision of anxiety and trauma causes stories to compete and unfold. In the process, the body turns into an allegory of survival. But whose survival?

To give but one example of bodily transgression through transience, consider the following passage from Winton's 1984 novel *Shallows*, in which Maureen Coupar dreams a haunting image of the female body:

> There…there is this little girl swimming like a fish –
> only there's no water and she's wriggling about in a
> patch of red dirt – and her ribs are all showing, she's got
> no clothes on, and you can tell she's hungry, she moves
> her mouth, it's all swollen and dry and the teeth are
> black. She wants food […] Then…then she bites herself
> and blood comes out like red dust […][25]

This bleak, grotesque and almost surreal expression of hunger
and self-mutilation is directly linked to the state of being mute,
of being unable to raise one's voice and communicate troubled
feeling. And yet the girl's body screams at us forcefully, articulat-
ing its power as a textual and metaphorical sign. The dream – in
conjunction with Maureen's question 'What's going to happen to
our Queenie? And me?'[26] – signifies an existential crisis, reflecting the perilous topography of Maureen's social, geographical and,
above all, emotional isolation in rural Western Australia. The
girl in the dream, carrying signs of death and decay on her body,
foreshadows Maureen's own death a few hours later, when she
falls off a cliff after experiencing the first moment of happiness
with her husband, Daniel Coupar, in thirty-four years.[27] The
personification of death through the image of the starving girl is
suggestive of the predicament facing most women in Winton's
fiction. They often feel displaced and alone, while the trauma of
fractured motherhood consistently underpins a destructive element attached to the female body. This incites a familiar Oedipal
struggle, laying the foundation for the male voices to emerge –
a point discussed later in this essay.

Maureen is only one of several women in Winton's work
aligned very closely with death and dying. Take *Dirt Music*, for
example. First, dying receives a face in the elderly woman Bess,

who suffers from bowel cancer and celebrates life (and death) with reckless abandon during one final road trip with her partner Horrie.[28] Second, there are a remarkable number of dead mothers in this novel. Debbie, Jim's wife and mother of his sons, dies prematurely of cancer. Mrs Fox is hit by a falling tree in front of Lu's eyes. Sally dies in the car accident that eradicates all of Lu's remaining family members. Jim's mother kills herself, and Mrs Jutland passes away as the result of a brain haemorrhage. Both Jim Buckridge and Luther Fox lose their mothers when they are young. In all of these stories, violence is a strong denominator of the deaths described, leaving the men in the stories in states of distress. 'Re-storying' and re-contextualising their ensuing crises, the male protagonists embark upon different journeys of recollection and confession, which precipitate a necessary redefinition of their position in the world to overcome their trauma. This process, however, is closely aligned with a constant 'othering' and stigmatisation of the women in the stories that seem to condition the ability of the men to speak but, at the same time, suffocate the same ability for the women.

Alleged suicide and accidental death: stories of confession I

The visualisation of violent death in Winton's work as dominantly linked to femininity often carries with it the echo of suicide, exemplifying stereotypes of mystification. Anne Sexton once remarked: 'When (to me) death takes you and puts you thru the wringer, it's a man, but when you kill yourself it's a woman'.[29] Winton's first novel, *An Open Swimmer*, reinforces the implication of suicide as the 'quiet', female death whose terrifying force is re-experienced through memories and dreams. Here, Jewel's body turns into a postmodern Ophelian symbolic, crudely staging the horrors of (self-)mutilation and desire on her dead skin:

Jerra hated. And he would not forgive – not even her – that grinning slit that cleaved open the skin of her throat which was cracked, black and green, with her seaweed clump of a head half-buried in the sand that the storm had heaved up. On the same beach.

'Didn't they know she would?' he called out to the darkness [...]

Green plastic peeled back to show her grins [...]

Jerra looked down at the naked legs and scarred, slack belly. A jade tinge to the blown fingers.[30]

This image of death evokes a traditional binary, displacing the woman from the corporeality of her decaying body while placing the male viewer (Jerra) on the side of life. The female corpse is a memory trail for Jerra: the 'non-visible [that] is given figure, visual presence'.[31] Jewel's body, apart from being a signifier of fractured maternity, becomes a decisive matrix of self-realisation for the male protagonist. Deeply troubled by his ambiguous feelings towards Jewel – theirs is a love–hate relationship – Jerra experiences lack and confusion, a periodically 'life-less' condition that, similar to Luther Fox in *Dirt Music*, forces him to come to terms with his past before he can move on. He learns to see himself as part of a systemic oppression that has driven Jewel to suicide.[32] The memory of Jewel's death pursues Jerra through his darkest dreams:

He went in darker and found something soft. It trembled, the skin almost tightening. He rolled it over, the legs fanning wide, and saw the open slit reflecting green on the backs of his hands [...] he was no different from

102

the others taking advantage, helping to destroy, helping her in the delusion.[33]

Confronted with Jewel's fate, revisiting her body in his dreams and memories, Jerra begins to understand society's gendered relations. As a result, he is able to distance himself from it and face his future, reopening himself to love.

With regard to prominent aspects of female displacement, Jewel's death mirrors Ida's in *In the Winter Dark*. Ida has been longing to get away from the place where she has never felt a sense of belonging. 'The Sink' is a place of imprisonment for her, which mirrors Maureen's predicament in *Shallows*: 'She was a stranger here, and they were impostors. There was just a hollowing wind and she was going'.[34] In complete opposition to her husband's strong sense of belonging to 'The Sink', Ida leaves Minchinbury House for the woods, where she meets the darkness. There she merges with the mysterious other that has become a threat to Maurice, Jacob and Ronnie. Consequently, Maurice shoots into the darkness to fight 'the other', thus claiming the life of his spouse.

The death of Ida functions as the trigger for the protagonist, Maurice Stubbs, to tell his story:

> Up in the mud and the furrows of light, my Ida drowned. She felt the heat and the wind in her throat. Blood was her only voice. For perhaps a second she had hold of a thought, a memory.[35]

Driven by guilt and regret, Maurice confesses his sins to the darkness, which has become a part of him, a quiet confidant that listens to his story, keeping it a secret. This darkness, however, is not an anonymous listener but rather is filled with the faces of the old woman at Minchinbury House and his love, Ida – two women who are interlinked with his own history, making him the lonely 'carrier of everyone's memories':

> So I'm the teller. But why don't I keep my mouth shut? Why? Because someone has to hear sooner or later. Because the bloody dreams don't go away […] I'm alone here on the farm, the carrier of everyone's memories. So when the dusk comes, in that gloaming time of confusion when you can't tell a tree-stump from a kangaroo, an owl-hoot from a question in the night, the dark begins to open up like the ear of God and I babble it all out, try to get it straight in my mind, and listen now and then for a sigh, a whisper, some hint of absolution and comfort on the way.[36]

Through the act of confession, he seeks the hope of absolution to put his past to rest. It creates a dialogue with apparitions that are both 'catalysts and substance of traumatic memory'.[37]

As Judith Herman argues, the survivor tells their story to reconstruct traumatic events and transform them, to integrate them into their life story. In order to do so successfully, and 'develop a full understanding of the trauma story, the survivor must examine the moral questions of guilt and responsibility'[38] while building up a belief system that adds sense to suffering. Maurice, for his part, accepts his guilt, understanding that he is unable to 'redeem himself'[39]:

> I have these dreams. Dead people, broken people bleed things into you, like there's some pressure point because

they can't get it out any more, can't get it told. It's as
though the things which need telling seep across to you
in your sleep.[40]

Paradoxically, the narrator's claim to speak for the dead – a
perceived punishment imposed upon him through his dreams –
eventually opens up a space for his own redemption, and
thus turns into a form of appropriation that uses the dead
female body – or rather its memory – to pave his own way to
possible recovery.

Referring to the controversial concept of a masculinity crisis,
Sally Robinson states that 'announcements of a crisis in white
masculinity, and a widely evidenced interest in wounded white
men, themselves perform the cultural work of *re*centering
white masculinity by *de*centering it'.[41] She indicates that men
need to claim a 'symbolic disenfranchisement, must compete with
various others for cultural authority bestowed upon the authentically disempowered, the visibly wounded',[42] in order to define
their position within existing identity politics. Representing the
male protagonist as victim, however, frequently re-establishes
hegemonic power relations instead of deconstructing them.[43] In
her study *The Privilege of Crisis*, Elahe Haschemi Yekani[44] indicates that the narrative representation of 'crises of masculinity' in
contemporary postcolonial fiction seems to have become a carefully designed mode of promoting and privileging 'hegemonic
masculinity': 'Accordingly, one could argue that there is no crisis
of masculinity but rather a continuing narrative production of
crisis tendencies with specific privileging effects'.[45]

Quite a few of Winton's characters fall into this category
of *re*centralising the 'man-in-crisis' through confessional storytelling. Another example of this tendency is demonstrated in

Shallows. Daniel Coupar voices his pain and generational guilt in a passionate letter to his granddaughter, Queenie, that she never receives. The ideal reader is his only listener:

> You have to inherit lots, Queenie, and I don't want you to. You're the last real Coupar. Funny how it ends up being a woman [...] Oh, there's lots've things I wish I'd never done. There's sins of inaction, too, you know.[46]

These confessions are the epitome of the wounded 'man-in-crisis' who, in the process of redefining himself and his position in society, seeks reconciliation with the world around him.[47] Confronted with the collapse of his own world view, Coupar realises his misgivings – especially in relation to his wife, Maureen: 'I have to tell you about her. I wasted her heart'.[48] This connects with the previous discussions of Jerra's and Maurice's stories, who equally refocus attention on their own states of crisis by recalling the dead, traumatising and traumatised bodies of their lovers.

In the light of the strong narrative position adopted by the protagonists, the question may be asked whether the stigmatisation of death as female can actually be seen as a form of possibility for the female characters that grants them some means of expression. Elisabeth Bronfen frequently points to the act of writing the self within the spheres of death and dying. She argues convincingly in *Over Her Dead Body* that '[d]ying is a move beyond communication yet also functions as these women's one effective communicative act, in a cultural or kinship situation otherwise disinclined towards feminine authorship'.[49] Such acts are defined by a considerable amount of self-reflexivity, as 'death is chosen and performed by the woman herself, in an act that makes her both object and subject of dying and of representation'.[50] The woman, therefore, constructs herself in an autobiographical fashion by 'undoing her body'.[51] But, too frequently, this merely allows fantasies of gender to re-emerge in the textual mythologisation and fetishisation of death and the female body.

The narrative focus in many of Winton's stories, predominantly *An Open Swimmer*, *Shallows*, *In the Winter Dark* and *Breath*, filters the perception of female death through the point of view of the male protagonist, creating a twofold cultural reclamation of the female body, in the signification of the event itself and in the memories of the male characters. For Bronfen, the female is thus literally positioned between self-inscription and an inscription of otherness.[52] And it is this form of controversial expression that is written into the images of Jewel's violent 'grinning slit', and the dying Ida who drowns in her own blood, feeling the wind and heat of freedom/death in her throat at the moment of her suffocation.

Out of *Breath*: stories of confession II

Allusions to female death through suffocation are plentiful in Winton's oeuvre, as illustrated in the 2008 novel *Breath*, in which the American anti-heroine Eva Sanderson introduces the fifteen-year-old narrator, Bruce Pike (Pikelet), to her dark obsession with erotic asphyxiation – an addiction that causes her death later in the novel. The encounter between Eva, her husband Sando and Pikelet induces a traumatic period of suffering in the young man from which he never recovers. But in the attempt to find relief, he, too, becomes a storyteller who confesses to the reader his own victimisation and involvement with (auto)erotic asphyxiation.

The story's dialectic between life and death is stressed in the sexual relationship between Eva and Pikelet – a binary depicting the destruction of innocence, the 'fall of (wo)man', the deviant and destructive nature of female sexuality, and the abuse of a teen-ager's naivety – of a boy who considers himself in love. Presented as a marginal figure, psychologically unstable and aggressive, Eva stands in complete contrast to her husband, with his happy-go-lucky attitude and New Age philosophy. In his own narcissistic way, Sando seduces Pikelet and his friend Loonie into entering the no-man's-land between life and death where fear, excitement and surrender take control of the body and accelerate the senses: 'It's like you come pouring back into yourself, said Sando one afternoon. Like you've exploded and all the pieces of you are reassembling themselves. You're new. Shimmering. Alive'.[53]

Both the act of breathing and the awareness of this act as the prime source of life are central to the actions of the characters. Gambling with the transience of their own existence, the char-acters feel empowered, reaching a sublime state of dominion that brings the illusion of 'not being ordinary', of achieving a 'state of grace'. Pikelet describes surfing as 'something graceful, as if dancing on water',[54] and Sando describes the thrill of surfing as being touched by the 'hand of God'.[55] Here, 'grace' implies a gift from God to man, and feeling 'alive' an escape from the numbing world of suppressed emotion.

Unlike her male counterparts, Eva cannot achieve the state of grace intermittently granted to Sando, Loonie and even Pikelet. She never feels alive. Her 'fall from grace' is eternalised in her ruined limbs and her desperate addiction to sexual asphyxiation – a suffocation exercise that constantly positions her between life and death. Daniel D. Cowell[56] describes one form of autoerotic asphyxiation as the outcome of the 'desire for control over the anxiety of life versus death: the closer the reenactor approximates yet cheats death, the greater the sexual excitement'.[57] Eva assigns control over her body and life to Pikelet, who is forced to offer both life-threatening and life-sustaining assistance.

Eva's sense of controlling and violating her own body is more complex than merely aspiring to an extraordinary ideal. Chantal Kwast-Greff observes that '[t]he female body is clearly the battlefield where a drama is enacted by an angry spirit'[58] – an observation that applies to Eva's (ab)use of her own and Pikelet's bodies. Eva's obsessive rehabilitation exercises, in which she seems to be completely overstraining herself, correlate with her asphyxiation practices during sex. Both acts go beyond the ambition to challenge the self and actually reach a status of desperate addiction, in which the distressing thoughts and memories are too painful to bear and need to be relieved by the actual or metaphorical scarring of the body through intoxication and violence.[59] Unlike Sando, whose body is also marked, albeit to serve his own self-expression in positive, life-affirming respects, Eva's body connotes a constant lack, a dooming negativity that foreshadows her death and eternally displaces her from her desired lifestyle of skiing adventurer. Although honest in her intentions, and thus arguably morally superior to her husband, Eva is still clearly presented as the perpetrator, whose destructive influence on Pikelet leaves fatal imprints on the boy's psyche.[60]

In relation to Eva, Roie Thomas highlights how death functions as a form of stimulant for a life not worth living.[61] Eva's drug-taking and asphyxiation practices are not simply attempts to regain power and control over somebody else, but also to escape the strangling effects of pain and loss of belief. Highly emotional disruptions in her life need to be muted in order for her to survive. Eva's erotic asphyxiation and strangulation reflect a restless, nomadic nature, driven by ambition, aspiration and mortal anxiety, all of which Eva herself describes as typically American attributes.[62] Eva is literally presented as the stereotype of a 'fallen' woman who is held partly accountable for Pikelet's downfall. This can lead to a misogynist reading of her character.[63]

Arguing that her role cannot be simply reduced to sinner or saviour, I regard Eva, and hence other women in Winton's fiction, as the personification of a strong desire for knowledge, ambition, progress and change. This is expressed through their sexuality and curtailed by their own downfall, which paradoxically leads them back to their own state of grace, previously denied, through death.[64] This is evident in Eva's 'suicide', its nature resembling a carefully planned act of tragic performance in the fashion of a celebrity – an act that publicly reveals the extent of her own troubles, imprinting itself onto the narrator's memory:

> Eva was found hanging naked from the back of a bathroom door in Portland, Oregon. A Salvadorean hotel employee discovered her with a belt around her neck. The deceased had been the sole occupant of her five-star room, the cause of death cardiac arrest as a result of asphyxiation.[65]

This is reminiscent of Jewel's death in *An Open Swimmer*, which appears equally staged in its gruesomeness, turning the beach into the performance space and the sea into a character itself. Jewel's return to the scene of the boating accident as the stage for her 'final performance' dramatically enacts her alienation and mental confusion. She is trapped between life and death, imagination and reality. The beach embodies this hybrid space, a mediating position between land-as-finite and ocean-as-infinite. As Alistair Rolls and Vanessa Alayrac argue, the beach functions not only as a 'bridge from self to alterity'[66] but also as an edge that leads the way into dreams, fantasy and evasion – a point well illustrated through Jewel's suicide.

Notwithstanding the inherent morbidity of what the sea washes up onto the shore, the body with the 'seaweed clump of a head'[67] evokes the curiosity of a show. This is the last 'Act' of Jewel's tragedy. A crowd of people gathers in the distance, watching intently while gulls circle the scene from above. Jewel's husband, Jim, cries into the coat of Jerra's father. Her death exposes order as a hypocritical farce, its unveiling serving as a source of catharsis for both bystanders and the reader. The novelty of the body discovered on the shore corresponds with the events of the ill-fated party on the boat and the '[h]urrahs and hoots on the beach'.[68] Affected by her near-death experience of the boating accident, Jewel chooses this beach for her final goodbye. She comes back to this environment to die and thus reconnects past and present; pain and desire; intoxication, fear and excitement in a final showdown, staging suicidal fantasies in the corporeal:

> Suicide, in turn, is both the literal attainment of alterity through death and the performance of an autobiographical desire. For suicide implies an authorship with one's own life, a form of writing the self and writing death that is ambivalently poised between self-construction and self-destruction; a confirmation that is also an annihilation of the self, and as such another kind of attempt to know the self as radically different and other from the consciously known self during life.[69]

As a result of the violence and ambiguity of their deaths, Eva and Jewel bear a heavy symbolic weight that is both corrupting and enlightening for the male protagonists. Both men are seduced by an older woman and heavily affected by her death.[70]

In *Breath*, the narrator's memory of the female body as traumatised and deeply traumatising not only opens up a space of reproach and self-investigation, but also morphs into a narrative platform for confession, similar to those granted to Maurice, Daniel and Jerra. Winton creates an outlet for the protagonist to declare his trauma as linked to a fragile and fractured idea of female sexuality and death. Kay Schaffer argues that a victim of traumatic experiences 'projects the trauma of the past forward through the story and assumes agency in the present through the necessary fiction of recovery'.[71] All the women in *Breath* (and in other Winton novels as well) become the signifier of lack for the male protagonist, who now tries to come to terms with his own tragedy by revisiting its origins. The act of telling and verbalising body memories can be contemplated as a final attempt to reconcile with the world and return fully to the self as a socially defined being.[72] Telling becomes 'a process of...demystifying'[73] memory, which also mirrors Foucault's concept[74] of sexuality and confession as part of a ritual, manifested in a discourse of power relations from below – a speech act that 'under some imperious compulsion, breaks the bonds of discretion or forgetfulness'.[75]

Pike therefore uses Eva's memory for the purpose of self-healing, empowerment, maturation and self-purification through confessional storytelling:

For a long and ruinous period of my later life I raged against Eva Sanderson, even as I grieved for her. In the spirit of the times I held her morally accountable for all my grown-up troubles.[76]

Despite remaining the angry, excessive and deeply unhappy femme fatale in Pike's memory, Eva is the agent of Pike's maturation, functioning as a source of knowledge that precipitates his realisation that '[p]eople are fools, not monsters'.[77] Hence she adopts an enlightened position that directs Pikelet's life from beyond the grave.

She also, however, symbolises the male malaise of not being able to read the woman and her private world. She therefore becomes the focus of an underlying criticism of the text that positions the woman as a continuous matrix of ambiguity and clues the man tries to interpret in a never-ending process: 'Nowadays, with the distance of the years, I wonder if I misread her. That disgust might have been reserved for herself'.[78] And it is her body that is presented as the material site of man's numerous attempts to gain access to the woman's world. At the same time, her body signifies an unbridgeable chasm between masculinity and femininity that Winton's novels lament. Pikelet epitomises this 'male malady' in his failure to read the women in his life adequately, and he is left stranded in speculations about their feelings, thoughts and intentions.[79] In his realisation that the women will not provide him with any answers to relieve his pain, Pikelet resorts to addressing his imagined audience in the act of using his 'breath' to tell his story – a privilege too frequently denied the female voices in Winton's novels.[80]

Conclusion

Giving prominence to the woman's body as a central trigger in the context of knowledge and realisation, Winton's texts create a controversial site of mnemonic and associative interactions between values and emotions, demonstrating the desire to understand and show sympathy for female suffering while only marginally acknowledging the male force behind it. Because he locates the narrative authority primarily with his male protagonists, the balance between male and female voices in his fiction vanishes, and calls into question the motives behind his ambivalent female portrayals. Filtered through the bias of confessional storytelling, the simultaneously destructive and constructive representation of the self-harming and suicidal women in Winton's works turns the body into a dialogical site of gender history and memory as a projection of male desire, and female 'dis-ease'. The representation of women's trauma is increasingly interspersed with the crisis and recentralisation of masculinity, which imprints itself onto female corporeality. The female body in its complexity becomes a central locale of traumatic memory and confession, an expression of a *lieu de mémoire* that not only reflects gender dissonances and power relations, but also evokes the close alliance between love and the desire for representation within a mnemonic struggle for emotional survival.

Notes

1   T. Winton, *In the Winter Dark*, Picador, London, 2003, p. 107.

2   T. Winton, *An Open Swimmer*, Picador, London, 2003.

3   T. Winton, *Shallows*, Penguin, Melbourne, 2009, p. 81.

4   T. Winton, *That Eye, the Sky*, Picador, London, 2003.

5   T. Winton, *Cloudstreet*, Simon & Schuster, New York, 2002.

6   T. Winton, *Breath*, Hamish Hamilton, Melbourne, 2008.

7   T. Winton, *Dirt Music*, Picador, Sydney, 2001.

8   Winton, *Breath*, pp. 201–2.

9   L. Hopkins, 'Sandy's story: re-storying the self', in D. L. Gustafson (ed.), *Unbecoming Mothers: The Social Production of Maternal Absence*, Haworth Clinical Practice Press, New York, 2005, pp. 103–16.

10 See also M. Foucault, *The History of Sexuality*, trans. R. Hurley, Vintage, New York, 1990.

11 E. Grosz, 'Feminist theory and the politics of art', in A. Jones (ed.), *The Feminism and Visual Culture Reader*, 2nd edn, Routledge, London and New York, 2010, p. 133.

12 E. Grosz, *Volatile Bodies: Toward a Corporeal Feminism*, Allen & Unwin, Sydney, 1994, p. 118.

13 P. Nora, 'Between memory and history: *les lieux de mémoire*', *Representations*, vol. 26, 1989, pp. 7–24.

14 M. Tumarkin, *Traumascapes*, Melbourne University Press, Melbourne, 2005.

15 Nora, 'Between memory and history', p. 8.

16 See also P. Nora, *Realms of Memory: Rethinking the French Past*, vol. 1, *Conflicts and Divisions*, trans. A. Goldhammer, Columbia University Press, New York, 1992, pp. 1–23.

17 Nora, 'Between memory and history', p. 8.

18 Ibid., p. 12.

19 K. Schaffer, *Women and the Bush: Forces of Desire in the Australian Cultural Tradition*, Cambridge University Press, Melbourne, 1988, p. 102.

20 See K. S. Guthke, *The Gender of Death: A Cultural History in Art and Literature*, Cambridge University Press, Cambridge, 1999; E. Bronfen, *Over Her Dead Body: Death, Femininity and the Aesthetic*, Manchester University Press, Manchester, 1992, pp. 395–434; and M. Worthington, 'Posthumous Posturing: the subversive power of death in contemporary women's fiction', *Studies in the Novel*, vol. 32, no. 2, 2000, pp. 243–63.

21 K. James, *Death, Gender and Sexuality in Contemporary Adolescent Literature*, Routledge, New York, 2009, p. 10.

22 J. Baudrillard, *Symbolic Exchange and Death*, trans. I. H. Grant, Sage, London, 2006, p. 5.

23 Bronfen, *Over Her Dead Body*, p. xi.

24 A. Kellehear and I. Anderson, 'Death in the country of Matilda', in K. Charmaz, G. Howarth and A. Kellehear (eds), *The Unknown Country: Death in Australia, Britain and the USA*, Macmillan, Basingstoke, 1997, p. 13.

25 Winton, *Shallows*, pp. 73–4.

26 Ibid., p. 74.

27 Ibid., pp. 81–2.

28 Winton, *Dirt Music*, pp. 243–52.

29 L. Sexton and L. Ames (eds), *Anne Sexton: A Self-Portrait in Letters*, Houghton Mifflin, Boston, Massachusetts, 2004, p. 231.

30 Winton, *An Open Swimmer*, p. 177.

31 Bronfen, *Over Her Dead Body*, p. 123.

32 M. McGirr, *Tim Winton: The Writer and His Work*, Macmillan, Melbourne, 1999, p. 24.

33 Winton, *An Open Swimmer*, p. 113.

34 Winton, *In the Winter Dark*, p. 99.

35 Ibid., p. 107.

36 Ibid., pp. 1–2.

37 L. Vickroy, *Trauma and Survival in Contemporary Fiction*, University of Virginia Press, Charlottesville, 2002, p. 208.

38 J. Herman, *Trauma and Recovery*, Basic Books, New York, 1997, p. 178.

39 Winton, *In the Winter Dark*, p. 110.

40 Ibid., p. 2.

41 S. Robinson, *Marked Men: White Masculinity in Crisis*, Columbia University Press, New York, 2000, p. 12.

42 Ibid.

43 Ibid., pp. 331–2.

44 In this context, see also H. Christian, *The Making of Anti-sexist Men*, Routledge, London, 1994, p. 7; R. W. Connell, *Gender and Power: Society, the Person, and Sexual Politics*, Stanford University Press, Stanford, California, 1987, pp. 183–90; C. Beasley, 'Rethinking hegemonic masculinity in a globalizing world', *Men and Masculinities*, vol. 11, no. 1, October 2008, pp. 86–103; M. Flood, 'Between men and masculinity: an assessment of the term "masculinity" in recent scholarship on men', in S. Pearce and V. Muller (eds), *Manning the Next Millennium: Studies in Masculinities*, Black Swan, Perth, 2002, pp. 203–14; and C. A. Vaccaro, 'Review of *Inclusive Masculinity: The Changing Nature of Masculinities* by Eric Anderson', *Gender & Society*, vol. 25, 2011, pp. 124–5.

45 E. H. Yekani, *The Privilege of Crisis: Narratives of Masculinities in Colonial and Postcolonial Literature, Photography and Film*, Campus Verlag, Frankfurt, 2011, p. 16.

46 Winton, *Shallows*, pp. 88–9.

47 In this context, see M. Kimmel, 'Men's responses to feminism at the turn of the century', *Gender & Society*, vol. 1, no. 3, September 1987, pp. 265–6; Yekani, *The Privilege of Crisis*, pp. 18–25; M. Dabakis, 'Douglas Tilden's *Mechanics Fountain*: labor and the "crisis of masculinity" in the 1890s', *American Quarterly*, vol. 47, no. 2, 1995, pp. 204–35; S. Robinson, *Marked Men: White Masculinity in Crisis*, Columbia University Press, New York, 2000; K. Bode, *Damaged Men / Desiring Women: Male Bodies in Contemporary Australian Women's Fiction*, VDM Verlag Dr. Müller, Saarbrücken, 2008;

E. Anderson, *Inclusive Masculinity: The Changing Nature of Masculinities*, Routledge, New York, 2009; and B. Arizti Martín, 'Fathercare in Tim Winton's fiction', *Hungarian Journal of English and American Studies*, vol. 12, nos 1–2, 2006, pp. 277–86.

48   Winton, *Shallows*, p. 89.

49   Bronfen, *Over Her Dead Body*, p. 141.

50   Ibid., pp. 141–2.

51   Ibid., p. 143.

52   Ibid.

53   Winton, *Breath*, p. 111.

54   Ibid., p. 24.

55   Ibid., p. 78.

56   See also S. Erman, 'Word games: raising and resolving the shortcomings in accident-insurance doctrine that autoerotic-asphyxiation cases reveal', *Michigan Law Review*, vol. 103, no. 8, August 2005, p. 2177.

57   D. Cowell, 'Autoerotic asphyxiation: secret pleasure – lethal outcome?', *Pediatrics*, vol. 124, no. 5, November 2009, p. 1322, pediatrics. aappublications.org/content/124/5/1319.full.

58   C. Kwast-Greff, 'Mad "mad" women: anger, madness, and suffering in recent white Australian fiction', in G. V. Davies, P. H. Marsden, B. Ledent and M. Delrez (eds), *Towards a Transcultural Future: Literature and Society in a 'Post'-colonial World*, Rodopi, Amsterdam, 2005, p. 164.

59   K. Skegg, 'Self-harm', *Lancet*, vol. 366, no. 9495, October 2005, p. 1473.

60   R. Thomas, 'Inspire, expire: masculinity, mortality and meaning in Tim Winton's *Breath*', *Journal of Men, Masculinities and Spirituality*, vol. 4, no. 2, June 2010, pp. 58–9.

61   Ibid., p. 59.

62   Winton, *Breath*, p. 136.

63   C. McGloin, 'Reviving Eva in Tim Winton's *Breath*', *Journal of Commonwealth Literature*, vol. 47, no. 1, 2012, pp. 113–14.

64   Thomas, 'Inspire, expire', pp. 59–60.

65   Winton, *Breath*, p. 206.

66   A. Rolls and V. Alayrac, 'Changing the tide and the tidings of change: Robert Drewe's *The Drowner*', *Southerly*, vol. 62, no. 3, Autumn 2002, p. 157.

67   Winton, *An Open Swimmer*, p. 176.

68   Ibid.

69   Bronfen, *Over Her Dead Body*, p. 142.

70   K. Goldsworthy/Pavlov's Cat, 'Biblical world legitimised: Australian feminist icon turns in grave', Still Life with Cat (blog), 18 June 2009, stilllifewithcat. blogspot.com.au/2009/06/biblical-world-view-legitimised.html.

71 K. Schaffer, 'What is haunting the nation? Responding to stolen generation testimony', in S. Williams, D. Lonergan, R. Hosking, L. Deane and N. Bierbaum (eds), *The Regenerative Spirit*, vol. 2, *(Un)settling, (Dis)location, (Post-)colonial, (Re)presentations – Australian Post-colonial Reflections*, Lythrum Press, Adelaide, 2004, pp. 129–30.

72 R. Culbertson, 'Embodied memory, transcendence, and telling: recounting trauma, re-establishing the self', *New Literary History*, vol. 6, no. 1, 1995, p. 179.

73 Ibid.

74 See also P. Ricoeur, 'Sorrows and the making of life-stories', *Philosophy Today*, vol. 47, no. 3, Fall 2003, p. 322.

75 Foucault, *The History of Sexuality*, p. 62.

76 Winton, *Breath*, p. 169.

77 Ibid., p. 171.

78 Ibid., p. 172.

79 As we see on pages 204 and 206 of *Breath*.

80 Allusions to the lack of voice materialise in the fact that many of Winton's female characters either die or are marked by suffocation: Jewel's throat is cut, Ida drowns in her own blood and Eva dies as a result of her asphyxiation.

Bibliography

Anderson, E., *Inclusive Masculinity: The Changing Nature of Masculinities*, Routledge, New York, 2009.

Arizti Martín, B., 'Fathercare in Tim Winton's fiction', *Hungarian Journal of English and American Studies*, vol. 12, nos 1–2, 2006, pp. 277–86.

Baudrillard, J., *Symbolic Exchange and Death*, Sage, London, 2006.

Beasley, C., 'Rethinking hegemonic masculinity in a globalizing world', *Men and Masculinities*, vol. 11, no. 1, October 2008, pp. 86–103.

Bode, K., *Damaged Men / Desiring Women: Male Bodies in Contemporary Australian Women's Fiction*, VDM Verlag Dr. Müller, Saarbrücken, 2008.

—— 'Aussie battler in crisis? Shifting constructions of white Australian masculinity and national identity', *ACRAWSA E-Journal*, vol. 2, no. 1, 2006, acrawsa.org.au/files/ejournalfiles/89KatherineBode.pdf.

Bronfen, E., *Over Her Dead Body: Death, Femininity and the Aesthetic*, Manchester University Press, Manchester, 1992.

Christian, H., *The Making of Anti-sexist Men*, Routledge, London, 1994.

Connell, R. W., *Gender and Power: Society, the Person, and Sexual Politics*, Stanford University Press, Stanford, California, 1987.

Cowell, D., 'Autoerotic asphyxiation: secret pleasure – lethal outcome?',

Pediatrics, vol. 124, no. 5, November 2009, pp. 1319–24, pediatrics.
aappublications.org/content/124/5/1319.full.

Culbertson, R., 'Embodied memory, transcendence, and telling: recounting
trauma, re-establishing the self', *New Literary History*, vol. 6, no. 1, 1995,
pp. 169–95.

Dabakis, M., 'Douglas Tilden's *Mechanics Fountain*: labor and the "crisis of
masculinity" in the 1890s', *American Quarterly*, vol. 47, no. 2, 1995,
pp. 204–35.

Doane, M. A., *Femmes Fatales: Feminism, Film, Theory, Psychoanalysis*, Routledge,
New York, 1991.

Erman, S., 'Word games: raising and resolving the shortcomings in accident-
insurance doctrine that autoerotic-asphyxiation cases reveal', *Michigan Law
Review*, vol. 103, no. 8, August 2005, pp. 2172–208.

Flood, M., 'Between men and masculinity: an assessment of the term
"masculinity" in recent scholarship on men', in S. Pearce and V. Muller (eds),
Manning the Next Millennium: Studies in Masculinities, Black Swan, Perth,
2002, pp. 203–14.

Foucault, M., *The History of Sexuality*, trans. R. Hurley, Vintage Books, New
York, 1990.

Goldsworthy, K., 'Biblical world legitimised: Australian feminist icon turns in
grave', Still Life with Cat (blog), 18 June 2009, stilllifewithcat.blogspot.
com.au/2009/06/biblical-world-view-legitimised.html.

Grosz, E., 'Feminist theory and the politics of art', in A. Jones (ed.), *The
Feminism and Visual Culture Reader*, Routledge, London and New York,
2010, pp. 128–38.

—— *Volatile Bodies: Toward a Corporeal Feminism*, Allen & Unwin, Sydney, 1994.

Guthke, K. S., *The Gender of Death: A Cultural History in Art and Literature*,
Cambridge University Press, Cambridge, 1999.

Herman, J., *Trauma and Recovery*, Basic Books, New York, 1997.

Hopkins, L., 'Sandy's story: re-storying the self', in D. L. Gustafson (ed.),
Unbecoming Mothers: The Social Production of Maternal Absence, Haworth
Clinical Practice Press, New York, 2005, pp. 101–16.

James, K., *Death, Gender and Sexuality in Contemporary Adolescent Literature*,
Routledge, New York, 2009.

Kellehear, A. and Anderson, I., 'Death in the country of Matilda', in
K. Charmaz, G. Howarth and A. Kellehear (eds), *The Unknown Country:
Death in Australia, Britain and the USA*, Palgrave Macmillan, Basingstoke,
1997, pp. 1–14.

Kimmel, M., 'Men's responses to feminism at the turn of the century,' *Gender
& Society*, vol. 1, no. 3, September 1987, pp. 265–6.

Kwast-Greff, C., 'Mad "mad" women: anger, madness, and suffering in recent white Australian fiction', in G.V. Davies, P. H. Marsden, B. Ledent and M. Delrez (eds), *Towards a Transcultural Future: Literature and Society in a 'Post'-colonial World*, Rodopi, Amsterdam, 2005, pp. 161–8.

McGirr, M., *Tim Winton: The Writer and His Work*, Macmillan, Melbourne, 1999.

McGloin, C., 'Reviving Eva in Tim Winton's *Breath*', *Journal of Commonwealth Literature*, vol. 47, no. 1, 2012, pp. 109–20.

Nora, P., *Realms of Memory: Rethinking the French Past*, vol. 1, *Conflicts and Divisions*, trans. A. Goldhammer, Columbia University Press, New York, 1992.

—— 'Between memory and history: *les lieux de mémoire*', *Representations*, vol. 26, Spring 1989, pp. 7–24.

Ricoeur, P., 'Sorrows and the making of life-stories', *Philosophy Today*, vol. 47, no. 3, Fall 2003, pp. 322–4.

Robinson, S., *Marked Men: White Masculinity in Crisis*, Columbia University Press, New York, 2000.

Rolls, A. and Alayrac, V., 'Changing the tide and the tidings of change: Robert Drewe's *The Drowner*', *Southerly*, vol. 62, no. 3, Autumn 2002, pp. 154–67.

Schaffer, K., 'What is haunting the nation?: responding to stolen generation testimony', in S. Williams, D. Lonergan, R. Hosking, L. Deane and N. Bierbaum (eds), *The Regenerative Spirit*, vol. 2, *(Un)settling, (Dis)location, (Post)colonial, (Re)presentations – Australian Post-colonial Reflections*, Lythrum Press, Adelaide, 2004, pp. 127–40.

—— *Women and the Bush: Forces of Desire in the Australian Cultural Tradition*, Cambridge University Press, Cambridge, 1988.

Sexton, L. and Ames, L. (eds), *Anne Sexton: A Self-Portrait in Letters*, Houghton Mifflin, Boston, Massachusetts, 2004.

Skegg, K., 'Self-harm', *Lancet*, vol. 366, no. 9495, October 2005, pp. 1471–81.

Thomas, R., 'Inspire, expire: masculinity, mortality and meaning in Tim Winton's *Breath*', *Journal of Men, Masculinities and Spirituality*, vol. 4, no. 2, June 2010, pp. 54–65.

Tumarkin, M., *Traumascapes*, Melbourne University Press, Melbourne, 2005.

Vaccaro, C. A., 'Review of *Inclusive Masculinity: The Changing Nature of Masculinities* by Eric Anderson', *Gender & Society*, vol. 25, 2011, pp. 124–5.

Vickroy, L., *Trauma and Survival in Contemporary Fiction*, University of Virginia Press, Charlottesville, 2002.

Winton, T., *Shallows*, Penguin, Melbourne, 2009.

—— *Breath*, Hamish Hamilton, Melbourne, 2008.

—— *An Open Swimmer*, Picador, London, 2003.

—— *In the Winter Dark*, Picador, London, 2003.

—— *That Eye, the Sky*, Picador, London, 2003.

—— *Cloudstreet*, Simon & Schuster, New York, 2002.

—— *Dirt Music*, Picador, Sydney, 2001.

—— *The Riders*, Picador, London, 1996.

Worthington, M., 'Posthumous posturing: the subversive power of death in contemporary women's fiction', *Studies in the Novel*, vol. 32, no. 2, Summer 2000, pp. 243–63.

Yekani, E. H., *The Privilege of Crisis: Narratives of Masculinities in Colonial and Postcolonial Literature, Photography and Film*, Campus Verlag, Frankfurt, 2011.

5

THE EDITING AND PUBLISHING OF TIM WINTON IN THE UNITED STATES

Per Henningsgaard

When writing about Tim Winton, it is de rigueur among academics to observe that relatively few scholarly articles or books have been published on the subject of Winton's work. For example, Robert Dixon writes, 'Winton…has had surprisingly few academic articles written about his books: Andrew Taylor's article in *Australian Literary Studies*[1] is a rare exception'.[2] Nathanael O'Reilly observes something similar in his review of Salhia Ben-Messahel's *Mind the Country: Tim Winton's Fiction*, touted on its back cover as 'the first book-length critical study'[3] of Winton:

> He is arguably the most popular Australian writer within Australia. Nevertheless, surprisingly little criticism has been published on Winton's work, especially when compared to Peter Carey and David Malouf, both of whom published their first novels not long before Winton.[4]

And while this observation may be losing its currency as more and more scholarly articles and books (not least the present volume) are published on the subject of Winton's work, it is still possible to claim that, simply by focusing on Winton, this chapter is swimming against the scholarly currents of Australian literary studies.

It is equally de rigueur among academics, when writing about the publication in America of books written by Australian authors, to observe that relatively few scholarly articles or books have been published on the subject. David Carter's research project 'America publishes Australia: Australian books and American publishers, 1890–2005',[5] which in 2006 received a three-year Australian Research Council grant, went some distance towards addressing this oversight. Nonetheless, Roger Osborne, a collaborator on Carter's research project, is quick to note,

> Due to the common perception that Australian publishing was a 'tale of three cities' with London dominating the smaller local markets of Sydney and Melbourne, most makers of Australian literature in the United States of America have escaped the attention of book historians.[6]

Therefore, by focusing on both Winton and the publication of his books in American editions, this chapter marks itself as exceptional – as in unusual or atypical. It follows that this chapter must necessarily content itself with providing an overview of its subject matter, thereby laying the groundwork for more specific inquiries into these topics by future researchers.

Drawing upon theories and methodologies associated with the field of textual criticism and scholarly editing, as well as those associated with the field of book history, this chapter examines the editing and publishing of Winton's books in the United States. All aspects of the publication process are surveyed, but this chapter devotes its greatest critical attention to the editorial process. In particular, it examines the sorts of editorial accommodations that occur while translating the work of a regional writer from the south-west corner of Western Australia for an American audience, which is to say the largest identifiable market segment in the English-language book-publishing industry.

Speaking of editorial accommodations – or, perhaps more precisely and judiciously, editorial variations between Australian and American editions of an Australian author's book – the following (rather lengthy) excerpt makes a singular contribution to this conversation:

> Relatively little attention has been paid to variant texts of Australian literary works and where that has occurred (in the work of the Scholarly Editions Centre and of individuals like the late Elizabeth Perkins) it has usually been for pre-twentieth and early twentieth-century literary works. There has been little awareness of textual variations in more contemporary literature; these are more common than is often supposed – for example, Christopher Koch has revised and rewritten parts of several of his earlier works, there are substantial differences between editions of Kate Grenville's *Lilian's Story* and between the American and British editions of [Katharine Susannah] Prichard's *Haxby's Circus*, and a chapter is missing from some editions of Carey's *Oscar and Lucinda*.[7]

So uncommon is the type of scholarly work described here, that the above excerpt from a chapter by Carol Hetherington is just about the only one of its kind – that is to say, the only analysis of 'variant texts of Australian literary works' published in the mid- to late twentieth century, much less the twenty-first century.

Indeed, even the chapter from which this excerpt comes does not *perform* this type of scholarly work; it merely *describes* it in a single paragraph. Paul Eggert's 'Case-study: Peter Carey's *True History of the Kelly Gang*' is another publication that has made a small contribution to this type of scholarly work. Eggert notes, for example,

> The moment UQP [University of Queensland Press] despatched its document files to [American publisher] Knopf for their separate typesetting, the novel's single line of textual descent split into two and it became inevitable that there would be many differences between the two editions.[8]

Eggert does not, however, document these differences for the purposes of analysis of 'variant texts of Australian literary works'; like Hetherington, he merely describes them in a cursory manner. Clearly, analysis of editorial variations between Australian and American editions of an Australian author's book, where that book happens to have been published in the mid- to late twentieth century, is almost completely unexplored territory – rarer by far than scholarly writing about Winton or writing about the publication in the United States of books written by Australian authors.

Nonetheless, closer examination of Hetherington's anecdotes in the excerpt above yields interesting insights. These anecdotes will later be shown to fail to account for a type of editorial variant that can be found in the Australian and American editions of Winton's books. Hetherington's first anecdote relates to Koch, who revised two of his novels following their original publication. Koch's *The Boys in the Island*,[9] first published in 1958, underwent two revisions by the author – in 1974[10] and 1987.[11] In the Author's Note that appears in the 1987 edition, Koch describes his revisions as 'considerable' and notes '[t]he shape of *The Boys in the Island* should now be finally clear; and this edition is the only one I wish to survive, or to be read'.[12] Koch makes a similar comment in his Author's Note to the 1982 edition of *Across the Sea Wall*,[13] a novel originally published in 1965.[14] Therefore, if we treat Hetherington's paragraph about 'variant texts of Australian literary works' as a sort of taxonomy of the types of editorial variation that exist between Australian and American editions of an Australian author's book, then the Koch example she provides is helpful to identify variations that are the result of changes made by the author.

Hetherington's second taxonomic category includes 'substantial differences between editions of Kate Grenville's *Lilian's Story* and between the American and British editions of Prichard's *Haxby's Circus*'. In these two cases, Hetherington is identifying substantial editorial changes that were made by the author at the behest of the publisher of an alternate (e.g. American) edition. In the case of Grenville's *Lilian's Story*,[15] the American edition[16] includes some minor textual changes as well as, more substantially, twelve extra pages that were the result of a suggestion made by Grenville's American editor.[17] The American edition of *Lilian's Story* has since become the standard form of the novel; the latest Australian edition[18] of *Lilian's Story*, for example, now carries the changes first introduced in the American edition. As for Prichard's *Haxby's Circus*, the novel was originally published in London in 1930 by Jonathan Cape.[19] When New York–based publisher W. W. Norton published the book in 1931 under the title *Fay's Circus*,[20] the title was not the only thing changed; the publisher also suggested a change designed to remedy a structural weakness, which resulted in Prichard writing 'twenty-seven and a half extra pages, one and a half chapters amounting to approximately 9,700 words'.[21] Following publication of the American edition, Prichard commented, 'I would rather use it myself than the English'.[22] Indeed, she even preferred the title of the American edition, *Fay's Circus*, to that of the English (and, subsequently, Australian) edition, *Haxby's Circus*.[23] Clearly, in Hetherington's taxonomy of the types of editorial variation that exist between Australian and American editions of an Australian author's book, both of these examples fit under the category of substantial editorial changes that were made by the author at the behest of the publisher of an alternate edition.

The third category in Hetherington's taxonomy consists of accidental changes introduced by the publisher. Eggert's discussion of Carey's *True History of the Kelly Gang*[24] fits in this category. Coincidentally, Hetherington also uses, as noted earlier, an example from Carey's oeuvre to illustrate her point: 'A chapter is missing from some editions of Carey's *Oscar and Lucinda*'. When a substantial change such as *Oscar and Lucinda*'s missing chapter[25] comes to the attention of either the author or the publisher, it is usually quickly remedied in the next printing. Many, more minor, changes of this sort go unnoticed, however, such as a missing comma or two words mistakenly inverted. Eggert describes how such differences occurred:

> Knopf faced a problem that dogs any such attempt to achieve identical texts of the same work. If a second publisher was to set from the 'same' files as the first, but in a different typesetting program, only word-processed 'document' files are usable. Given that UQP's Ventura typesetting file was not used by Knopf, the only way the text could have remained identical in the two editions would be if Knopf had kept a log of all UQP's changes,

Table 1: Publishers of Tim Winton's books as recorded on the title pages of the first Australian and US editions

Title	Genre	First Australian edition	First US edition
An Open Swimmer	novel	Allen & Unwin, 1982	n/a
Shallows	novel	Allen & Unwin, 1984	Atheneum, 1986
Scission	short stories	McPhee Gribble, 1985	n/a
That Eye, the Sky	novel	McPhee Gribble, 1986	Atheneum, 1987[a]
Minimum of Two	short stories	McPhee Gribble, 1987	Atheneum, 1988
In the Winter Dark	novel	McPhee Gribble, 1988	n/a
Jesse	children's book	McPhee Gribble, 1988	n/a
Lockie Leonard, Human Torpedo	children's book	McPhee Gribble, 1990	Little, Brown, 1991[b]
Cloudstreet	novel	McPhee Gribble, 1991	Graywolf Press, 1992
The Bugalugs Bum Thief	children's book	Puffin, 1991	n/a
Lockie Leonard, Scumbuster	children's book	Piper, 1993	Margaret K. McElderry Books, 1999[c]
Land's Edge[d]	memoir	Pan Macmillan, 1993	n/a
Local Colour: Travels in the Other Australia[e]	photo book	The Guidebook Company, 1994	Amphoto Art, 1998
The Riders	novel	Macmillan, 1994	Scribner, 1995
Lockie Leonard, Legend	children's book	Pan Macmillan, 1997	n/a
Blueback: A Fable for All Ages[f]	children's book	Macmillan, 1997	Scribner, 1997

Title	Genre	First Australian edition	First US edition
The Deep	children's book	Sandcastle Books, 1998	Tricycle Press, 2000[g]
Down to Earth: Australian Landscapes	photo book	Fremantle Arts Centre Press in association with Sandpiper Press, 1999	n/a
Dirt Music	novel	Picador, 2001	Scribner, 2002
The Turning	short stories	Picador, 2004	Scribner, 2005
Breath	novel	Hamish Hamilton, 2008	Farrar, Straus and Giroux, 2008
Smalltown	photo book	Hamish Hamilton, 2009	n/a
Eyrie	novel	Hamish Hamilton, 2013	Farrar, Straus and Giroux, 2014

[a] AustLit does not list this edition in its records.
[b] A note on the imprint (copyright) page of this edition specifies that it has been 'modified for American readers'. This piece of information is missing from the AustLit record for this title.
[c] A note on the imprint page of this edition specifies that it has been 'modified for American readers'.
[d] Subtitled *A Coastal Memoir* when Hamish Hamilton published a new Australian edition in 2010.
[e] Published in the United States as *Australian Colors: Images of the Outback*.
[f] Published in the United States as *Blueback: A Contemporary Fable*.
[g] A note on the imprint page of this edition specifies that it has been 'modified for American readers'.

and vice versa, and if both sides had incorporated them successfully.[26]

Clearly, there was a lot of potential for accidental changes to be introduced by the publisher when the book originally published in an Australian edition was later (or concurrently) published in an American edition, and, indeed, examples of variations belonging to this third category in Hetherington's taxonomy are quite common.

As noted above, by studying the editorial variations between Australian and American editions of Winton's books, one finds a type of variant unaccounted for in Hetherington's taxonomy. Before discussing this variant, however, it is important first to examine Winton's publishing history. Table 1 lists all of Winton's books and details the Australian and US publishers of these books as recorded on the title pages of the first Australian edition and first American edition.

Based only on the information provided in Table 1, it would seem that Winton frequently switched publishers. This was not the case, however, as is demonstrated in Table 2. This table lists all of Winton's books and details the companies that either owned at the time or would soon own the imprints/publishers responsible for publishing Winton's books in their first Australian edition and first American edition.

Table 2 clearly demonstrates that Winton's publishing history, at least as concerns the Australian editions of his books, proceeded through four distinct stages. In the first stage, Winton published his first two books – the novels *An Open Swimmer*[27] and *Shallows*[28] – with Allen & Unwin. Since publication by Allen & Unwin is one of the prizes associated with *The Australian*/Vogel's Literary Award for an unpublished manuscript – which Winton

Table 2: Companies that either owned at the time or would soon own the publishers/imprints responsible for publishing Winton's books in their first Australian and US editions

Title	Genre	First Australian edition	First US edition
An Open Swimmer	novel	Allen & Unwin, 1982	n/a
Shallows	novel	Allen & Unwin, 1984	Simon & Schuster, 1986
Scission	short stories	Penguin, 1985	n/a
That Eye, the Sky	novel	Penguin, 1986	Simon & Schuster, 1987
Minimum of Two	short stories	Penguin, 1987	Simon & Schuster, 1988
In the Winter Dark	novel	Penguin, 1988	n/a
Jesse	children's book	Penguin, 1988	n/a
Lockie Leonard, Human Torpedo	children's book	Penguin, 1990	Hachette, 1991
Cloudstreet	novel	Penguin, 1991	Graywolf Press, 1992
The Bugalugs Bum Thief	children's book	Penguin, 1991	n/a
Lockie Leonard, Scumbuster	children's book	Pan Macmillan, 1993	Simon & Schuster, 1999
Land's Edge	memoir	Pan Macmillan, 1993	n/a
Local Colour: Travels in the Other Australia	photo book	The Guidebook Company, 1994	Random House, 1998
The Riders	novel	Pan Macmillan, 1994	Simon & Schuster, 1995
Lockie Leonard, Legend	children's book	Pan Macmillan, 1997	n/a
Blueback: A Fable for All Ages	children's book	Pan Macmillan, 1997	Simon & Schuster, 1997
The Deep	children's book	Fremantle Arts Centre Press, 1998	Random House, 2000
Down to Earth: Australian Landscapes	photo book	Fremantle Arts Centre Press, 1999	n/a
Dirt Music	novel	Pan Macmillan, 2001	Simon & Schuster, 2002
The Turning	short stories	Pan Macmillan, 2004	Simon & Schuster, 2005
Breath	novel	Penguin, 2008	Macmillan, 2008
Smalltown	photo book	Penguin, 2009	n/a
Eyrie	novel	Penguin, 2013	Macmillan, 2014

won in 1981 for *An Open Swimmer* – the fact that Allen & Unwin published his first two books is hardly surprising.

Winton then changed publishers, however, starting with his collection of short stories *Scission*[29] in 1985. Hilary McPhee, co-founder of the McPhee Gribble publishing house, recalls Winton's reasons for changing publishers in the following excerpt from her memoir:

> We were pleased but not too surprised when literary agent Caroline Lurie rang one morning and asked if we'd like to talk about Tim Winton, the youngest-ever recipient of the Miles Franklin Award for his second novel, *Shallows*. What did surprise us was that Tim's initial publishers were willing to let him go. Apparently he'd wanted to publish a collection of stories next – and Allen & Unwin 'didn't want him to', Caroline Lurie said.[30]

So began the second stage in Winton's Australian publishing history. He remained with McPhee Gribble – which, at the time it published his first book, had already entered into a co-publishing agreement with Penguin – from 1985 through to the publication of *Cloudstreet*[31] in 1991. By 1989, however, McPhee Gribble had become an imprint of Penguin.[32]

Not long thereafter, in 1992,

> McPhee Gribble folded, [and] Hilary McPhee joined Pan Macmillan Australia as publishing director, bringing many of McPhee Gribble's authors with her – Drusilla Modjeska, Helen Garner, Tim Winton, Richard

Flanagan – and publishing them through Picador, Pan Macmillan's literary imprint.[33]

Ken Gelder and Paul Salzman, in their book *After the Celebration: Australian Fiction 1989–2007*, note that 'these authors all stayed with Picador/Pan Macmillan into the new millennium'.[34] This is the third – and by far the longest – stage in Winton's Australian publishing history: his first book connected with the Macmillan name was the children's book *Lockie Leonard, Scumbuster*[35] in 1993, while his final book with Macmillan was the collection of short stories *The Turning*[36] in 2004. It is certainly not uncommon for writers to follow publishers when they change publishing houses, so the shift from the second to third stages in Winton's Australian publishing history – like the shift from the first to second stages – is hardly surprising.

The fourth and final stage (to date, at least) in Winton's Australian publishing history has been with Penguin since it published his novel *Breath*[37] in 2008. Once again, the reason for Winton's change of publishers is quite a common one:

> [Winton] said the catalyst for his move was his previous publisher's departure from Pan Mac. [Jenny] Darling [Winton's literary agent] said she sent the manuscript to the major publishers. After sifting through the deals, Winton opted for Penguin.[38]

Presumably, the size of the advance (rumoured to be anywhere from a 'high six-figure amount' all the way up to 'about $1 million'[39]) offered by Penguin played a role in Winton's decision, though so, too, did the fact that 'Penguin keeps six of his earlier books, including the ever-popular *Cloudstreet*, in print'.[40] So the four stages in Winton's Australian publishing history have spanned only three companies: beginning with Allen & Unwin, then the Penguin family of imprints/publishers, followed by the Macmillan family, and finally back to Penguin.

The only books not accounted for in this overview are *Local Colour: Travels in the Other Australia*,[41] published by the Guidebook Company in 1994; *The Deep*,[42] published in 1998 under Fremantle Arts Centre Press's short-lived Sandcastle Books imprint (used for children's books); and *Down to Earth: Australian Landscapes*,[43] published by Fremantle Arts Centre Press in 1999. While these three books would seem to throw into chaos Winton's afore-mentioned four-stage Australian publishing history, it is possible to regard them as curious exceptions to an otherwise very stable journey. After all, none of the three books is in the genres upon which Winton's reputation as a writer has been built. *Down to Earth*, for example, is a photo book with photography by Richard Woldendorp and an accompanying essay by Winton titled 'Strange passion: a landscape memoir'.[44] Clive Newman of Fremantle Press (the publishing house formerly known as Fremantle Arts Centre Press) recalls how *Down to Earth* came about:

> The book was commissioned [by] photographer Richard Woldendorp, who showed the proposed content to Tim. Richard's environmental concerns matched those of Tim's, and he agreed to provide an essay for inclusion in the book.[45]

Newman gives a similar account of the gestation of *The Deep*, the children's picture book published by Fremantle Arts Centre Press:

> *The Deep* is another example of Tim's generosity in supporting the works of emerging artists whose talents he admires. We were offered the book as a package which included first time illustrator Karen Louise by Tim's then agent.[46]

In both cases, Winton was supporting the work of another artist rather than initiating a book himself. And while very little information is available about the publishing history of *Local Colour*, a photo book featuring photography and text by Bill Bachman with additional text provided by Winton, the fact that the publisher of its first edition is listed as the Guidebook Company in Hong Kong, suggests that its publication may have been financed by the author/photographer; that is to say, it may have been self-published. If this is true, then the Guidebook Company is simply the book's printer. Australian publishers regularly use offshore printers for illustrated books, as these printers offer significant cost savings where colour printing is involved. The suggestion that Winton collaborated on a self-published book is not completely far-fetched, as *Down to Earth* was published by Fremantle Arts Centre Press in association with Sandpiper Press, which is photographer Woldendorp's own publishing imprint. But even if *Local Colour* was not self-published, it seems likely that this is again a case of Winton supporting the work of another artist rather than initiating a book himself. The only other example in Winton's oeuvre that fits this characterisation is *Smalltown*,[47] a photo book featuring photography by Martin Mischkulnig with an accompanying essay by Winton, which was published by Hamish Hamilton in 2009. Clearly *Smalltown*, unlike the other books surveyed in this paragraph, fits Winton's aforementioned four-stage Australian publishing history. The fact that it is the most recent of the books surveyed in this paragraph, and that it fits this publishing history, is arguably a testament to the success of Winton's earlier experiments, which had to occur outside the parameters of his very stable publishing history in order to demonstrate his potential to succeed in new genres.

Of course, Winton had published several children's books before publishing *The Deep*, so it is not exactly an example of Winton having to demonstrate his potential to succeed in new genres. After all, *Jesse*,[48] *The Bugalugs Bum Thief*[49] and the *Lockie Leonard* series of books[50] had already earned him a proven track record as a children's book author. Nonetheless, before publishing *The Deep*, Winton had always initiated his children's book projects; first he wrote the manuscript and only later, if illustrations were required, was it matched with an artist. Involving an illustrator from the start tested, in effect, Winton's influence as a co-star rather than the leading man. The photo books on which Winton collaborated represented a similar test.

Moving now from the imprints/publishers responsible for publishing Winton's books in their first Australian edition to those who published Winton's books in their first American edition, Table 1 once again makes it seem that Winton frequently switched publishers. Table 2, unfortunately, does little to clarify the situation; nothing like the clear pattern of Winton's Australian publishing history emerges. Indeed, one of the few conclusions it is possible to draw from the evidence presented in Table 2 is that Simon & Schuster dominates the publishing history of Winton's books in their first American edition. This conclusion is not immediately apparent in Table 1, since Table 1 obscures the fact that Atheneum, Winton's original publisher in the United States, had merged with Scribner in 1978, several years before publishing Winton. Scribner is an imprint of Simon & Schuster, and while this particular acquisition did not occur until 1994, it is still convenient to list in Table 2 the books published by both Atheneum and Scribner (no matter their publication date) under the banner of Simon & Schuster. Doing so highlights what is really a small measure of consistency in an otherwise random publishing history. After all, when Winton was publishing the American edition of his books with Atheneum, Scribner and Simon & Schuster, there is a very good chance that he was dealing with some of the same people.

Another conclusion it is possible to draw from the evidence presented in Table 2 is that there is little to no connection between the imprints/publishers responsible for publishing Winton's books in their first Australian edition and those that published Winton's books in their first American edition. For example, Picador, which is owned by Macmillan, published *Dirt Music*[51] and *The Turning* in Australia, while Scribner, which is owned by Simon & Schuster, published these two books in the United States.[52] Macmillan and Simon & Schuster are two of what are known in the United States as the Big Six book publishers. The Big Six are the result of a 'phase of mergers and acquisitions in trade publishing, which began in the early 1980s and has continued to the present';[53] indeed, this group recently shrank to the Big Five, in light of the merger of Penguin and Random House. The Big Six/Five currently 'publish about two-thirds of books in the United States'.[54] The fact that there appears to be little or no connection between which Big Six/Five publisher published a book in Australia and that book's American publisher, accords with Louise Poland and Ivor Indyk's observations about the publication of American editions of books by Australian authors in the period from the mid-1970s to the late 1980s; Poland and Indyk observe 'the promising but limited role played by the multinational publisher...offering Australian titles through its US affiliate'.[55] It seems likely the multinational publishers Winton published with in Australia did not offer his books to their American affiliates, though it is possible they were offered and refused. It is also clear that, as Carter describes it,

> [F]ollowing the collapse of the Traditional Markets Agreement…the new rights regime created a separate Australasian publishing territory, so authors and agents could negotiate Australasian rights and *then* US or UK rights.[56]

McPhee, as well as many other Australian publishers, had argued throughout much of the 1980s for exactly this outcome, claiming 'that it was better for authors and the books to have separate contracts and, if necessary, separate publishers in the British, American and Australian markets'.[57] Winton's literary career and international reputation benefited enormously from these new contract terms, as evidenced by his publishing history.

Editorial variations in Winton's early work

Having discussed Winton's publishing history, it is time to return to the editorial variations between Australian and American editions of Winton's books. Thirteen of Winton's twenty-three books have been published in American editions (and a fourteenth, *Eyrie*, is due for publication in 2014). Of these thirteen, four are children's books (*Lockie Leonard, Human Torpedo*;[58] *Lockie Leonard, Scumbuster*;[59] *Blueback: A Fable for All Ages*,[60] which was published in the United States as *Blueback: A Contemporary Fable*;[61] and *The Deep*)[62] and one is a photo book (*Local Colour: Travels in the Other Australia*, which was published in the United States as *Australian Colors: Images of the Outback*).[63] Setting aside for the moment these five books, that leaves eight novels or short story collections that have been published in American editions; in the order of their publication, they are as follows: *Shallows*;[64] *That Eye, the Sky*;[65] *Minimum of Two*;[66] *Cloudstreet*;[67] *The Riders*;[68] *Dirt Music*; *The Turning*; and *Breath*.[69]

The American editions of the first five of these eight books share a similar editorial history and, thus, similar types of editorial variations. Specifically, the American publishers of these five books opted to print them from film taken of the Australian editions. In other words, the American editions of *Shallows*; *That Eye, the Sky*; *Minimum of Two*; *Cloudstreet* and *The Riders* are photographic reproductions of their respective Australian editions, with a few relatively minor variations. Consequently, by at least one definition, the American editions of these books are not new editions at all:

> An *edition*, first of all, is all the copies of a book printed at any time (or times) from substantially the same setting of type…As to the meaning of 'substantially the same setting of type', there are bound to be ambiguous cases, but we may take it as a simple rule of thumb that there is a new edition when more than half the type has been reset.[70]

In the case of the five aforementioned books, nowhere near half of the type was reset for the production of the American edition. Indeed, only the front matter of each of these books was reset, while the body of the book remains the same. In the case of *Shallows*, for example, this means the American edition has a reset half-title page, list of works by the same author, title page, dedication, epigraph, imprint page and contents page. Even though these pages of reset type are not enough to qualify the book as a 'new edition', according to the bibliographical definition of that term, common parlance suggests that it is acceptable to continue to refer to, for example, 'the American edition of *Shallows*'.

Indeed, it is important to discuss these books because their very existence has, to date, gone largely unremarked by scholars in the field. Deborah Jordan is perhaps the only scholar to mention the existence of books by Australian authors that were published overseas using the film from the Australian edition:

> The second way for UQP to sell into the North American market was by selling the rights after their Australian edition had been published. Again there were a number of printing options and UQP could sell the American publisher the film, or allow them to re-photograph the book itself for use in their manufacture of the books in the US.[71]

Since Winton has published five books that fit this description, and more than one publisher was involved, it would appear that this practice is (or was) fairly widespread.

Of course, a likely reason scholars have failed to note this practice is that they assume it means the American edition is unremarkable – that no changes were made to the text in the movement from an Australian edition to an American edition. This is not entirely true, however, as editorial variations crept into the reset front matter. *Shallows*, for example, uses a stanza from the John Dryden poem *Annus Mirabilis* as one of its two epigraphs. The chosen stanza appears in the first Australian edition as follows:

So close behind some promotory lie
The huge leviathans to attend their prey,
And give no chace, but shallow in the fry,
Which through their gaping jaws mistake the way.[72]

In the first American edition, however, two changes were made. Firstly, 'promotory' was changed to 'promontory',[73] which is a clear-cut case of correcting a spelling mistake that was made in the first Australian edition. Secondly, and more significantly, the word 'chace' (an archaic spelling of the more familiar 'chase') was changed to 'chance',[74] thus completely changing the meaning of the epigraph. This editorial difference might be dismissed as simply another example of the third type of variant in Hetherington's taxonomy: accidental changes introduced by the publisher. After all, where Dryden's poem *Annus Mirabilis* has appeared in critical editions of his poetry, the word in question is consistently represented as either 'chace'[75] or 'chase'.[76] Yet the opening pages of Herman Melville's *Moby-Dick; or, The Whale* feature exactly the same stanza from Dryden, and in some editions the word in question is printed 'chance'.[77] Since the characters in Winton's *Shallows* repeatedly reference Melville's novel, it is not hard to imagine that Winton first encountered this particular stanza of the Dryden poem through an edition of *Moby-Dick* that used the word 'chance'. Clearly, this is not a simple case of an accidental change introduced by the publisher. Ironically, however, both the first Australian edition and the first American edition feature the word 'shallow' in the third line of the stanza; everywhere else Dryden's poem appears, including in the opening pages of Melville's novel, this word is 'swallow'. Later editions of *Shallows*, in both Australia and the United States, correct this error[78] – if, indeed, it is an error (the coincidence of a novel titled

Shallows containing a typo that reads 'shallow' is too great to dismiss out of hand).

Another example of an editorial variation that crept into the reset front matter of one of the five early American editions involves a most prominent feature: the title of *That Eye, the Sky*. In the first Australian edition of *That Eye, the Sky*,[79] the title on the front cover, the title on the half-title page, and the title on the title page all appear in the same format:

THAT

EYE

THE SKY

Meanwhile, the title on the inside jacket flap and the imprint page appears as follows: 'That Eye, the Sky'. Of course, the inside jacket flap and the imprint page are much less obvious parts of the book than the front cover, the half-title page and the title page. It is therefore reasonable to assume that readers of the first Australian edition of this book understand the title as a sequence of four words with no punctuation. In the first American edition, by contrast, the comma appears everywhere, including the front cover, the half-title page and the title page:

THAT

EYE,

THE SKY

Clearly, this is no accidental change introduced by the publisher. The effects of this change on readers, while ultimately unknowable, are not insignificant.

A third and final example of an editorial variation that crept into the reset front matter of these five books involves the use of quotation marks. This example is once again taken from the front matter of *Shallows*. The book's second epigraph is a verse from a Bruce Cockburn song; in the Australian edition, this song is listed as 'Grim Travellers'[80] (with single quotation marks), while in the American edition it appears as "Grim Travellers"[81] (with double quotation marks).

What do these three examples – 'chace' versus 'chance'; 'THAT EYE THE SKY' versus 'THAT EYE, THE SKY'; and 'Grim Travellers' versus "Grim Travellers" – have in common? As alluded to earlier, in examining these variations one finds a type of variant unaccounted for in Hetherington's taxonomy. These variations are not the result of changes made by the author; they are not substantial editorial changes made by the author at the behest of the publisher of an alternate (e.g. American) edition; and, finally, they are not accidental changes introduced by the publisher. Rather, they are intentional changes introduced by the publisher that are meant to either remedy perceived errors (e.g. 'chace' versus 'chance') or failings (e.g. 'THAT EYE THE SKY' versus 'THAT EYE, THE SKY') in the first Australian edition, or translate a detail of the first Australian edition for an American audience (e.g. 'Grim Travellers' versus "Grim Travellers").

Of course, it is difficult to say with absolute certainty that any given change is the publisher's doing rather than the author's, as decades of scholarly editors and textual critics will attest. As G. Thomas Tanselle has observed of the scholarly editor's role, they 'must distinguish authorial alterations from alterations made by someone else and must decide what constitutes "authorial intention" at such times'.[82] Tanselle further observes,

> What the editor must attempt to assess is whether the author genuinely preferred the changes made by the publisher's reader or whether he merely acquiesced in them...It is possible for someone other than the 'author' to make alterations which are identical with the intention of the 'author', when the relationship partakes of the spirit of collaboration.[83]

In this excerpt, Tanselle suggests that scholarly editors consider only those changes made by the author, or on which the author collaborated, while all other types of changes (such as changes made by an editor or publisher without any authorial input) can be disregarded. Tanselle's opinions are, of course, far from the last word on this subject. For example, Jerome J. McGann later advocated for 'a socialized concept of authorship and textual authority',[84] which rejects the 'hypnotic fascination with the isolated author'[85] who possesses a single, clear line of authorial intention. McGann and other textual critics of his ilk are responsible for throwing open the discipline's doors to the idea of 'texts as social products'.[86] In doing so, they called attention to the deceivingly simplistic notion that 'authors do not generally act alone to bring their works to the public'.[87] Consequently, textual critics for the last two or three decades have increasingly focused on 'the nonauthorial contributions to textual constitution',[88] such as the contributions made by editors and publishers.

Editorial variations in Winton's later work

In the case of Winton's books, where editorial variations between the Australian and American editions are apparent, it is possible to say with reasonable confidence that these variations are the result of the publisher's actions, with little or no input from

Winton himself. After all, the variations that exist in the first American editions are reproduced in later American editions but never in later Australian editions. If Winton had suggested any of these changes, it seems likely he would have suggested that his Australian publisher make some of the same changes when reprinting or publishing new editions. Just because they are not Winton's changes does not, however, allow for their dismissal; as Hans Walter Gabler writes, '[t]he object of scholarly and critical analysis and study...is not the final product of the writer's art alone, but beyond this, the totality of the Work in Progress'.[89] The American edition of each of Winton's books is part of 'the totality of the Work in Progress' for that book, and as such is deserving of 'scholarly and critical analysis and study'.

The particular type of editorial variant identified in *Shallows*; *That Eye, the Sky*; *Minimum of Two*; *Cloudstreet* and *The Riders* can also be found in Winton's three other novels or short story collections that have been published in American editions: *Dirt Music*, *The Turning* and *Breath*. After *The Riders*[90] was shortlisted for the 1995 Booker Prize, however, Winton's American publishers started resetting the type in the American editions of his books. This decision by Scribner (and later by Farrar, Straus and Giroux) was likely driven by a desire to more clearly identify Winton as a Scribner (or Farrar, Straus and Giroux) author, and thus benefit from the accumulation of cultural capital that comes with publishing a prize-winning author.[91] Of course, resetting the type in a book also requires a greater financial investment on the part of the publisher, which has to pay a designer, a typesetter and a proofreader for the labour involved. Clearly, Winton's American publishers believed this investment could be justified after *The Riders* was shortlisted for the Booker Prize.

Because Winton's American publishers reset the type in the

American editions of *Dirt Music*, *The Turning* and *Breath*, there are more editorial variations between these editions and their respective Australian editions than for the other five books. It is interesting to note, however, that Winton's American publishers have left unchanged almost all of the things one might expect an American publisher to change during the process of resetting type. For example, Winton's American publishers retained the British/Australian spellings in all three novels. Also, the poem quoted in the epigraph to *The Turning*[92] has single quotation marks around its title, which is contrary to the American standard of using double quotation marks.

Another example of Winton's American publishers leaving unchanged something one might expect an American publisher to change during the process of resetting type is the use of Australian slang. The frequency of Winton's use of Australian slang is reflected in the reviews of the American editions of his books in the American print media. For example, the *New York Times* review of the Atheneum edition of *That Eye, the Sky* begins,

> If you don't know Australian slang you might stop reading this novel after coming upon words like 'ute' (pickup truck or van), 'crook' (sick or broken), 'bowser' (gasoline pump), 'plonk' (red wine) and 'dag' (sloppy or slovenly person).[93]

A review in the *New York Times Book Review* of the Graywolf Press edition of *Cloudstreet* also mentions Australian slang in its opening paragraph: 'It offers the most wonderful linguistic delicacies, words such as "chiack" (tease) and "larrikin" (hooligan)'.[94] And while both of these examples come from books the American publishers chose not to reset, the same could be said for Winton's more recent books, since his American publishers did not change any of the Australian slang during the process of resetting type.

Instead, the American publishers of *Dirt Music*, *The Turning* and *Breath* made a different sort of intentional change designed to remedy perceived errors or failings in the first Australian edition. For example, where the Australian edition of *The Turning* reads, '[h]e was very short with a rodent's big eyes and narrow teeth',[95] in the American edition this was changed to '[h]e was very short, with a rodent's big eyes and narrow teeth'.[96] As mentioned earlier, if Winton had suggested any of these changes, it seems likely he would have suggested to his Australian publisher that they make some of the same changes when reprinting, or in a new edition. Thus, because the variations that exist in the first American editions are reproduced in later American, but never later Australian editions, it is possible to say with reasonable confidence that the addition of the comma noted above is the result of a change made by the publisher rather than the author. It is also clear that this is not an accidental change introduced by the publisher, because this sort of thing is repeated throughout the American edition of the book. Just a few pages after this sentence, for example, the Australian edition of *The Turning* reads, '[s]he's tall and not very beautiful with long, shiny brown hair and big knees';[97] in the American edition this was changed to '[s]he's tall and not very beautiful, with long, shiny brown hair and big knees'.[98]

Similar editorial variations can be found in *Breath*. The Australian edition of *Breath* reads, for example,

> [T]he only approach was to bash out across the bush track from the Point to the cliffs, and crab your way down the rock-face until you got within jumping range.[99]

In the American edition, this was changed to

> [T]he only approach was to bash out across the bush track
> from the Point to the cliffs and crab your way down the
> rock-face until you got within jumping range.[100]

Yet again, it is clear that the omission of this comma is not an accidental change introduced by the publisher, because this sort of thing is repeated throughout the American edition. It would seem that American publishers perceive errors or failings in comma usage in books originally published by Australian publishers.

It may be tempting to dismiss these editorial variations as inconsequential – after all, it is just a few commas. Even among textual critics and scholarly editors there is a tendency to dismiss such variations, as exemplified in the following excerpt from W. W. Greg's classic essay 'The rationale of copy-text':

> We need to draw a distinction between the significant,
> or as I shall call them 'substantive', readings of the text,
> those namely that affect the author's meaning or the
> essence of his expression, and others, such in general
> as spelling, punctuation, word-division, and the like,
> affecting mainly its formal presentation, which may be
> regarded as the accidents, or as I shall call them 'acciden-
> tals', of the text.[101]

By labelling comma placement and usage as 'accidentals', Greg is clearly dismissive of the (potential) meaningfulness of these editorial variations. Of even greater concern is the fact that the terms 'substantives' and 'accidentals' have been widely accepted, and are still regularly employed by textual critics and scholarly editors more than sixty years after Greg first coined them; indeed, they are a go-to concept for scholarly editors responsible for producing so-called 'critical editions'. Some more recent textual critics and scholarly editors, however, remind us why each comma is important.

According to eminent textual critic Tanselle, in his 2001 assessment of the state of textual criticism as a scholarly field, '[d]uring the last part of the twentieth century...a focus on texts as social products came to characterize the bulk of the discussion of textual theory, if not editions themselves'.[102] The editions to which Tanselle refers are, of course, the 'critical editions' produced by scholarly editors who are reliant on the concepts of 'substantives' and 'accidentals'. The critical and theoretical consensus within the scholarly field of textual criticism, however, has moved away from these concepts. In their place, textual critics have begun to focus on 'the forms of texts that emerged from the social process leading to public distribution, forms that were therefore accessible to readers'.[103] Clearly, then, in the case of Winton's books, since the 'forms that were...accessible to readers' differed in, for example, comma placement and usage, this difference is significant in the eyes and minds of some more recent textual critics and scholarly editors. Furthermore, it is not hard to believe that it also matters to readers; while they may not notice the subtle difference in rhythm, tone and style created by adding or deleting a single comma, readers generally assume the book they are reading is identical to the book read by their friend or relative, even if that person is on the other side of the world, as long as the two copies share an author and title.

Editorial variations in Winton's books for children

One does not have to work nearly so hard to make a case for the relevance of editorial variations when discussing Winton's children's books that appeared in American editions. In stark contrast to his eight novels and collections of short stories that have been published in American editions, Winton's four children's books contain abundant examples of editorial variations designed not merely to remedy perceived errors or failings in the first Australian edition (though there is plenty of that, as well), but to translate a detail of the first Australian edition for an American audience. Still, these appear to be intentional changes introduced by the publisher as opposed to the author, and thus reside outside Hetherington's taxonomy of editorial variations. There is insufficient space in this chapter to detail all of these variations, but they include, for example, changing Lockie Leonard's age so that it is in line with when most Americans begin high school,[104] specifying 'surfboard'[105] where Winton simply wrote 'board'[106] and changing 'chooks'[107] to 'chickens'.[108]

It is possible to assert with almost complete certainty that it was the editor or publisher, rather than the author, who made these changes, because the Americanisation of some of the Australian slang or cultural references is so misguided that it is highly unlikely an Australian introduced the change. A single example of this phenomenon will have to suffice: In *Lockie Leonard, Human Torpedo*, the sentence 'Lockie's little brother looked at him, pegging off his nose with his fingers'[109] was changed in the American edition to 'Lockie's little brother looked at him, thumbing his nose with his fingers'.[110] If any Australian – or, for that matter, Winton himself – had been responsible for changing this sentence for the American edition, they would have understood that 'pegging off his nose' refers to squeezing his nose in the manner of a clothes peg. But Americans don't call them 'clothes pegs' – they call them 'clothespins' – so 'pegging off his nose' means nothing to an American audience. Indeed, the American editor or publisher who changed this phrase to 'thumbing his nose' clearly had no idea that someone 'pegging off his nose' involves a motion employing both thumb and forefinger. Accordingly, it is reasonable to conclude that the author is not responsible for this editorial variation.

This and similar editorial variations led the publishers of the American editions of three of Winton's children's books (*Lockie Leonard, Human Torpedo*; *Lockie Leonard, Scumbuster* and *The Deep*) to note on these books' imprint pages that they had been 'modified for American readers'. But even this was not enough to satisfy some critics. The *Publishers Weekly* review of the American edition of *Lockie Leonard, Human Torpedo*, for example, mentions Winton's 'use of alien, sometimes challenging Australian slang'.[111] And while this same reviewer goes on to claim that Winton's use of slang will 'charm young readers', it is hard not to feel that this is a backhanded compliment.[112]

Conclusion

In this chapter's broad overview of the sorts of editorial accommodations that occurred while translating Winton's work for an American audience, the most significant insight involves intentional changes introduced by the publisher that are meant to either remedy perceived errors or failings in the first Australian edition, or translate a detail of the first Australian edition for an American audience. This may not seem like much until one considers that there has been a 'surge of references in Australian literary studies over the last few years to the transnational dimensions of the national literature'.[113] Nonetheless, it is an undeniable fact that literary critics in Australia premise their critical interpretations of books by Australian authors almost exclusively on the Australian editions of these books. Even those Australian literary critics who are most interested in exploring 'the transnational dimensions of the national literature' use Australian editions to produce their critical interpretations. Yet it is an equally undeniable fact that 'literary works and their interpretation depend, to a great extent, upon which text or combination of texts one reads'.[114]

Surely, if these same Australian literary critics read the American editions of books by Australian authors, the editorial variations introduced by the publishers of these American editions would alter the Australian literary critic's interpretation of the book. This point becomes especially acute when it is acknowledged that Winton's latest book with an American edition, *Breath*, has sold more than 14,000 copies in the United States since its publication in 2008.[115] *The Turning*'s American edition, published in 2005, has sold more than 5,000 copies in the United States. Meanwhile, the American edition of *Dirt Music*, published in 2002, has sold more than 21,000 copies in the United States.[116] Clearly, as Australian scholars work to develop 'a transnational practice of Australian literary criticism',[117] the editorial variations between American and Australian editions of books by Australian authors are an important factor to consider.

Notes

1   A. Taylor, 'What can be read, and what can only be seen in Tim Winton's fiction', *Australian Literary Studies*, vol. 17, no. 4, 1996, pp. 323–31.

2   R. Dixon, 'Tim Winton, *Cloudstreet* and the field of Australian literature', *Westerly*, no. 50, 2005, p. 249.

3   S. Ben-Messahel, *Mind the Country: Tim Winton's Fiction*, University of Western Australia Press, Perth, 2006.

4   N. O'Reilly, 'Review of *Mind the Country: Tim Winton's Fiction* by Salhia Ben-Messahel', *Australian Literary Studies*, vol. 23, no. 3, 2008, p. 360.

5   'Professor David Carter', ARC Cultural Research Network, University of Queensland, 2008, www.uq.edu.au/crn/participants/carter.html.

6   R. Osborne, 'Australian literature in a world of books: a transnational history of Kylie Tennant's *The Battlers*', in K. Bode and R. Dixon (eds), *Resourceful Reading: The New Empiricism, eResearch, and Australian Literary Culture*, Sydney University Press, Sydney, 2009, p. 105.

7   C. Hetherington, 'Old tricks for new dogs: resurrecting bibliography and literary history', in Bode and Dixon (eds), *Resourceful Reading*, p. 80.

8   P. Eggert, 'Case-study: Peter Carey's *True History of the Kelly Gang*', in C. Munro and R. Sheahan-Bright (eds), *Paper Empires: A History of the Book in Australia, 1946–2005*, University of Queensland Press, Brisbane, 2006, p. 197.

9   C. Koch, *The Boys in the Island*, Hamish Hamilton, London, 1958.

10   C. Koch, *The Boys in the Island*, Angus & Robertson, Sydney, 1974.

11   C. Koch, *The Boys in the Island*, Sirius Books, Sydney, 1987.

12   Ibid., p. xv.

13   C. Koch, *Across the Sea Wall*, Sirius Books, Sydney, 1982.

14   C. Koch, *Across the Sea Wall*, Heinemann, London, 1965.

15   K. Grenville, *Lilian's Story*, Allen & Unwin, Sydney, 1985.

16   K. Grenville, *Lilian's Story*, Viking, New York, 1986.

17   AustLit work record, *Lilian's Story*, AustLit, www.austlit.edu.au/austlit/page/C179649, accessed 18 September 2013.

18   K. Grenville, *Lilian's Story*, Allen & Unwin, Sydney, 1997.

19   K. S. Prichard, *Haxby's Circus*, Jonathan Cape, London, 1930.

20   K. S. Prichard, *Fay's Circus*, W. W. Norton, New York, 1931.

21   C. Hetherington, 'Authors, editors, publishers: Katharine Susannah Prichard and W. W. Norton', *Australian Literary Studies*, vol. 22, no. 4, 2006, p. 424.

22   K. S. Prichard, 'Letter to Norton', 4 June 1931, Prichard papers, National Library of Australia, NLA MSS 6201, Series 10, Folder 9.

23   Hetherington, 'Authors, editors, publishers', p. 418.

24   P. Carey, *True History of the Kelly Gang*, University of Queensland Press, Brisbane, 2000; P. Carey, *True History of the Kelly Gang*, Knopf, New York, 2000.

25   The chapter in question is missing from some of the earliest editions of the novel, including the first Australian edition (P. Carey, *Oscar and Lucinda*, University of Queensland Press, Brisbane, 1988) but is included in the first American edition (P. Carey, *Oscar and Lucinda*, Harper and Row, New York, 1988).

26   Eggert, 'Case-study', p. 197.

27   T. Winton, *An Open Swimmer*, Allen & Unwin, Sydney, 1982.

28   T. Winton, *Shallows*, Allen & Unwin, Sydney, 1984.

29   T. Winton, *Scission*, McPhee Gribble, Melbourne, 1985.

30   H. McPhee, *Other People's Words: The Rise and Fall of an Accidental Publisher*, Picador, London, 2003, pp. 233–4.

31   T. Winton, *Cloudstreet*, McPhee Gribble, Melbourne, 1991.

32   K. Gelder and P. Salzman, *After the Celebration: Australian Fiction 1989–2007*, Melbourne University Press, Melbourne, 2009, p. 1.

33   Ibid., p. 2.

34   Ibid.

35   T. Winton, *Lockie Leonard, Scumbuster*, Piper, Sydney, 1993.

36   T. Winton, *The Turning*, Picador, Sydney, 2004.

37   T. Winton, *Breath*, Hamish Hamilton, Melbourne, 2008.

38   J. Steger, 'With a deep *Breath*, Winton looks and leaps', *Age*, 25 April 2008, www.theage.com.au/articles/2008/04/24/1208743153682. html?s_cid=rss_.

39   Ibid.

40   Ibid.

41   B. Bachman, *Local Colour: Travels in the Other Australia*, The Guidebook Company, Hong Kong, 1994.

42   T. Winton, *The Deep*, Sandcastle Books, Fremantle, 1998.

43   R. Woldendorp, *Down to Earth: Australian Landscapes*, Fremantle Arts Centre Press in association with Sandpiper Press, Fremantle, 1999.

44   T. Winton, 'Strange passion: a landscape memoir', in Woldendorp, *Down to Earth*, pp. ix–xxxii.

45   C. Newman, personal correspondence, 13 September 2013.

46   Ibid.

47   M. Mischkulnig and T. Winton, *Smalltown*, Hamish Hamilton, Melbourne, 2009.

48   T. Winton, *Jesse*, McPhee Gribble, Melbourne, 1988.

49   T. Winton, *The Bugalugs Bum Thief*, Puffin, Melbourne, 1991.

50   T. Winton, *Lockie Leonard, Human Torpedo*, McPhee Gribble, Melbourne, 1990; Winton, *Lockie Leonard, Scumbuster*, Piper; and T. Winton, *Lockie Leonard, Legend*, Pan Macmillan, Sydney, 1997.

51   T. Winton, *Dirt Music*, Picador, Sydney, 2001.

52   T. Winton, *Dirt Music*, Scribner, New York, 2002; T. Winton, *The Turning*, Scribner, New York, 2005.

53   J. B. Thompson, *Merchants of Culture: The Publishing Business in the Twenty-first Century*, Polity Press, Cambridge, 2010, p. 107.

54   B. Kachka, 'Book publishing's big gamble', *New York Times*, 9 July 2013, www.nytimes.com/2013/07/10/opinion/book-publishings-big-gamble. html?_r=0.

55   L. Poland and I. Indyk, 'Rejected by America? Some tensions in Australian–American literary relations', in R. Dixon and N. Birns (eds), *Reading Across*

the Pacific: Australia–United States Intellectual Histories, Sydney University Press, Sydney, 2010, p. 309.

56 D. Carter, 'Transpacific or transatlantic traffic? Australian books and American publishers', in Dixon and Birns (eds), *Reading Across the Pacific*, p. 356.

57 McPhee, *Other People's Words*, p. 174.

58 T. Winton, *Lockie Leonard, Human Torpedo*, Little, Brown, Boston, Massachusetts, 1991.

59 T. Winton, *Lockie Leonard, Scumbuster*, Margaret K. McElderry Books, New York, 1999.

60 T. Winton, *Blueback: A Fable for All Ages*, Macmillan, Sydney, 1997.

61 T. Winton, *Blueback: A Contemporary Fable*, Scribner, New York, 1997.

62 T. Winton, *The Deep*, Tricycle Press, Berkeley, California, 2000.

63 B. Bachman, *Australian Colors: Images of the Outback*, Amphoto Art, New York, 1998.

64 T. Winton, *Shallows*, Atheneum, New York, 1986.

65 T. Winton, *That Eye, the Sky*, Atheneum, New York, 1987.

66 T. Winton, *Minimum of Two*, Atheneum, New York, 1988.

67 T. Winton, *Cloudstreet*, Graywolf Press, Saint Paul, Minnesota, 1992.

68 T. Winton, *The Riders*, Scribner, New York, 1995.

69 T. Winton, *Breath*, Farrar, Straus and Giroux, New York, 2008.

70 P. Gaskell, *A New Introduction to Bibliography*, Oak Knoll Press, New Castle, Delaware, 1995, p. 313.

71 D. Jordan, 'American dreams and the University of Queensland Press', in Dixon and Birns (eds), *Reading Across the Pacific*, p. 329.

72 Winton, *Shallows*, Allen & Unwin, p. vii.

73 Winton, *Shallows*, Atheneum, p. vii.

74 Ibid.

75 J. Dryden, *Dryden: Poetry, Prose and Plays*, in D. Grant (ed.), Harvard University Press, Cambridge, Massachusetts, 1952, p. 67.

76 J. Dryden, *John Dryden*, in K. Walker (ed.), Oxford University Press, Oxford, 1987, p. 57.

77 See, for example, H. Melville, *Moby-Dick; or, The Whale*, Penguin (Penguin Drop Caps series), New York, 2013, p. xxv; and H. Melville, *Moby-Dick; or, The Whale*, Pocket Books, New York, 1999, p. 11. By way of comparison, the word in question is printed as 'chace' in the first American edition (H. Melville, *Moby-Dick; or, The Whale*, Harper & Brothers, New York, 1851, p. xiv).

78 T. Winton, *Shallows*, Penguin, Melbourne, 1998.

79 T. Winton, *That Eye, the Sky*, McPhee Gribble, Melbourne, 1986.

80 Winton, *Shallows*, Allen & Unwin, p. vii.

81 Winton, *Shallows*, Atheneum, p. vii.

82 G. T. Tanselle, 'The editorial problem of final authorial intention', *Studies in Bibliography*, no. 29, 1976, p. 170.

83 Ibid., pp. 190–1.

84 J. J. McGann, *A Critique of Modern Textual Criticism*, University of Chicago Press, Chicago, 1983, p. 8.

85 Ibid., p. 122.

86 G. T. Tanselle, 'Textual criticism at the millennium', *Studies in Bibliography*, no. 54, 2001, p. 1.

87 Ibid.

88 Ibid.

89 H. W. Gabler, 'The synchrony and diachrony of texts: practice and theory of the critical edition of James Joyce's *Ulysses*', *Text*, no. 1, 1981, p. 325.

90 T. Winton, *The Riders*, Macmillan, Sydney, 1994.

91 J. F. English, *The Economy of Prestige: Prizes, Awards, and the Circulation of Cultural Value*, Harvard University Press, Cambridge, Massachusetts, 2009.

92 Winton, epigraph, *The Turning*, Scribner.

93 G. Epps, 'In short: fiction', *New York Times*, 17 May 1987, www.nytimes.com/1987/05/17/books/in-short-fiction-108187.html.

94 J. Olshan, 'See Perth and perish', *New York Times Book Review*, 23 August 1992, p. 15.

95 Winton, *The Turning*, Picador, p. 7.

96 Winton, *The Turning*, Scribner, p. 7.

97 Winton, *The Turning*, Picador, p. 11.

98 Winton, *The Turning*, Scribner, p. 11.

99 Winton, *Breath*, Hamish Hamilton, p. 82.

100 Winton, *Breath*, Farrar, Straus and Giroux, p. 84.

101 W. W. Greg, 'The rationale of copy-text', *Studies in Bibliography*, no. 3, 1950–1, p. 21.

102 Tanselle, 'Textual criticism at the millennium', p. 1.

103 Ibid.

104 Winton, *Lockie Leonard, Human Torpedo*, McPhee Gribble, p. 6; Winton, *Lockie Leonard, Human Torpedo*, Little, Brown, p. 6.

105 Winton, *Lockie Leonard, Scumbuster*, Margaret K. McElderry Books, p. 1.

106 Winton, *Lockie Leonard, Scumbuster*, Piper, p. 1.

107 Winton, *Blueback: A Fable for All Ages*, Macmillan, p. 20.

108 Winton, *Blueback: A Contemporary Fable*, Scribner, p. 21.

109 Winton, *Lockie Leonard, Human Torpedo*, McPhee Gribble, p. 5.

110 Winton, *Lockie Leonard, Human Torpedo*, Little, Brown, p. 5.

111 'Review of *Lockie Leonard, Human Torpedo* by Tim Winton', *Publishers Weekly*, 1 January 1992, www.publishersweekly.com/978-0-316-94753-4.

112 Ibid.

113 M. Jacklin, 'The transnational turn in Australian literary studies', *JASAL Special Issue: Australian Literature in a Global World*, 2009, p. 1.

114 P. Cohen, 'Introduction', in P. Cohen (ed.), *Devils and Angels: Textual Editing and Literary Theory*, University Press of Virginia, Charlottesville, 1991, p. xiv.

115 At the time of writing, the American edition of *Eyrie*, due for publication in 2014, had not yet appeared.

116 The sales figures in this paragraph come courtesy of Nielsen BookScan, which provided me complimentary academic access to its data. Nielsen BookScan data is, according to its own promotional materials, 'Point-of-Sales data…acquired from a growing list of retailers who send Nielsen scanned data on 500,000 ISBNs/14 million units from 16,000 locations a week. This data covers roughly 85% of the US trade physical book market'.

117 R. Dixon, 'Australian literature – international contexts', *Southerly*, vol. 67, nos 1–2, 2007, p. 22.

Bibliography

AustLit work record, *Lilian's Story*, AustLit, www.austlit.edu.au/austlit/page/ C179649, accessed 18 September 2013.

Bachman, B., *Australian Colors: Images of the Outback*, Amphoto Art, New York, 1998.

—— *Local Colour: Travels in the Other Australia*, The Guidebook Company, Hong Kong, 1994.

Ben-Messahel, S., *Mind the Country: Tim Winton's Fiction*, University of Western Australia Press, Perth, 2006.

Carey, P., *True History of the Kelly Gang*, University of Queensland Press, Brisbane, 2000.

—— *True History of the Kelly Gang*, Knopf, New York, 2000.

—— *Oscar and Lucinda*, University of Queensland Press, Brisbane, 1988.

—— *Oscar and Lucinda*, Harper and Row, New York, 1988.

Carter, D., 'Transpacific or transatlantic traffic?: Australian books and American publishers', in R. Dixon and N. Birns (eds), *Reading Across the Pacific: Australia–United States Intellectual Histories*, Sydney University Press, Sydney, 2010, pp. 339–59.

Cohen, P., 'Introduction', in P. Cohen (ed.), *Devils and Angels: Textual Editing and Literary Theory*, University Press of Virginia, Charlottesville, 1991, pp. ix–xviii.

Dixon, R., 'Australian literature – international contexts', *Southerly*, vol. 67, nos 1–2, 2007, pp. 15–27.

—— 'Tim Winton, *Cloudstreet* and the field of Australian literature', *Westerly*, no. 50, 2005, pp. 245–60.

Dryden, J., *John Dryden*, in K. Walker (ed.), Oxford University Press, Oxford, 1987.

—— *Dryden: Poetry, Prose and Plays*, in D. Grant (ed.), Harvard University Press, Cambridge, Massachusetts, 1952.

Eggert, P., 'Case-study: Peter Carey's *True History of the Kelly Gang*', in C. Munro and R. Sheahan-Bright (eds), *Paper Empires: A History of the Book in Australia, 1946–2005*, University of Queensland Press, Brisbane, 2006, pp. 195–8.

English, J. F., *The Economy of Prestige: Prizes, Awards, and the Circulation of Cultural Value*, Harvard University Press, Cambridge, Massachusetts, 2009.

Epps, G., 'In short: fiction', *New York Times*, 17 May 1987, www.nytimes. com/1987/05/17/books/in-short-fiction-108187.html.

Gabler, H. W., 'The synchrony and diachrony of texts: practice and theory of the critical edition of James Joyce's *Ulysses*', *Text*, no. 1, 1981, pp. 305–26.

Gaskell, P., *A New Introduction to Bibliography*, Oak Knoll Press, New Castle, Delaware, 1995.

Gelder, K. and Salzman, P., *After the Celebration: Australian Fiction 1989–2007*, Melbourne University Press, Melbourne, 2009.

Greg, W. W., 'The rationale of copy-text', *Studies in Bibliography*, no. 3, 1950–1, pp. 19–36.

Grenville, K., *Lilian's Story*, Allen & Unwin, Sydney, 1997.

—— *Lilian's Story*, Viking, New York, 1986.

—— *Lilian's Story*, Allen & Unwin, Sydney, 1985.

Hetherington, C., 'Old tricks for new dogs: resurrecting bibliography and literary history', in K. Bode and R. Dixon (eds), *Resourceful Reading: The New Empiricism, eResearch, and Australian Literary Culture*, Sydney University Press, Sydney, 2009, pp. 70–83.

—— 'Authors, editors, publishers: Katharine Susannah Prichard and W. W. Norton', *Australian Literary Studies*, vol. 22, no. 4, 2006, pp. 417–31.

Jacklin, M., 'The transnational turn in Australian literary studies', *JASAL Special Issue: Australian Literature in a Global World*, 2009, pp. 1–14.

Jordan, D., 'American dreams and the University of Queensland Press', in R. Dixon and N. Birns (eds), *Reading Across the Pacific: Australia–United States Intellectual Histories*, Sydney University Press, Sydney, 2010, pp. 323–8.

Kachka, B., 'Book publishing's big gamble', *New York Times*, 9 July 2013, www.nytimes.com/2013/07/10/opinion/book-publishings-big-gamble. html?_r=0.

Koch, C., *The Boys in the Island*, Sirius Books, Sydney, 1987.

—— *Across the Sea Wall*, Sirius Books, Sydney, 1982.

—— *The Boys in the Island*, Angus & Robertson, Sydney, 1974.

—— *Across the Sea Wall*, Heinemann, London, 1965.

—— *The Boys in the Island*, Hamish Hamilton, London, 1958.

McGann, J. J., *A Critique of Modern Textual Criticism*, University of Chicago Press, Chicago, 1983.

McPhee, H., *Other People's Words: The Rise and Fall of an Accidental Publisher*, Picador, London, 2003.

Melville, H., *Moby-Dick; or, The Whale*, Penguin (Penguin Drop Caps), New York, 2013.

—— *Moby-Dick; or, The Whale*, Pocket Books, New York, 1999.

—— *Moby-Dick; or, The Whale*, Harper & Brothers, New York, 1851.

Mischkulnig, M. and Winton, T., *Smalltown*, Hamish Hamilton, Melbourne, 2009.

Olshan, J., 'See Perth and perish', *New York Times Book Review*, 23 August 1992, p. 15.

O'Reilly, N., 'Review of *Mind the Country: Tim Winton's Fiction* by Salhia Ben-Messahel', *Australian Literary Studies*, vol. 23, no. 3, 2008, pp. 359–61.

Osborne, R., 'Australian literature in a world of books: a transnational history of Kylie Tennant's *The Battlers*', in K. Bode and R. Dixon (eds), *Resourceful Reading: The New Empiricism, eResearch, and Australian Literary Culture*, Sydney University Press, Sydney, 2009, pp. 105–18.

Poland, L. and Indyk, I., 'Rejected by America? Some tensions in Australian–American literary relations', in R. Dixon and N. Birns (eds), *Reading Across the Pacific: Australia–United States Intellectual Histories*, Sydney University Press, Sydney, 2010, pp. 309–22.

Prichard, K. S., *Fay's Circus*, W. W. Norton, New York, 1931.

—— 'Letter to Norton', 4 June 1931, Prichard papers, National Library of Australia, NLA MSS 6201, Series 10, Folder 9.

—— *Haxby's Circus*, Jonathan Cape, London, 1930.

'Professor David Carter', ARC Cultural Research Network, University of Queensland, 2008, www.uq.edu.au/crn/participants/carter.html.

'Review of *Lockie Leonard, Human Torpedo* by Tim Winton', *Publishers Weekly*, 1 January 1992, www.publishersweekly.com/978-0-316-94753-4.

Steger, J., 'With a deep *Breath*, Winton looks and leaps', *Age*, 25 April 2008, www.theage.com.au/articles/2008/04/24/1208743153682.html?s_cid=rss_.

Tanselle, G. T., 'Textual criticism at the millennium', *Studies in Bibliography*, no. 54, 2001, pp. 1–80.

—— 'The editorial problem of final authorial intention', *Studies in Bibliography*, no. 29, 1976, pp. 167–211.

Taylor, A., 'What can be read, and what can only be seen in Tim Winton's fiction', *Australian Literary Studies*, vol. 17, no. 4, 1996, pp. 323–31.

Thompson, J. B., *Merchants of Culture: The Publishing Business in the Twenty-first Century*, Polity Press, Cambridge, 2010.

Winton, T., *Eyrie*, Hamish Hamilton, Melbourne, 2013.

—— *Breath*, Hamish Hamilton, Melbourne, 2008.

—— *Breath*, Farrar, Straus and Giroux, New York, 2008.

—— *The Turning*, Scribner, New York, 2005.

—— *The Turning*, Picador, Sydney, 2004.

—— *Dirt Music*, Scribner, New York, 2002.

—— *Dirt Music*, Picador, Sydney, 2001.

—— *The Deep*, Tricycle Press, Berkeley, California, 2000.

—— *Lockie Leonard, Scumbuster*, Margaret K. McElderry Books, New York, 1999.

—— 'Strange passion: a landscape memoir', in R. Woldendorp, *Down to Earth: Australian Landscapes*, Fremantle Arts Centre Press in association with Sandpiper Press, Fremantle, 1999, pp. ix–xxxii.

—— *The Deep*, Sandcastle Books, Fremantle, 1998.

—— *Shallows*, Penguin, Melbourne, 1998.

—— *Blueback: A Fable for All Ages*, Macmillan, Sydney, 1997.

—— *Blueback: A Contemporary Fable*, Scribner, New York, 1997.

—— *Lockie Leonard, Legend*, Pan Macmillan, Sydney, 1997.

—— *The Riders*, Scribner, New York, 1995.

—— *The Riders*, Macmillan, Sydney, 1994.

—— *Land's Edge*, Macmillan, Sydney, 1993.

—— *Lockie Leonard, Scumbuster*, Piper, Sydney, 1993.

—— *Cloudstreet*, Graywolf Press, Saint Paul, Minnesota, 1992.

—— *The Bugalugs Bum Thief*, Puffin, Melbourne, 1991.

—— *Cloudstreet*, McPhee Gribble, Melbourne, 1991.

—— *Lockie Leonard, Human Torpedo*, Little, Brown, Boston, Massachusetts, 1991.

—— *Lockie Leonard, Human Torpedo*, McPhee Gribble, Melbourne, 1990.

—— *In the Winter Dark*, McPhee Gribble, Melbourne, 1988.

—— *Jesse*, McPhee Gribble, Melbourne, 1988.

—— *Minimum of Two*, Atheneum, New York, 1988.

—— *Minimum of Two*, McPhee Gribble, Melbourne, 1987.

—— *That Eye, the Sky*, Atheneum, New York, 1987.

—— *Shallows*, Atheneum, New York, 1986.

—— *That Eye, the Sky*, McPhee Gribble, Melbourne, 1986.

—— *Scission*, McPhee Gribble, Melbourne, 1985.

—— *Shallows*, Allen & Unwin, Sydney, 1984.

—— *An Open Swimmer*, Allen & Unwin, Sydney, 1982.

Woldendorp, R., *Down to Earth: Australian Landscapes*, Fremantle Arts Centre Press in association with Sandpiper Press, Fremantle, 1999.

6

FROM FATHER TO SON: FATHERHOOD AND FATHER–SON RELATIONSHIPS IN *SCISSION*

Nathanael O'Reilly

Father–son relationships have been a recurrent motif in the Western literary canon for millennia, from Abraham and Isaac to Odysseus and Telemachus, and Hamlet and his father's ghost. Within Australian literature, famous father–son relationships are harder to find. Rolf Boldrewood's *Robbery Under Arms*,[1] Louis Stone's *Jonah*,[2] George Johnston's *My Brother Jack*[3] and Peter Carey's *Oscar and Lucinda*[4] all address father–son relationships, but those relationships are rarely the primary focus of the novel. Father–son relationships are addressed far more frequently in shorter literary forms, such as poems and short stories, but such shorter works rarely garner the degree of visibility within the culture that novels enjoy. Exceptions might include Henry Lawson's 'His Father's Mate',[5] Tim Winton's 'My Father's Axe'[6] and Peter Carey's 'Do You Love Me?'.[7] Similarly, the body of criticism on father–son relationships in Australian literature is remarkably slight. Such relationships are, however, quite prominent in life writing, including memoirs and autobiographies, such as Hal Porter's *The Watcher on the Cast-iron Balcony*,[8] Raimond Gaita's *Romulus, My Father*[9] and Peter Rose's *Rose Boys*,[10] all of which are examined in Stephen Mansfield's *Australian Patriography*.[11]

Fatherhood and father–son relationships have been a pre-occupation in Tim Winton's fiction throughout his career. Winton began exploring the themes in early works such as *Scission*, *That Eye, the Sky*[12] and *Minimum of Two*,[13] and continued to address them in his mid-career novels *Cloudstreet*[14] and *The Riders*.[15] More recent works, including *The Turning*[16] and *Breath*,[17] have also addressed fatherhood and father–son relationships. Since Winton is both a son and a father, it is no surprise that fatherhood and father–son relationships recur in his work. What is most interesting, however, is not the fact that Winton repeatedly returns to subject matter closely related to his own roles in life, but the plethora of father–son relationships he presents and the ways he interrogates fatherhood and masculinity. As Bárbara Arizti Martín notes, Winton depicts a wide variety of fathers in his fiction, from those who assume the traditional breadwinner role to those who stay home while their wives work.[18] This chapter focuses on Winton's depiction of fatherhood and father–son relationships in his first collection of short fiction, *Scission*. I argue that Winton presents non-traditional fathers and complex father–son relationships in order to question and challenge Australian cultural norms regarding fatherhood and masculinity.

Søren Kierkegaard, in his parable 'The Quiet Despair',[19] writes,

> A son is like a mirror in which the father beholds himself, and for the son the father too is like a mirror in which he beholds himself in the time to come [...] And the father believed that he was to blame for the son's melancholy, and the son believed that he was the occasion of the father's sorrow – but they never exchanged a word on the subject.[20]

Although Kierkegaard was not writing about Australian fathers and sons, the father–son relationship he describes is remarkably universal, and thus in Winton's short fiction readers encounter father–son relationships in which the fathers and sons look for themselves in each other, believe themselves to be a disappointment to the other party in the relationship, and, in a typically Australian masculine fashion, often remain silent regarding their emotions. In *Masculinity in Crisis*, Roger Horrocks argues that traditional conceptions of masculinity require 'a self-destructive identity, a deeply masochistic self-denial, a shrinkage of the self, [and] a turning away from whole areas of life', to such an extent 'that the man who obeys the demands of masculinity…become[s] only half-human'.[21] Winton depicts fathers and sons who struggle to resist the self-destructive traditional conception of masculinity outlined by Horrocks. Furthermore, as Arizti Martín argues, Winton's fiction provides 'models of alternative fatherhood'.[22]

This chapter addresses three stories in *Scission* that focus closely on fatherhood and father–son relationships:[23] 'A Blow, a Kiss',[24] 'My Father's Axe'[25] and 'Wake'.[26] The first two of these deal with boys and the relationships they have with their fathers. Brian Matthews argues that Winton's depictions of childhood contain 'an extraordinary poetic power and richness', comparing them to 'the kind of uncalculating depth that Blake and Wordsworth… sensed in the pronouncements and perceptions of children'.[27] Winton has two sons and a daughter, and has declared that he is fascinated by children.[28] In an interview with Andrew Taylor, Winton notes that for most of the time he has been writing he has also been raising children, and since he 'started very young both as a writer and a father', children 'were probably [his] chief influence'.[29]

'A Blow, a Kiss' focuses on a pair of father–son relationships. In the story's second sentence, Winton provides a positive depiction of the primary father–son relationship: 'Just the pipe smell of his father and the warmth of him in the truck's cab beside him was enough'.[30] Albie, a young boy, and his father are driving home after a night of fishing. A speeding motorcyclist overtakes their truck then crashes in front of them. Albie's father stops to assist the man, who is badly injured, but disoriented by shock, the motorcyclist fights Albie's father, who then manages to subdue him. Since they are in a remote location, Albie's father realises he needs to drive to the nearest farmhouse for help, and instructs Albie to sit on top of the now-unconscious motorcyclist and restrain him if he regains consciousness. While Albie's father seeks assistance, Albie sits on the stranger, wondering 'how he should behave towards [...a] man who had struck his father'.[31]

Waiting for his father to return, Albie intones, '[c]ome on, Dad. Come on, Dad. Come on, Dad'.[32] The third-person narrator states that Albie

> [O]ften prayed to his father in his absence. God, he decided, was just like his Dad, only bigger. It was easier to pray to him and hope God got the message on relay.[33]

Bruce Bennett argues that Winton's 'shrewdly humorous observation of the adolescent male sensibility' in this scene 'is complemented by a sense of the mystery of an intimacy that can be so easily shattered'.[34] Albie is young enough to still be in awe of his father and has not yet experienced an event that might cause a schism in the father–son relationship. Salhia Ben-Messahel argues that Albie 'is in complete symbiosis with his father', who is 'a shelter against fear, worry and pain'.[35] Bennett suggests that '[s]cission, or at least separation, seems endemic' to the father–son relationship, which 'is full of mysteries, secrets, uncertainties and, sometimes, betrayals'.[36] In Winton's fiction, such scissions usually occur during the son's adolescence or early adulthood.

As Albie prays to his father, the motorcyclist regains consciousness and twice asks, '[d]ad?'[37] Unsure how to reply, Albie whispers, '[y]es?'[38] The motorcyclist then states, '[o]h. Oh, Dad, I'm sorry. Was coming back',[39] before weeping. Thus Winton adds another layer to a story that initially seems to be about the father–son relationship between Albie and his father, juxtaposing the two relationships. Playing the role of the motorcyclist's father, Albie comforts the injured man, repeatedly stating, '[i]t's alright', before kissing 'the wet, prickled face',[40] an act that causes the injured man's sobbing to cease moments before Albie's father returns. The role-playing allows Albie to express emotion in a manner that would be unacceptable between Australian males conforming to cultural norms of heterosexual masculinity.

Seeing blood on his son's face, Albie's father sweeps him up into his arms to make sure he is unharmed. Albie yields to the embrace, savouring the sensation of his father's fingers on his cheeks and the comforting familiarity of his breath. Having been unable to find a house with a telephone, Albie's father drives the injured man to town. When they arrive, Albie's father encounters a friend at the petrol station who informs him that the injured man is Wilf Beacon's son, and Beacon is in the pub. Albie's father goes into the pub and soon emerges locked in a tussle with Beacon, who is subdued by a blow. The drunken Beacon accuses Albie's father of hurting his son. Albie observes the altercation from the truck's cab, wanting 'the man to see his son, and to weep like the son had wept out on the road'.[41] In defiance of cultural norms of masculinity, Albie yearns for the open expression of emotion between fathers and sons. When Beacon reaches his son, he calls him a coward for leaving his father alone, and then beats his son's head against the truck's tray.

Unable to bear Beacon's abuse of his son, Albie gets out of the cab, grabs a lamp, and whacks Beacon with it so forcefully that he falls unconscious onto his son. Later, as Albie and his father pull into their driveway, Albie asks his father why Beacon hit his son for getting hurt. When Albie's father replies that he does not know, Albie asks if his father would ever do that to him. Albie's father stops the truck suddenly, exclaiming, 'Lord, no. God A'mighty, no!'[42] before reaching out and pressing his knuckles gently against Albie's cheek. The story concludes with Albie revelling in his father's love: 'Albie felt those knuckles on his cheek still and knew, full to bursting, that that was how God would touch someone'.[43] Thus the narrative ends with a complicated image conveying love, comfort and the subtle suggestion of violence. The narrative's primary father–son relationship remains intact and sacred.

Although Winton presents a troubled father–son relationship through Wilf Beacon and his son, the narrative mostly focuses on Albie's positive, close and comforting relationship with his father, affirming the father–son relationship as central to Australian masculinity while simultaneously highlighting the difficulty of expressing emotions within such relationships. This positive depiction of the primary father–son relationship is no anomaly. As Arizti Martín has shown in her work on fathers in Winton's fiction, 'caring fathers, who challenge patriarchal norms and show a high degree of involvement with their children, outnumber... negative figures'.[44]

'My Father's Axe' provides a much more complex portrayal of father–son relationships than 'A Blow, a Kiss'. One of Winton's most anthologised stories, 'My Father's Axe' is a first-person narrative focusing on the loss of the axe belonging to the unnamed narrator's father. The adult narrator is deeply troubled by the loss of the axe, not because of any practical need for the tool, which can be replaced, but due to the symbolic function it serves, representing the narrator's relationship with his father. During the narrator's childhood, he watched his father use the axe to cut wood on the outskirts of town. The narrator and his mother watched the father fell trees and cheered when he succeeded, cementing his masculine status in his son's eyes. A master axeman, the narrator's father would skilfully 'dismember' the trees with 'graceful swings';[45] this combination of violence and grace foreshadows the nightmares the narrator experiences later in the story, while highlighting binaries inherent within the narrator's perception of his father's masculinity.

As a child, the narrator was not merely an observer of his father's axemanship. The narrator's father taught his son the art of woodcutting, and thus the axe became a tool that strengthened their relationship, uniting them through a shared activity. Although the narrator's skill with the axe does not equal his father's, cutting wood becomes an important part of his life and a skill he hopes to pass on to his own son. During the narrator's childhood, his father often had to leave for long periods due to his work as a salesman. While his father was absent, the narrator was responsible for cutting wood to fuel the home, and took pride in knowing that the hot water, his mother's cooking and the living room fire all depended upon him.

One of the most significant scenes in 'My Father's Axe' concerns the narrator as a boy, witnessing his father weeping. Distraught at having to leave his family to go on a long trip for work, the narrator's father sits on the front step of the house sobbing. The father is so upset that he bites a balled-up handkerchief in order to stifle his sobs. The narrator is deeply affected by observing his father expressing such powerful emotion, especially since up until this moment he has perceived his father as the epitome of traditional Australian masculinity, a man who is strong, brave, stoic, physically skilled, hardworking and a good provider. Sarah Zapata argues that by presenting males who express their emotions, Winton 'seeks to undermine and subvert' conventions of masculinity.[46] The narrator's initial reaction to seeing his father weep is to run into the backyard, pick up the axe, and begin shattering 'great blocks of sheoak' until darkness falls.[47] Rather than comfort his father, the narrator's instinctual reaction is to resort to physical violence in order to exorcise his anger and confusion. Having witnessed his father behave in a 'feminine' manner, the narrator attempts to exert and confirm his masculinity by utilising his physical strength violently, unconsciously immersing himself in the stereotypically hyper-masculine.

The scene is important, not merely because it reveals how threatened the narrator is by the sight of his father behaving in a manner that contradicts masculine norms, but also because it is one of the many instances in Winton's fiction in which male characters exhibit behaviour that may be considered feminine[48] (*Cloudstreet*'s Lester Lamb is probably the best known example). In interviews, Winton repeatedly addresses his depiction of non-traditional male characters, especially fathers, and the relationship between his male characters and the men in his own family who served as models. Winton tells Taylor that his childhood experience was of 'benign males' who were 'non-violent [and] sometimes ineffectual'.[49] Winton describes his father as 'a gentle man who did the ironing, the washing, and was, I guess, not very manly by Australian standards'.[50] In another interview, Winton notes that other writers 'have written about men in a traditional way', and describes his approach as writing about men 'from an orthodox female point of view'.[51]

In her essay on representations of class and gender in Winton's work, Lekkie Hopkins argues that Winton 'constantly plays with notions of masculinity in ways which appear to undermine conventional gender stereotypes', and notes that a great deal of his early fiction explores what it might mean 'to be a son, a father, a husband, a male friend', arguing that Winton's male characters 'are often psychic, always intuitive, often emotional and sensitive'.[52] Hopkins takes issue, however, with Winton's depiction of male characters possessing stereotypically feminine characteristics, not because she favours depictions of stereotypical masculinity, but because she finds it 'disturbing' as a feminist that Winton's 'male characters are positioned as odd and different precisely because of their "feminine" qualities'.[53] She goes on to argue that it is the feminine qualities of the male characters that render them powerless, and concludes that the equation of 'powerlessness with feminine attributes…does not subvert, but rather reinforces, the patriarchal ideology which insists that power properly rests with the masculine'.[54] The problem Hopkins identifies, however, is not one Winton has created or that exists solely within his fictional worlds. Rather, the equation of strength with masculinity and powerlessness with femininity is a dominant construct within Australian society. Blaming Winton for depicting the existence of gender norms and power relationships within realistic works of fiction seems unfair. Rather, he deserves praise for creating characters that question gender norms and refuse to conform to them.

Despite the narrator's desire to emulate his father, especially during his childhood, he notes that he often falls short of his father's standards. His use of the axe is 'less graceful'[55] than his father's, and he often accidentally breaks and damages his father's tools. The narrator admits that he had 'never been a handyman like [...his] father', and, as a boy, 'did not see the need to learn' because he believed his father would always be around: 'If I needed something built, something done, there was my father and he protected me'.[56] Like Albie in 'A Blow, a Kiss', the narrator in 'My Father's Axe' perceives his father as a God-like protector. Describing a childhood fishing trip, the narrator recalls his father teaching him to 'brace' himself 'side-on to the waves and find footholds in the reef': 'I hugged his leg and felt his immovable stance and moulded myself to him'.[57] Here, the verbs 'hugged' and 'moulded' suggest that the son attempts to become one with his father, while 'immovable' portrays strength and longevity.

The role of the narrator's father as protector is emphasised during the fishing trip section of 'My Father's Axe', especially through a scene where a rat sets off a trap in the rafters above the boy's bed in the middle of the night. The narrator recalls that he 'lay still and did not scream because [...he] knew [...his] father would come'.[58] As expected, the father removes the rat and fulfils his role as protector. Following the rat incident, the narrator often has dreams in which he is rescued by his father. In one of these dreams, the family home is on fire and the narrator is 'trapped inside, hair and bedclothes afire'; the father splinters 'the door with an axe blow',[59] fights his way in and carries his son to safety. This depiction of the father as protector could be read as a characterisation that conforms to societal norms for masculinity and fatherhood. Likewise, the father is drawn as a quiet man who says little and does not seem to value words – in short, a prime example of what Mansfield terms 'the reticent-laconic Australian father'.[60] The narrator converses often with his mother, but the father–son relationship lacks verbalisation, privileging action and emulation. But while the narrator's father certainly conforms to the role of 'the strong silent type', he is a non-traditional father in that he is emotional, sensitive and highly affectionate, kissing his son 'goodnight and goodbye and hello',[61] until the narrator reaches the age of fourteen and begins to evade his father's kisses out of shame.

As the narrator's father ages, he chops wood less often, and his son gradually replaces him as the primary woodcutter in the family. Part of the role reversal entails the father sitting and watching his son cut wood, whereas the son previously watched the father. Eventually, as the son becomes a man with a busy life, he cuts the wood more quickly, 'often finishing before the old man had a chance to come out and sit down'.[62] Thus, the father–son relationship alters to a state in which the father has been made redundant as well as no longer worthy of emulation and admiration. After the narrator leaves home and marries, he visits his parents once a week to cut wood for his father, who has refused to have electric heating and cooking facilities installed. As time passes, the narrator's father becomes 'a frail, old man'.[63] The narrator thinks his father looks at him 'in disappointment every week',[64] but the cause of the disappointment is unspecified. Nevertheless, here Winton depicts the father–son relationship as one in which the son's admiration for the father decreases over time and ultimately ceases to exist, a process coinciding with the father's inevitable physical decline and the son's perception that his father is disappointed in him. Winton suggests that even the strongest father–son relationships deteriorate over time as an inevitable consequence of ageing.

The narrator becomes a father himself, and once his son, Jamie, is old enough to use an axe, the narrator teaches his son just as his father taught him. Jamie is 'careless'[65] with the axe, however, blunting its edge, which angers the narrator. Thus the narrator is disappointed in his son, just as he perceives himself to be a disappointment to his own father. Winton suggests here that sons are unable to fulfil their father's expectations, perhaps because those expectations are unrealistic. Once Jamie is competent enough with the axe, the narrator drops his son at his grandfather's house on Sunday afternoons so that Jamie can assume his father's role as the extended family's primary woodcutter. Thus the notion of sons replacing their fathers is carried through to the third generation.

After the narrator's mother suffers a stroke, Jamie demands to be paid for chopping wood, and the narrator's wife Elaine visits her in-laws twice a week to cook and clean. The narrator's response to the difficult situation is to move his parents into a nursing home, sell his own house, and move back into his parents' house with his wife and son. Eventually, Jamie refuses to chop wood at all, leading the narrator to declare, '[h]e is lazier than me',[66] once again emphasising the narrator's disappointment in his son.

Winton divides 'My Father's Axe' into six numbered sections, and frequently shifts the narrative between past and present. The story's second section presents a dream in which the narrator chops wood. As he chops harder and harder, his feet lift a little further off the ground each time he swings the axe until he feels he will float away. As the narrator attempts to control his actions within the dream and push himself back down to the ground, the axe-head comes off the handle and, in a 'slow, tumbling trajectory [...] sails across the woodheap',[67] beheading the narrator's father. The father's head rolls onto the woodpile, eyes facing the narrator, 'transfixed at the moment of scission in a squint of disappointment'.[68] The nightmare obviously displays the narrator's guilt over putting his parents in a home, guilt that is exacerbated by the loss of his father's axe, which serves as the most important physical reminder of the close father–son relationship that once existed. As Bennett argues, the narrator has 'relegated his parents to a "Home"',[69] and displaced them by moving into theirs.

In the fifth section of 'My Father's Axe', the guilt-plagued narrator experiences another nightmare. In this second nightmare, the narrator dreams his body is 'dissected, raggedly sectioned up and battered and crusted black with blood'.[70] His father's axe is 'embedded' in his trunk 'right through the pelvis', his 'severed limbs'[71] scattered about, and his head lies to one side, facing the ceiling. If the nightmare is not already horrific enough, the narrator then sees his son pick up his severed head and hold it 'like a bowling ball',[72] carrying it to the chopping block in the backyard where he splits the head in two with the missing axe. Jamie then takes the two halves of his father's head to the street in front of their house and skids them 'into the paths of oncoming cars',[73] where they are reduced to pulp. Thus, while the narrator kills his father in the first nightmare, his son kills him in the second. Clearly, the narrator is deeply disturbed by the state of both father–son relationships in which he plays a role, and feels that he is not adequately performing either the role of son or father. Moreover, the axe embedded in the narrator's pelvis in the second nightmare clearly symbolises castration, suggesting that his son is removing his ability to father another child. Here, Winton depicts complex father–son relationships fraught with psychological peril and emotional turmoil.

The morning after the second nightmare, the narrator decides he must replace the missing axe in order to gain closure and halt his psychological torment. Coming home from the hardware store with the replacement axe, the narrator is met on the front verandah by his crying wife, who informs him his father has

173

passed away. Not only does the narrator's father die in the nursing home, displaced from his family home, he dies before the narrator can heal the father–son relationship. Readers now must reconsider the narrator's first nightmare in which he kills his father; in addition to being a symptom of guilt and fear, the nightmare may also be interpreted as a premonition.

The day after his father's funeral, while the narrator sits on his verandah contemplating the likelihood of his mother's imminent death, a man and a boy approach and give him a hessian bag. The narrator opens the bag to find his father's axe. In response, the narrator runs inside and quickly returns with the new axe, which he gives to the boy, declaring, '[t]his is yours'.[74] By concluding 'My Father's Axe' with a father leading his son to return the stolen axe, Winton presents another father–son relationship, one in which the father plays the traditional role of authority figure and moral guide, leading the wayward son to atone for his crime. The father and son of the story's conclusion also serve to provide closure to the narrator, reuniting him with his father's axe, the absence of which has caused guilt, regret and fear. Although the return of the axe cannot make up for the loss of the narrator's father, nor repair his relationship with his own son, the story's conclusion does symbolise closure. Bennett argues that the symbolism employed by Winton is 'never wholly resolved',[75] but Winton might leave the conclusion somewhat unresolved in order to suggest that the main father–son relationships in the story cannot have neat resolutions. 'My Father's Axe' clearly demonstrates Winton's ability to depict non-traditional fathers and complex father–son relationships. Moreover, Winton's use of dreams and nightmares demonstrates the psychological complexity of the father–son relationship and emphasises the centrality of the relationship to the characters' conceptions of masculinity.

'Wake', the fifth story in *Scission*, is a third-person narrative focusing on a week in the life of an unnamed protagonist. The week depicted is anything but normal, however; it is the week immediately after the protagonist's girlfriend leaves him. The protagonist is in a precarious mental state and has not accepted his loss. When a friend stops by the morning after the abandonment with a gift and asks where his 'lady'[76] is, the protagonist lies and says she is in bed. Later that morning, the protagonist telephones his father and asks, '[s]he there?'[77] The protagonist's father 'sounds surprised and perplexed',[78] but the son does not explain the situation. Thus, in 'Wake', Winton introduces a father–son relationship in which the father is the first person the son calls in a crisis, initially suggesting intimacy, but in which the son refrains from open communication with his father during a time of great distress, indicating emotional repression.

On the second day after being abandoned, the protagonist eats dinner with his parents but 'avoids any conversation concerning her'.[79] Late in the evening, the protagonist's father asks him if he would like to go for a run to the beach and back. The son agrees to run with his father, and manages to keep pace for the first block, but then falls behind. The protagonist watches his father 'pull away from him',[80] until his father slows down to let him catch up. When the son declares his father is 'too good', the father tells his son he is 'damned unfit'[81] and will be dead by the time he is forty. Here, Winton focuses on the competitive element often present within father–son relationships, positioning the son as physically inferior, even though he is a young man and his father is middle-aged. As in 'My Father's Axe', this father–son relationship contains disappointment; in this case, the father is disappointed in his son. Later during the father–son run, the father asks, '[d]o you think she'll come back?'[82] The son replies, '[y]eah.

Yes. I suppose',[83] unwilling to admit the relationship is over, and the conversation ends. The father speeds up again, and the son is left to follow; clearly, Winton uses the run as a metaphor for the distance between the father and son.

Winton's primary focus in 'Wake' is on the difficulty of extended, meaningful conversations between fathers and sons, which he presents through a series of short, shallow dialogues. Bennett argues that when the father and son run together, 'the moment of emotional truth is between them'.[84] This 'emotional truth' remains unspoken, however, haunting the relationship. Both father and son conform to a code of masculinity that does not allow them to be emotionally open and honest. On the third evening, the father and son run together, but this time the father does not speak. Not only is there no dialogue between father and son in this scene, there is not even an attempt at communication. Again, Winton emphasises the difficulty of communication between fathers and sons trapped within the norms of Australian masculinity.

On the fourth evening, the father and son run again, and this time engage in brief conversation. The conversation avoids any mention of the departed girlfriend or any other meaningful topic, however, focusing solely on a three-eyed squid the protagonist was given that day but threw away rather than eating. The father declares his son a 'wasteful bastard', before speeding up until he is 'twenty or thirty yards ahead',[85] a distance he maintains for the rest of the run. The physical distance the father puts between himself and his son echoes the emotional distance in the relationship, while labelling his son a 'wasteful bastard' perpetuates the theme of disappointment and suggests the father thinks the son is to blame for losing his girlfriend.

During their run on the fifth evening, the father and son are both 'quiet in the darkness', and '[n]either lets the other ahead'.[86] During the final stretch, the father asks his son, '[h]ave you ever wept? Cried, I mean'.[87] The son does not reply and '[n]othing more is said'.[88] In this scene, Winton recalls the image of the father weeping in 'My Father's Axe' and raises the possibility of both father and son engaging in non-traditional behaviour: namely, openly expressing deep emotion through a physical act. The mere mention of an act that does not conform to masculine norms is enough to end the conversation. The fact the son does not reply does not mean he has never wept, of course, but it certainly indicates that if he has wept, he is unable to admit it. Both father and son repress their emotions and fail to communicate effectively with each other. Zapata argues that through this scene, Winton demands for men 'the right to cry...to stop restraining themselves and let emotions flow naturally'.[89] Winton suggests that father–son relationships in which the norms of masculinity are upheld lack depth, understanding and intimacy; this story can certainly be read as a critique of masculine norms and traditional father–son relationships.

Winton's detailed depictions of fatherhood and complex father–son relationships in *Scission* consistently critique masculine norms and illuminate common dysfunctional behaviours exhibited by both fathers and sons. As Arizti Martín has argued, Winton calls for a revision of 'traditional masculinity',[90] and questions 'traditional notions of fatherhood'.[91] Simultaneously, Winton demonstrates how masculine norms damage father–son relationships. Furthermore, as Zapata contends, Winton's non-traditional representations of males challenge 'dominant patriarchal practices'[92] that are prevalent in Australian culture. Through his early works of short fiction, Winton challenges cultural norms, highlights dysfunction, celebrates intimacy and encourages new ways of being for both fathers and sons.

Notes

1   R. Boldrewood (T. A. Browne), *Robbery Under Arms*, Remington, London, 1888.
2   L. Stone, *Jonah*, Methuen, London, 1911.
3   G. Johnston, *My Brother Jack*, Collins, Sydney, 1964.
4   P. Carey, *Oscar and Lucinda*, University of Queensland Press, Brisbane, 1988.
5   H. Lawson, 'His Father's Mate', *While the Billy Boils*, Angus & Robertson, Sydney, 1896, pp. 146–60.
6   T. Winton, 'My Father's Axe', *Scission*, McPhee Gribble, Melbourne, 1985, pp. 23–33.
7   P. Carey, 'Do You Love Me?', *Collected Stories*, University of Queensland Press, Brisbane, 1994, pp. 1–10.
8   H. Porter, *The Watcher on the Cast-iron Balcony*, Faber & Faber, London, 1963.
9   R. Gaita, *Romulus, My Father*, Text Publishing, Melbourne, 1998.
10 P. Rose, *Rose Boys*, Allen & Unwin, Sydney, 2001.
11 S. Mansfield, *Australian Patriography: How Sons Write Fathers in Contemporary Life Writing*, Anthem Press, London, 2013.
12 T. Winton, *That Eye, the Sky*, McPhee Gribble, Melbourne, 1986.
13 T. Winton, *Minimum of Two*, McPhee Gribble, Melbourne, 1987.
14 T. Winton, *Cloudstreet*, McPhee Gribble, Melbourne, 1991.
15 T. Winton, *The Riders*, Macmillan, Sydney, 1994.
16 T. Winton, *The Turning*, Picador, Sydney, 2004.
17 T. Winton, *Breath*, Hamish Hamilton, Melbourne, 2008.
18 B. Arizti Martín, 'Fathercare in Tim Winton's fiction', *Hungarian Journal of English and American Studies*, vol. 12, nos 1–2, 2006, p. 280.
19 I am indebted to Stephen Mansfield's *Australian Patriography* for bringing this passage to my attention.
20 S. Kierkegaard, 'The Quiet Despair', *The Parables of Kierkegaard*, edited by T. C. Oden, Princeton University Press, Princeton, New Jersey, 1989, p. 79.
21 R. Horrocks, *Masculinity in Crisis: Myths, Fantasies and Realities*, Macmillan, London, 1994, p. 25.
22 Arizti Martín, 'Fathercare in Tim Winton's fiction', p. 277.
23 Readers interested in Winton's depiction of fatherhood and father–son relationships should also consult his second collection of short fiction, *Minimum of Two*, which contains five stories that focus closely on

fatherhood and father–son relationships: 'No Memory Comes' (pp. 11–21), 'Gravity' (pp. 23–32), 'The Strong One' (pp. 95–104), 'More' (pp. 117–31) and 'Blood and Water' (pp. 139–53).

24 Winton, 'A Blow, a Kiss', *Scission*, pp. 7–13.

25 Winton, 'My Father's Axe', pp. 23–33.

26 Winton, 'Wake', *Scission*, pp. 35–9.

27 B. Matthews, 'Childhood in Tim Winton's fiction', in R. Rossiter and L. Jacobs (eds), *Reading Tim Winton*, Angus & Robertson, Sydney, 1993, p. 69.

28 R. Rossiter, 'In his own words: the life and times of Tim Winton', in Rossiter and Jacobs (eds), *Reading Tim Winton*, p. 1; A. Taylor, 'An interview with Tim Winton', *Australian Literary Studies*, vol. 17, no. 4, 1996, p. 375.

29 Winton, cited in Taylor, 'An interview with Tim Winton', p. 375.

30 Winton, 'A Blow, a Kiss', p. 7.

31 Ibid., p. 9.

32 Ibid.

33 Ibid.

34 B. Bennett, 'Nostalgia for community: Tim Winton's essays and stories', in D. Haskell (ed.), *Tilting at Matilda: Literature, Aborigines, Women and the Church in Contemporary Australia*, Fremantle Arts Centre Press, Fremantle, 1994, p. 66.

35 S. Ben-Messahel, *Mind the Country: Tim Winton's Fiction*, University of Western Australia Press, Perth, 2006, p. 45.

36 Bennett, 'Nostalgia for community', p. 66.

37 Winton, 'A Blow, a Kiss', p. 9.

38 Ibid.

39 Ibid.

40 Ibid., p. 10.

41 Ibid., p. 12.

42 Ibid., p. 13.

43 Ibid.

44 Arizti Martín, 'Fathercare in Tim Winton's fiction', p. 280.

45 Winton, 'My Father's Axe', p. 24.

46 S. Zapata, 'Rethinking masculinity: changing men and the decline of patriarchy in Tim Winton's short stories', *ATENEA*, vol. 28, no. 2, 2008, p. 98.

47 Winton, 'My Father's Axe', p. 25.

48 As Arizti Martín notes, '[t]he list of traditionally feminine attitudes and tasks carried out by fathers in Winton's work is indeed long' ('Fathercare in Tim Winton's fiction', p. 281).

49 Winton, cited in Taylor, 'An interview with Tim Winton', p. 377.

50 Winton, cited in E. Wachtel, 'Eleanor Wachtel with Tim Winton', *Malahat Review*, vol. 121, 1997, p. 68.

51 Winton, cited in E. Guy, 'A conversation with Tim Winton', *Southerly*, vol. 56, no. 4, 1997, p. 129.

52 L. Hopkins, 'Writing from the margins: representations of gender and class in Winton's work', in Rossiter and Jacobs (eds), *Reading Tim Winton*, p. 46.

53 Ibid., p. 47.

54 Ibid., p. 49.

55 Winton, 'My Father's Axe', p. 24.

56 Ibid., p. 25

57 Ibid., p. 26.

58 Ibid.

59 Ibid., p. 27.

60 Mansfield, *Australian Patriography*, p. 12.

61 Winton, 'My Father's Axe', p. 27.

62 Ibid.

63 Ibid., p. 28.

64 Ibid.

65 Ibid.

66 Ibid.

67 Ibid., p. 29.

68 Ibid.

69 Bennett, 'Nostalgia for community', p. 64.

70 Winton, 'My Father's Axe', p. 31.

71 Ibid.

72 Ibid.

73 Ibid., p. 32.

74 Ibid., p. 33.

75 Bennett, 'Nostalgia for community', p. 64.

76 Winton, 'Wake', p. 35.

77 Ibid.

78 Ibid.

79 Ibid., p. 36.

80 Ibid.

81 Ibid.

82 Ibid., p. 37.

83 Ibid.

84 Bennett, 'Nostalgia for community', p. 66.

85 Winton, 'Wake', p. 38.

86 Ibid.

87 Ibid.

88 Ibid.
89 Zapata, 'Rethinking masculinity', p. 98.
90 Arizti Martín, 'Fathercare in Tim Winton's fiction', p. 277.
91 Ibid., p. 284.
92 Zapata, 'Rethinking masculinity', p. 97.

Bibliography

Arizti Martín, B., 'Fathercare in Tim Winton's fiction', *Hungarian Journal of English and American Studies*, vol. 12, nos 1–2, 2006, pp. 277–86.

Ben-Messahel, S., *Mind the Country: Tim Winton's Fiction*, University of Western Australia Press, Perth, 2006.

Bennett, B., 'Nostalgia for community: Tim Winton's essays and stories', in D. Haskell (ed.), *Tilting at Matilda: Literature, Aborigines, Women and the Church in Contemporary Australia*, Fremantle Arts Centre Press, Fremantle, 1994, pp. 60–73.

Boldrewood, R. (T. A. Browne), *Robbery Under Arms*, Angus & Robertson, Sydney, 1990.

Carey, P., *Collected Stories*, University of Queensland Press, Brisbane, 1994.

—— *Oscar and Lucinda*, University of Queensland Press, Brisbane, 1988.

Gaita, R., *Romulus, My Father*, Text Publishing, Melbourne, 1998.

Guy, E., 'A conversation with Tim Winton', *Southerly*, vol. 56, no. 4, 1997, pp. 127–33.

Hopkins, L., 'Writing from the margins: representations of gender and class in Winton's work', in R. Rossiter and L. Jacobs (eds), *Reading Tim Winton*, Angus & Robertson, Sydney, 1993, pp. 45–58.

Horrocks, R., *Masculinity in Crisis: Myths, Fantasies and Realities*, Macmillan, London, 1994.

Johnston, G., *My Brother Jack*, Collins, Sydney, 1964.

Kierkegaard, S., *The Parables of Kierkegaard*, edited by T. C. Oden, Princeton University Press, Princeton, New Jersey, 1989.

Lawson, H., *While the Billy Boils*, Angus & Robertson, Sydney, 1896.

Mansfield, S., *Australian Patriography: How Sons Write Fathers in Contemporary Life Writing*, Anthem Press, London, 2013.

Matthews, B., 'Childhood in Tim Winton's fiction', in Rossiter and Jacobs (eds), *Reading Tim Winton*, pp. 59–71.

Porter, H., *The Watcher on the Cast-iron Balcony: An Australian Autobiography*, Faber & Faber, London, 1963.

Rose, P., *Rose Boys*, Allen & Unwin, Sydney, 2001.

Rossiter, R., 'In his own words: the life and times of Tim Winton', in Rossiter and Jacobs (eds), *Reading Tim Winton*, pp. 1–14.

Stone, L., *Jonah*, Methuen, London, 1911.

Taylor, A., 'An interview with Tim Winton', *Australian Literary Studies*, vol. 17, no. 4, 1996, pp. 373–7.

Wachtel, E., 'Eleanor Wachtel with Tim Winton', *Malahat Review*, vol. 121, 1997, pp. 63–81.

Winton, T., *Breath*, Hamish Hamilton, Melbourne, 2008.

—— *The Turning*, Picador, Sydney, 2004.

—— *The Riders*, Macmillan, Sydney, 1994.

—— *Cloudstreet*, McPhee Gribble, Sydney, 1991.

—— *Minimum of Two*, McPhee Gribble, Melbourne, 1987.

—— *That Eye, the Sky*, McPhee Gribble, Melbourne, 1986.

—— *Scission*, McPhee Gribble, Melbourne, 1985.

Zapata, S., 'Rethinking masculinity: changing men and the decline of patriarchy in Tim Winton's short stories', *ATENEA*, vol. 28, no. 2, 2008, pp. 93–106.

7

WRITING CHILDHOOD IN TIM WINTON'S FICTION

Tanya Dalziell

In Tim Winton's novel *The Riders*, young Billie Ann Scully admits that '[i]t's hard to think of your father as a kid'.[1] At first blush akin to something out of a fairy story filled with magical mirrors and secret chambers permitting crossings into parallel worlds, 'a tea-chest somewhere'[2] stores objects that remain from her father's childhood and are now in Billie's possession, 'a whole snake-skin, a stick for finding water, and an old bag with books and papers in it'.[3] Together with 'all his old comics and his Biggles books (which are plain stupid, really) and *The Magic Pudding*',[4] a copy of '*The Hunchback of Notre Dame*, with its gaudy pictures and forests of exclamation marks', and 'all his old *Classics Illustrated* [...] *Moby Dick*, *Huckleberry Finn*, *The Count of Monte Cristo*',[5] these are objects that survive as witnesses to the passing of time. Yet as inherited things, their meanings are not immediately apparent; they offer no clear access to or knowledge of her father's boyhood, and as such prompt Billie's attempts to grapple with how to comprehend and narrate his childhood: 'Milking cows. With no TV. Before space rockets, even',[6] she muses. Stacked in the way of children's graduated building blocks (two words, three words, four words), the impressionistic effect of these sentences, in addition to affording Billie an inner life and marking out apparent differences between her father's imagined childhood and her own, leads to a turn to stories in order to make some sense of what is otherwise 'hard', if not inaccessible: 'Living like Tom Sawyer, that's how Billie thinks of it',[7] Winton writes of his child character's satisfied apprehension of her father's childhood. In multiple ways, childhoods are bound up with storytelling.

This chapter takes its cue from this single moment in a much larger narrative, to begin to examine the complex representations of childhood and storytelling in Winton's work. It does not claim to be a complete survey of Winton's ever-expanding oeuvre, or indeed a comprehensive account of childhood, as it is variously expressed across the genres in which Winton writes and the texts he has authored. Its aims are more modest insofar as it offers a pause to think about what is routinely acknowledged as a feature of Winton's texts but rarely discussed at length, namely that Winton's writing is marked by repeated references to childhood.

This feature is arguably as true of the books Winton writes for children (even as the category of 'children's literature' is by no means an uncontested one)[8] and for which Winton is well known, particularly the *Lockie Leonard* series, as it is of novels and short stories not marketed expressly to young readers. Some texts entertain more obvious references to childhood: *That Eye, the Sky* is told from the point of view of Ort Flack, a young boy who at one point in the novel confides, Peter Pan–like, '[g]eez, I don't want to grow up';[9] *The Deep*, with its illustrations by Karen Louise, focuses on the young girl Alice who is 'scared of the deep'[10] but whose eventual defeat of her fear of swimming beyond the shallows, with the help of some friendly dolphins, evokes an idea of childhood as a terrain of frightening but improving adventures. An unnamed boy is at the centre of the short story 'No Memory

Comes' from the collection *Minimum of Two*;[11] in *Breath*[12] an older man reflects on his adolescence.

Yet childhood also takes on a special charge in texts that do not, on first reading, have much to do with it at all. In *Dirt Music*, for instance, two young boys serve as an incidental part of the backdrop to Georgie Jutland's story of midlife chaos, which occupies a good portion of the narrative; yet, as a work of mourning, the text turns very much on certain ideas of childhood, with Luther Fox, Georgie's would-be lover and the novel's protagonist, consumed by the death of his beloved niece, Bird, whom he considers to be 'perfect'.[13] Fox spends part of the narrative in the north-western Australian coastal region trying to escape as part of his 'project of forgetting'[14] the deaths in a car accident of his brother, sister-in-law, niece and nephew. In memory, this child is rendered innocent, beatific even, and invokes an apprehension of childhood assisted by Fox's reading of Wordsworth and Blake.[15] Broadly speaking, then, childhood is neither evenly imagined nor 'put to use' in any consistent manner in Winton's work, and a focus on it in this chapter is therefore an invitation to consider its reach and composite relationships with themes and formal characteristics that preoccupy Winton's writing.

Yet such an enterprise is not as straightforward as these introductory intentions might suggest. At the very least, there is the matter of what might be meant by 'childhood'. In her study of representations of childhood in modern fiction, Susan Honeyman identifies two strands of thinking on the topic. One she nominates is the developmentalist view, which sees childhood as a series of stages in the movement towards an ideal of adulthood; the other is Romantic, insofar as adulthood is conceived as a fall from a childhood state modelled as original, innocent and natural.[16]

In a similar cast, Chris Jenks, along with many other literary scholars, presents childhood taxonomically – the 'Dionysian child' and the 'Apollonian child' in the instance of Jenks's work[17] – in part to suggest varying meanings of childhood, but with the result that such categories come to look rigid and ahistorical in the face of the discourses (legal, political, sociological, literary – the list goes on) that proliferate and produce varying ideas of childhood in any specific historical or cultural context. Such a limitation vexes the schema of childhood Reinhard Kuhn has posed, resting on categories such as 'The Redemptive Child' and 'The Menacing Child'.[18] Philippe Ariès's provocative claim that in 'medieval society the idea of childhood did not exist',[19] while raising the eyebrows if not the ire of many historians, nevertheless emphasises the historical contingency of childhood and the role representation has in its multiple imaginings. In this vein, recent scholarly collections such as *The Child in British Literature* map out childhood within chronological periods that might not have been meaningful for those now seen to be writing within them but are thought to offer contemporary readers 'prominent trends in literary constructions of childhood'.[20]

While recognising the insights these and other accounts of literary childhood provide, this chapter is interested less in suggesting that Winton's works register some recognisable national or temporal 'trend' or 'taxonomy' of childhood, or applying categories of childhood a priori to Winton's fictions, than in taking seriously the ways childhood is debated and narrated within the worlds of these texts. This approach seems especially important for thinking about childhood in the short story, a mode in which Winton has frequently written. After all, with its requirement of economy in narrative and characterisation, the short story form cannot easily entertain the narrative sequencing that would seem to give rise to the ideas of childhood as the series of stages Honeyman identifies at work in modern *long* fiction. In other words, the short story genre carries the possibility, in formal terms, of producing other versions of childhood that a focus on novels alone cannot recognise. When considering Winton's novels, it is equally clear that the application of received frameworks for conceiving of literary childhood are not entirely adequate in attending to the multiple ways it is represented.

'Secrets'[21] is the first story in Winton's first collection of short narratives, *Scission*, and its ostensible subject is a young girl, Kylie, whose domestic life has altered dramatically; she is, at the start of the story, in a new house with her mother's 'new husband, only they weren't married'.[22] Her father haunts the story; the photographs Kylie turns to for comfort and company attest to his ghostly presence, as 'he was always out of the picture, behind the camera'.[23] Largely ignored by the adults with whom she lives, Kylie defies the directive of Philip, her mother's 'husband', to keep clear of a bore well in the backyard, and takes the photographs with her into its depths of 'thirty-six feet'.[24] Eventually discovered, she is physically punished; in turn, Kylie throws down the well the newly hatched chicks she has been anticipating since the beginning of the story and commits an act of violence against an image of herself by cutting off her head in a photograph and poking it 'through a hole in the flyscreen of the window'.[25]

In many ways, this is a story that is implicitly indebted to familiar fairy-tale tropes: the wicked step-parent, the forbidden space, transgression, a fairly strict division between the world of adults (and sexuality) and that of the child. But if fairy tales are also often tales of morality, this short story is morally ambiguous and resists efforts to slot Kylie crudely into any imagined child 'type'. Is Kylie's determination to climb down the well wilful disobedience or an instance of a child's 'natural' curiosity? Is her treatment of the newly born chicks a sure indication of her innate wickedness or a sign of some deeper psychological injury that her descent into the womb-like subterranean cavern symbolises? Of course, these questions themselves produce or presuppose certain ideas of childhood (as well as critical tropes), and they are not the questions the text arguably raises in the first instance, anyway.

A feature of the story, one that becomes notable in the context of the volume in which it appears, is the absence of dialogue, leading to other sorts of questions about childhood and narrative. The stories that follow 'Secrets' in the collection – 'A Blow, a Kiss'[26] and 'Getting Ahead'[27] – also have a focus on childhood, as does the next story in the collection's linear sequence, 'My Father's Axe',[28] which is written in the first person (as is 'Getting Ahead'). In this story (as with the short story 'Aquifer'[29] that appears in *The Turning*, another collection), the narrator's childhood is mediated by memory, in this instance as a means of giving shape to the protagonist's preoccupation in the present (tense) with a lost axe that once belonged to his father. By contrast, 'A Blow, a Kiss' sees Albie, a young boy, and his father unintentionally attend an accident, an event that lends itself to a meditation, by means of a third-person limited point of view, on the bewildering physical violence adults can commit against children, a concern that 'Secrets' powerfully conveys in its briefest of sentences: 'He hit her'.[30] 'Getting Ahead' focuses the narrative through Maxford, 'old enough to understand and too young to contradict',[31] whose mother sets in motion (failed) plans, including the recruitment of her son to kill the cats of a recalcitrant tenant, to improve the family's financial situation following the death of her husband. Both 'A Blow, a Kiss' and 'Getting Ahead' have their fair quota of dialogue, 'My Father's Axe' less so, but the complete absence of it in 'Secrets' (as both the first story in this sequence and as a self-contained narrative) prompts some consideration of the role the short story form has in narrating childhood.

The absence of dialogue in 'Secrets' would seem to have the effect of rendering Kylie voiceless, not to silence childhood but rather to represent it in terms of limited power and knowledge. Unlike the reader, presumably, Kylie is uncomprehending of Philip and her mother 'locked in the big bedroom, laughing and making the bed bark on the boards',[32] for example. Yet, at the same time, the refusal to put words directly into Kylie's mouth, as it were, while still telling her story, which is only ever partly known to and about her as an effect of the limited third-person narration, might also be read as an opening statement on the ethics of the short story form (and the collection itself), and its ability to produce and represent ideas of childhood. In this first story of the collection, there is recognition that narrating childhood is a complicated undertaking, one that runs the risk of enforcing the very power structures it seeks to critique by telling that story in the first place. That Kylie herself spends much of the (written) story contemplating a wordless mode of representation – the photograph – upon which she performs her own intervention at the conclusion of the story, by cutting up an image of herself taken a year before when she was at kindergarten, suggests a silent protest at any claims to unmediated transparency and self-evident knowledge that both representational modes might presume, despite – or perhaps because of – the slice of childhood they both aim to capture.

If 'Secrets' can be interpreted at least in part as a comment on the role a particular narrative form plays in its (necessarily limited) imagining of childhood, then Lockie Leonard's father, the Sarge, in *Lockie Leonard, Human Torpedo*[33] has a more upfront apprehension of what childhood is about, where its limits lie. In this novel for younger readers, the first in a series of books that has been adapted for television, Lockie is adjusting to a new life in the town of Angelus. In the eighth chapter of the book he has his thirteenth birthday – school that day 'went fine';[34] his parents give him a 'new neoprene vest [in] Australian colours';[35] and he realises he is in love with Vicki Streeton, the rich, popular girl from school. The narrative from that point largely traces his on-again off-again relationship with Vicki. When Lockie is beaten up for refusing to fight with some older boys who are Vicki's friends, he is prompted to contemplate the ethics of violence. His father's response to his probing thoughts is one of the longer moments of dialogue in the novel:

> Listen, you're already worried about the Greenhouse Effect, the whales, the seals, the dolphins, uranium, nuclear war and South Africa. Don't worry about the ethics of when to kill people until it arises. You'll give yourself a flamin' ulcer. The adult world isn't that fabulous you have to hurry for it. Enjoy being a kid.[36]

Adopting here an educational relationship that would not be altogether unfamiliar to John Locke and his privileging of supervisory pedagogy in *Some Thoughts Concerning Education*,[37] Lockie's father conceives of childhood and the 'adult world' in binary terms, as relatively distinct spheres. It is an apprehension of childhood very different from that imagined in *Blueback*,[38] another of Winton's novels for younger readers. That text begins with the protagonist, Abel Jackson, diving for abalone as a young boy and encountering Blueback, a huge groper; it ends with him, now a marine biologist of some international note, returning home to Longboat Bay 'where he lived the life of his boyhood every day'.[39] Here the *Bildungsroman* narrative is linearly conceived, with each chapter clearly marking out Abel's life in, and as, a series of 'stages' – Chapter 11 relates in its first sentence that 'Abel Jackson went to university to figure out the sea';[40] Chapter 12 begins 'Abel Jackson became a marine biologist married to another marine biologist'[41] – but it is also circular insofar as Abel ends up where he began, both physically and existentially. This double structure of the narrative produces an idea of childhood as idyllic and desired, one on which the positive return to boyhood rests.

By contrast, in foregrounding Lockie and his experiences, and in marginalising adult figures, *Lockie Leonard, Human Torpedo* formally supports the Sarge's demarcations between an adult world and childhood. As the kindly Sarge would have it, childhood is not to be rushed (as it was for Locke, who thought children should be moulded into adults as soon as possible) and is something in which to take (certain) pleasure, as this period, imagined as one of relative innocence and non-responsibility, will soon pass. For Lockie, though, demarcations of childhood turn around sexuality and are produced through the heterosexual romance narrative that partly structures the novel. While Vicki is presented as sexually active and demanding (or at least the text construes her as conceiving of sex as a means by which to win attention), Lockie responds to her advances by marking out a distinction between love and sex, aligning himself with the former and explaining in an echo of his father's earlier advice, '[g]eez, Vicki, six months ago I was in primary school. I'm a kid. I'm not in a hurry for all this stuff. We're not grown up'.[42] 'This stuff' is a line between being grown up and being a kid, even as the very presence of Vicki in the novel promises to complicate the categories that structure and give meaning to Lockie's understanding of, and identification with, childhood.

As such, Vicki has a perhaps unexpected parallel in Ort Flack, the protagonist–narrator of *That Eye, the Sky*, a novel not marketed to young readers. Ort, like Vicki and Lockie, turns thirteen and starts high school during the course of this novel, admitting four weeks into the new educational regime and towards the end of the novel,

> I'm kind of stuck. I don't feel like a kid anymore. I'm not even a proper teenager. I'm not a grown-up adult. I'm not in the city. I'm not properly in the country. I dunno what the hell to do with meself.[43]

The present tense, combined with the first-person narration and the realist form (at least at this moment; the novel combines narrative styles in a way that reaches for aspects of experience for which realism, and reason, cannot account), does not invite any extended rumination within the narrative on childhood and its meanings. These modes mean that childhood is not reflected on deeply by the thirteen-year-old narrator, who is preoccupied instead with things metaphysical: the shining cloud that stretches over his house at night and that only he can see. Indeed, like Fish in *Cloudstreet*,[44] who is afforded luminous insight in that novel, Ort suffers an incident in childhood that makes others wonder if 'there's something wrong'[45] with him but that the novel suggests offers other ways of being in the world. All of which is why Ort's uncertainty at this moment is striking; it is a marking out of a beginning of not-childhood, although what gives meaning to that receding childhood is not known or identified easily by Ort, stalled by the hanging question of futurity.

The opposite is the case in the novel (for adults) *Breath*. Most of this text is a long flashback narrated by Bruce 'Pikelet' Pike; this retrospective narrative revolves in memory around friendships the narrator had with Loonie, a boy his own age; and an older couple, Sando and Eva: 'It was a boyhood that now seems so far away I can understand why people doubt such days ever existed',[46] Pike says. Pike is a middle-aged paramedic, and what prompts this reflection is his attendance at the scene of an accidental death. Despite Pike's assurance in the first-person present tense that 'I'm not a nostalgic man. I can go for weeks without thinking about my boyhood',[47] the pages that follow suggest otherwise, with the narrative detailing, in past tense, that very boyhood and its effects into adulthood, prompted by 'tonight's asphyxiation'.[48] The incident stands in for, or even eclipses, the individual who has died; the accidental death, or rather Pike's response to it, prompts and frames his account of a boyhood remembered. If not focused through a nostalgic lens, much of the story is filled with familiar boys'-own-adventure and coming-of-age narratives: Loonie and Pike take risks, push the limits; friendships are built and broken; Pike's first sexual experiences are predictably with Eva, the wife of his mentor–friend Sando. Her predilection for 'a strap and a pink cellophane bag'[49] is, however, perhaps less expected (as is the specific detailing of the bag's colour), at least for the younger Pike the narrator recreates: 'As a kid I didn't know what respiratory acidosis was'.[50] 'The kid' presented is not so much 'far away' or in doubt, as mediated by the knowledge (and professional vocabulary) of an older man as well as literary tropes.

Yet this boyhood is not the only one in the novel. As Pike relates his boyhood from a position of adulthood, one that is cemented as such because of the reflection on a younger self it presumes, this possibility is denied the 'nice-looking kid' who is 'tonight's asphyxiation'.[51] Pike enters this 'kid's' room after the fact; his mother has 'cut him down and dressed him and tidied everything up'.[52] Unlike his ambulance-driving partner who suspects suicide, Pike knows what the kid's mother, June, cannot say. Instead, when asked if there is anyone Pike can call for her, she replies, '[c]all? [...] You can call my son back. As you can see, he's not listening to his mother'.[53] At this moment of intense shock and grief, June is curiously imagined here, from Pike's narrative point of view, as narcissistic and domineering. Her bitter, sad, impossible request signals her son's transgression of her apparent idea of childhood, one that is sexually innocent and marked by obedience, one that the novel subsequently calls into question.

Indeed, if Pike cannot call back June's son, then the narrative calls back another son, another childhood, and another mother who offers an intriguing bookend to June. In the last pages of the novel, Pike recalls that he learns from his mother of Eva's death, which resulted from circumstances similar to that of June's son. She sends him a 'news clipping' with the details, but 'I still don't know why she did'.[54] It is possible that Pike's mother apprehends her son's childhood in terms very different from those associated with June. The adult Pike recalls his younger self as imagining his parents as 'so insubstantial that I hardly knew them anymore. I didn't know what they thought, what they suspected, what their lives had become'.[55] If Pike, in effect, places his story of childhood in contrast to the one June seems to evoke, then he needs not to know his parents and their adult inner lives for his childhood to take shape and meaning. His mother's seemingly incidental relaying of the news of Eva's death, which might well carry a trace of 'suspicion', suggests that the premise on which Pike's narrative turns – experimental, risk-taking youth cordoned off from the world of (asexual) adults (Eva, Pike relates, 'was no longer a girl, but not a woman in the way that my mother was a woman',[56] while the glimpse afforded of June is a study in repression) – is more involved than he might otherwise acknowledge or indeed can admit to within the necessary limitations of the first-person point of view by which the story is told.

This complexity is also testimony to the spirit of Billie Scully's remarks opening this essay, namely that efforts to imagine childhood are difficult. And while it is understandable that publishers might want to promote certain ideas of childhood as attractive selling points – the back-cover blurb of *Lockie Leonard, Human Torpedo* promises 'trouble, worry, mega-embarrassment and some wild, wild times', while the blurb for the UK edition of *Breath* highlights two boys 'intoxicated by the treacherous power of the waves and by the immortality of youth' – the glance across Winton's writing offered in this chapter suggests it produces various imaginings of childhood bound up with storytelling, and settles on none of them.

Notes

1   T. Winton, *The Riders*, Macmillan, Sydney, 1994, p. 83.
2   Ibid.
3   Ibid.
4   Ibid.
5   Ibid., p. 56.
6   Ibid., p. 83.
7   Ibid.
8   See, for example, J. Rose, *The Case of Peter Pan or the Impossibility of Children's Fiction*, University of Pennsylvania Press, Philadelphia, 1984; and

P. Hunt, *An Introduction to Children's Literature*, Oxford University Press, Oxford, 1994.

9 T. Winton, *That Eye, the Sky*, Scribner, New York, 2002, p. 63.

10 T. Winton, *The Deep*, Sandcastle Books, Fremantle, 1999, n.p.

11 T. Winton, 'No Memory Comes', *Minimum of Two*, Penguin, New York, 1989, pp. 11–21.

12 T. Winton, *Breath*, Picador, London, 2009.

13 T. Winton, *Dirt Music*, Picador, Sydney, 2010, p. 105.

14 Ibid., p. 103.

15 See also B. Matthews, 'Childhood in Tim Winton's fiction', in R. Rossiter and L. Jacobs (eds), *Reading Tim Winton*, Angus & Robertson, Sydney, 1993, pp. 59–71.

16 S. Honeyman, *Elusive Childhood: Impossible Representations in Modern Fiction*, Ohio State University Press, Columbus, 2005.

17 C. Jenks, *Childhood*, Routledge, London, 1996.

18 R. Kuhn, *Corruption in Paradise: The Child in Western Literature*, Brown University Press, Hanover, New Hampshire, 1982.

19 P. Ariès, *Centuries of Childhood*, trans. R. Baldick, Knopf, New York, 1962, p. 128.

20 A. E. Gavin, 'The child in British Literature: an introduction', in A. E. Gavin (ed.), *The Child in British Literature*, Palgrave Macmillan, Basingstoke, 2012, p. 3.

21 T. Winton, 'Secrets', *Scission*, Penguin, Melbourne, 2007, pp. 1–6.

22 Ibid., p. 1.

23 Ibid., p. 3.

24 Ibid.

25 Ibid., p. 6.

26 Winton, 'A Blow, a Kiss', *Scission*, pp. 7–13.

27 Winton, 'Getting Ahead', *Scission*, pp. 15–22.

28 Winton, 'My Father's Axe', *Scission*, pp. 23–33.

29 T. Winton, 'Aquifer', *The Turning*, Picador, Sydney, 2004, pp. 37–53.

30 Winton, 'Secrets', p. 5.

31 Winton, 'Getting Ahead', p. 16.

32 Winton, 'Secrets', p. 4.

33 T. Winton, *Lockie Leonard, Human Torpedo*, McPhee Gribble, Melbourne, 1990.

34 Ibid., p. 37.

35 Ibid., p. 36.

36 Ibid., p. 100.

37 J. Locke, *Some Thoughts Concerning Education*, A. and J. Churchill, London, 1693.

38 T. Winton, *Blueback*, Penguin, Melbourne, 2009.

39 Ibid., p. 149.

40 Ibid., p. 109.

41 Ibid., p. 117.

42 Winton, *Lockie Leonard, Human Torpedo*, p. 122.

43 Winton, *That Eye, the Sky*, p. 121.

44 T. Winton, *Cloudstreet*, Penguin, Melbourne, 1992.

45 Winton, *That Eye, the Sky*, p. 136.

46 Winton, *Breath*, p. 18.

47 Ibid.

48 Ibid.

49 Ibid., p. 207.

50 Ibid., p. 219.

51 Ibid., p. 3.

52 Ibid., p. 2.

53 Ibid., p. 5.

54 Ibid., p. 236.

55 Ibid., p. 199.

56 Ibid., pp. 199–200.

Bibliography

Ariès, P., *Centuries of Childhood*, trans. R. Baldick, Knopf, New York, 1962.

Gavin, A. E. (ed.), *The Child in British Literature*, Palgrave Macmillan, Basingstoke, 2012.

Honeyman, S., *Elusive Childhood: Impossible Representations in Modern Fiction*, Ohio State University Press, Columbus, 2005.

Jenks, C., *Childhood*, Routledge, London, 1996.

Kuhn, R., *Corruption in Paradise: The Child in Western Literature*, Brown University Press, Hanover, New Hampshire, 1982.

Locke, J., *Some Thoughts Concerning Education*, A. and J. Churchill, London, 1693.

Rossiter, R. and L. Jacobs (eds), *Reading Tim Winton*, Angus & Robertson, Sydney, 1993.

Winton, T., *Dirt Music*, Picador, Sydney, 2010.

—— *Blueback*, Penguin, Melbourne, 2009.

—— *Breath*, Picador, London, 2009.

—— *Scission*, Penguin, Melbourne, 2007.

—— *The Turning*, Picador, Sydney, 2004.

—— *That Eye, the Sky*, Scribner, New York, 2002.

—— *The Deep*, Sandcastle Books, Fremantle, 1999.

—— *The Riders*, Macmillan, Sydney, 1994.

—— *Cloudstreet*, Penguin, Melbourne, 1992.
—— *Lockie Leonard, Human Torpedo*, McPhee Gribble, Melbourne, 1990.
—— *Minimum of Two*, Allen & Unwin, Sydney, 1987.

8

THE CYCLE OF LOVE AND LOSS: MELANCHOLIC MASCULINITY IN *THE TURNING*

Bridget Grogan

Short fiction has been noted as an exemplary genre for the exploration of grief. As Rochelle Almeida observes, it 'enables the writer and the reader to distil the very essence of personal loss by boiling human emotion down to the barest bones'.[1] Indeed, the short story goes hand in hand with a literary minimalism that paradoxically achieves an affective maximalism: description is pared down and, as Cynthia J. Hallett notes, an 'aesthetic of exclusion' reigns such that 'the unstated is present as a cogent force'.[2] More than the short story, the short story cycle may provide a sustained focus on affective themes, elaborating these emotions while retaining the practice of literary minimalism. Structurally, moreover, the story cycle enacts loss in the spaces between stories: a sense of absence is inherent in a structure defined by disjunctions in narrators and narrative time. Yet the short story cycle, defined in Forrest L. Ingram's seminal study of the genre, is 'a set of stories so linked to one another that the reader's experience of each one is modified by his experience of the others'.[3] Consisting of seemingly discrete stories typically linked by recurring characters, settings and themes rather than chronology or development, the cycle is a complex genre constantly balancing specificity and unity. Ingram explains its dynamic complexity:

Like the moving parts of a mobile, the interconnected parts of some story cycles seem to shift their positions with relation to the other parts, as the cycle moves forward in its typical pattern of recurrent development. Shifting internal relationships, of course, continually alter the originally perceived pattern of the whole cycle. A cycle's form is elusive.[4]

The Turning,[5] Tim Winton's third collection of stories after *Scission*[6] and *Minimum of Two*,[7] is a cycle of seventeen stories. Interlinked by recurring characters in and from the fictional working-class harbour town of Angelus on the southern coast of Australia, the stories are also thematically interwoven: each story 'turns' on the experience of disappointment and/or loss. Taken together, they circle family memories, mysteries and traumas: absent fathers, lost loves, the death of a child and the memory of deceased parents enter the collection, not as central foci but as marginal glimmerings of loss and sorrow.

Although *Minimum of Two* is also a cycle, in *The Turning* Winton deploys the form to its best effect, marrying its structurally paradoxical disjunctions and unity to the disruptions of subjectivity implicit in the experience of loss. Winton also deploys the relational dimension of the short story cycle – dependent, as Ingram has noted, upon the 'shifting internal relationships' between stories – to mirror the relational affect of grief. According to Judith Butler:

What grief displays...is the thrall in which our relations with others holds us, in ways that often interrupt the self-conscious account of ourselves we might try to provide, in ways that challenge the very notion of ourselves as autonomous and in control. I might try to tell a story here, about what I am feeling, but it would have to be a story in which the very 'I' who seeks to tell the story is stopped in the midst of the telling; the very 'I' is called into question by its relation to the Other, a relation that does not precisely reduce me to speechlessness, but does nevertheless clutter my speech with signs of its undoing. I tell a story about the relations I choose, only to expose, somewhere along the way, the way I am gripped and undone by these very relations. My narrative falters, as it must…Let's face it. We're undone by each other.[8]

Winton's collection of intersecting stories is itself a 'story about relations', which reveals the way subjectivity, and in this instance the narrative that describes it, is 'gripped and undone by these very relations'. Accordingly, despite its shifts in narrative, narrator and narrative time, *The Turning* does have a central protagonist of sorts: Vic Lang (or a member of his family) appears in the majority of the stories in a substantial way. His character is refracted through the narration of formative moments in his life, a narration shifting from third to first to second person and from the past to the present tense. Each of these stories is related to aspects of masculinity, including puberty, paternal relations, the rivalry between brothers, the role of the husband, desire, and the masculine virtue of protection versus the vice of violence.

'Abbreviation',[9] narrated in third-person past tense, describes Vic's first brief experience of romantic love as a twelve-year-old. 'Damaged Goods',[10] narrated in the present tense by Vic's wife, Gail, elaborates on his high-school infatuation with a girl who has a facial birthmark. 'On her Knees'[11] is Vic's own past-tense narration of his mother Carol's struggle to support him during his university years, after her policeman husband, Bob (Vic's father), has left. In present-tense narration in the second person, 'Long, Clear View'[12] describes Vic's adolescent unease as his family begins to fall apart shortly before his baby sister dies and his father abandons them for good. In 'Reunion',[13] Gail recalls the aborted attempt she, Carol and Vic make one Christmas to reunite with Bob Lang's brother Ernie and his family, long after Bob has left. 'Commission',[14] Vic's past-tense narration, centres on his reunion with his father after twenty-seven years when his mother, sick with cancer, requests his presence at her bedside. 'Fog'[15] continues the focus on Bob Lang, describing in third-person past tense his involvement in a mountain rescue at the height of his despondency and the beginning of his alcoholism in Angelus. Although 'Boner McPharlin's Moll'[16] – told in past tense by a female narrator – deals only peripherally with Bob Lang, it provides a context for his unhappiness in what is revealed as a corrupt police force deeply implicated in Angelus's burgeoning drug scene, and gives further insight into his eventual abandonment of the town and his family. 'Immunity'[17] is told from the past-tense perspective of a female narrator who remembers meeting the teenage Vic on a train shortly before the death of his sister, at a time when she had an adolescent crush on him. In 'Defender',[18] voiced in third-person past-tense narration, Vic and Gail visit friends for the weekend – after both Vic's parents have died – and address various aspects of the past.

The shifting narration of these stories, along with the way they disrupt the chronology of Vic's life, suggest that in loss, the 'very "I" who seeks to tell the story' is indeed 'stopped in the midst of the telling', as Butler suggests. Vic's memory of the girl with a birthmark, for example, encapsulates the collection as a whole as 'a story he used to tell against himself'.[19] Moreover, a number of other stories not devoted to the Lang family make up the collection, and so the narrative expands to provide a broader view of the community of Angelus. These stories also reflect in significant ways on some of the themes raised in the narration of Vic's experience. In the middle of the text, a trio of stories – 'The Turning',[20] 'Sand'[21] and 'Family'[22] – is devoted to the brothers Frank and Max, and their toxic and competitive relationship. 'The Turning' presents Raelene, Max's wife, as its focus, exploring her violent and abusive marriage, her fascination with two new-found Christian friends, and her eventual conversion to a pitiful and personal form of Christianity. 'Sand' explores the childhood relationship of Max and Frank, focusing on Max's incipient violence and Frank's naive yet loving acceptance. 'Family' is devoted to Frank's uncomfortable surfing reunion with Max and his eventual attempt to save him from a shark attack. This meeting occurs after Frank has abandoned his position as a star footballer known to fans as 'Leaper', his courage having failed him during a major game. Not only do these stories stand on their own, but they reflect on the dysfunctional relationship between the brothers Bob and Ernie Lang. Moreover, Max and Frank embody two potentials for Vic's character: violent anger or the role of the protector or defender of family.

The four remaining stories link obliquely to the aforementioned pieces. 'Big World',[23] the first story of the collection, describes in the first person the narrator's teenage friendship with a working-class boy called 'Biggie', a road trip that they take and the narrator's desperation to leave the confinement of Angelus behind him. He recalls a party at Massacre Point at the end of his final school year, connecting the story to 'Damaged Goods' and 'Boner McPharlin's Moll', both of which mention it too. 'Aquifer',[24] also in the words of an anonymous first-person narrator, explores the themes of the possibility of violence behind the bland surface of suburbia, and the effects of the past upon the present, a major theme in *The Turning*. The narrator, after seeing a news report of a police team carrying human bones from a familiar swamp, follows his curiosity back from Angelus to the suburbs of Perth where he was raised, simultaneously immersing himself in the past. In the third-person narration of 'Small Mercies',[25] Peter Dyson returns with his young son to Angelus, where he grew up, after his wife's suicide. Here he encounters his high-school sweetheart, diminished by years of prior drug use (drugs presumably linked to Bob Lang's unhappiness in the Angelus police force) and still seeking his affection. Dyson's son's favourite footballer is Leaper, linking the story to those dealing with Max and Frank. 'Cockleshell'[26] describes a character like Vic Lang: Brakey, an adolescent boy who also comes from a broken home and develops a crush on a tantalisingly distant girl (as Vic does in 'Abbreviation' and 'Damaged Goods').

Although *The Turning* moves seamlessly between male, female and third-person narrators, one of its primary concerns is Vic's coming of age and the losses that shape his character. Each of these losses occurs during his adolescence, indicating the role they play in constructing his adulthood. Indeed, *The Turning* implies that the very passing of time entails a loss around which a melancholic subjectivity, and Vic's particular notion of masculinity, is constructed. As the narrator of 'Aquifer' informs the reader, 'the past is in us, and not behind us. Things are never over'.[27]

Arguably the most famous discussion of grief, Freud's 1917 essay 'Mourning and melancholia', defines psychical responses to loss. Mourning, Freud argues, is a complete acknowledgement of loss whereby energy is gradually disinvested from a lost person, object or ideal, thereby allowing for new attachments: 'when the work of mourning is completed the ego becomes free and uninhibited again'.[28] Melancholia, by contrast, involves internalising and thereby keeping alive what is lost ('the past is in us', as Winton suggests: 'Life moves on, people say, but I doubt that. Moves in, more like it').[29] This process has its price: ambivalence towards the lost object (both missed and resented) is turned inward and directed toward the self. Thus melancholia, a directionless feeling of sadness no longer attached to an external source, is also characterised by self-loathing, shame and guilt. Because energy is redirected rather than gradually disinvested, the bereaved cannot move healthily into new attachments. In mourning, then, 'it is the world which has become poor and empty; in melancholia it is the ego itself'.[30] By the end of *The Turning*, Vic's melancholia is clear. In 'Defender', structurally and chronologically the last story of the collection, Gail has taken to calling him 'the fucking Book of Lamentations'.[31] Indeed, Vic is 'preoccupied with memories'; they are 'a swarm he could neither evade nor disperse'.[32] 'You're stuck',[33] Gail tells him. 'Nothing you do now holds your attention like the past'.[34]

As Melanie Klein observes, 'early mourning is revived whenever grief is experienced in later life'.[35] Vic's accumulating losses, as well as *The Turning*'s narrative structure, suggest the kind of collapse of time that grief involves, and that contradicts Freud's argument that mourning is eventually psychically concluded. As Klein suggests and others have argued, mourning must to some extent involve a melancholic response. Judith Butler, for example, argues that the process of mourning cannot involve a simple disinvestment from the object of loss. For Butler, mourning implies transformation, a turning point in the process that is subjectivity:

> [O]ne mourns when one accepts that by the loss
> one undergoes one will be changed, possibly forever.
> Perhaps mourning has to do with agreeing to undergo
> a transformation (perhaps one should say *submitting*
> to a transformation) the full result of which one cannot
> know in advance. There is losing, as we know, but there
> is also the transformative effect of loss, and this latter
> cannot be charted or planned.[36]

The Turning suggests that loss is inherent in character formation, and that one of the transformative aspects of loss is therefore the ongoing construction of the self. Specifically, loss and masculinity are linked: Vic's father leaves during his teenage years, shortly after his baby sister's death and just as he comes into his manhood. Without any other siblings, he is forced to become his mother's protector, the 'defender' to which the collection so often refers. Yet in 'Long, Clear View', as his parents' relationship deteriorates, the teenage Vic takes to standing at the window, watching the world through the crosshairs of his father's rifle. The ambiguity of the image suggests that, poised at the brink of manhood, Vic will go one of two possible ways: he will become the defender of others, or he will resort to violence to stem his pain – he will become like either Frank or Max in *The Turning*'s central stories. In 'Defender', a title with sporting connotations recalling Frank/Leaper, Vic realises how close he once came to the latter: 'He was only a breath away from something hideous. He was a ticking bomb'.[37] Vic makes his choice, however, after his sister has died and his father has left, to 'battl[e] on with his mother, feeling responsible for her as the only man, the only child in her life'.[38] Later, as his wife realises, '[i]n any dispute, Vic will instinctively seek out a victim to defend. That's his nature and it's become his work as a labour lawyer'.[39] While grief leaves him desperate, the opposing side of this emotion, love – without which grief would not eventuate – keeps him together and shapes his character.

The cohesive force of love versus the fragmentary affect of grief is thematised throughout *The Turning*, where the fragile construction of the self from familial and social bonds, and the corresponding threat of loss, are mirrored in its narrative structure. Out of a number of fragmented episodes that move backwards and forwards in time, as well as between different narrating conscious-nesses, the reader can construct a fuller narrative of characters' lives, particularly Vic's. Simultaneously, the themes that inform these lives are fleshed out, thus informing the narrative itself. Vic's association of love with absence, for example, is thematised in 'Abbreviation', but this theme intensifies as the reader sees love and loss oscillating throughout Vic's experience. In this story, a twelve-year-old Vic meets and falls in love with a girl called Melanie on the beach during a holiday at White Point. She has an unusual physical affliction, having lost her ring finger in an accident with a hay baler. Although she calls the remaining stump of her finger her 'abbreviation', the name also attaches to Vic's feelings for her, abbreviated when he goes to look for her family's campsite and realises they have gone. Melanie's earlier response to Vic's question of whether losing her finger hurt has broader implications within the collection: 'Like a total bastard, she said. But, you know, all the big things hurt, the things you remember. If it doesn't hurt it's not important'.[40] What Vic experiences as her sudden abandonment is the first of his disappointments registered within the text. Melancholy settles upon him in the story's concluding description: 'the sea and the sky were as pale and blue and blank as sleep, as empty as he felt standing there on the lapping shore'.[41]

'Damaged Goods' continues *The Turning*'s interest in the theme of the oscillation of love and loss, and in corporeal signifiers: Vic Lang's wife, Gail, describes her husband's teenage fascination with a girl with a birthmark. Vic's interest in 'Strawberry Alison' is directly related to her facial discolouration: 'in time he came to admit that he loved Alison because of the mark, not just despite it'.[42] Vic, according to Gail, is attracted to physical disfiguration, an external index, it would seem, of his inner condition. Indeed, a description of Vic and Alison on either side of the library window at school suggests that Alison reflects him. As she stares at herself in the reflective glass, unaware of his proximity, he looks into her face and is 'struck by the sadness of her gaze'.[43] Gail is aware of how potent a pull Vic's past has on his life, and so she takes to driving to Angelus on weekends, 'like some biographer sniffing around in vain for one, final, telling detail that will complete the psychological puzzle at the centre of Vic's life'.[44] In her attempt to interpret her husband, Gail stands in for the reader who is involved in a similar act of decoding.

Alison, with the burning mark across her face, symbolises damage and loss for Vic, not only in her facial marking, which reminds him of Melanie, his other elusive love, but because she dies in a car accident after Boner McPharlin's party at Massacre Point. Vic, it seems, will subsequently associate this lost and elusive love with the other losses of his life, compelling his wife, unbeknown to him, to return to the scene of the story. The closing words of her narrative reveal the infectious quality of loss, transferred not only to Gail but also to the reader. Like the relational aspect of the short story cycle, the transfer of emotion that makes *The Turning* so powerful contributes to the humanity of Winton's vision. As Moira Gatens argues, emotion exposes 'the breaches in the borders between self and other evidenced by the contagiousness of "collective" affects'.[45] Because Vic is lost to some degree to Gail, she contracts his melancholy:

> I've seen photos of the girl and read her poem and both seem unremarkable except for the fact that they entranced the boy who became my husband. I sit in a motel like a woman waiting for a man to show up. I go out to the cliffs with binoculars to see whales find their way in from the southern mist and I walk here in this paddock, stubbornly, wondering at the heat each of us leaves in our wake.[46]

The melancholic conclusions of 'Abbreviation' and 'Damaged Goods', both quoted above, suggest in their imagery of absence and emptiness a feeling of loss transferred to the reader. This sense of melancholy is emphasised by the finality of each story's conclusion, the silence each ending implies, and the break in interpretation required before the next story commences. Not every story ends with absence, however. Some conclude with images of elation and love, emphasising the collection's thematisation of the interrelation of love and grief. In 'On Her Knees', for example, after Vic has helped his proud mother clean for the last time the home of a woman who has unjustly fired her, the closing image suggests renewed strength and the engulfing affect of sudden love:

> My mother stood silhouetted in the open doorway. It seemed that the very light of day was pouring out through her limbs. I had my breath back. I followed her into the hot afternoon.[47]

Despite the sense of resolve or silence created by the conclusion of each story, narrative details span the divisions between them: the broader picture of Vic's life does not emerge simply from the accumulation of knowledge gleaned from each story as a whole, but mainly from the cumulative effect of small oblique details that occur in each story as seemingly casual asides or as brief references to names, places or events. In fact, these small details constitute the story of the collection, mirroring the ways the significant events of a life may not constitute much time within the everyday process of living but become repetitive focuses of attention in comprehending one's personhood. Perhaps the most poignant example of this gradually accruing character information pertains to the death of Vic's sister, an element of his past that becomes increasingly evident through glimmering references in the text. The toddler succumbs to meningitis, her death the harshest of Vic's early traumas. Vic is twelve years older than his sister, and so – perhaps because his focus would not have been on her entirely or, more likely, because her death constitutes unspeakable trauma – she barely exists in the stories that concern him, and enters the narrative merely as a tiny presence whose brief mention is nevertheless increasingly wrenching.

Vic's sister is first referred to in 'Damaged Goods', when his wife, Gail, referring in an aside to Vic's teenage unhappiness, effectively articulates the crux of the collection by touching on the traumas of his past:

I used to think he exaggerated this stuff but his mother Carol put me straight. That town, Angelus, wasn't such a quaint place in those days. It crushed her husband. Something happened there which caused him to lose his way. He began to drink. Bob Lang, the proverbial

straightshooter, became a local joke. And then their
infant daughter died of meningitis. Vic was fifteen.
He never mentioned a sister, never once said a word. I
couldn't believe it – I was incensed – and when I confronted him about it he told me that he'd forgotten. A
sick look came over his face. I pressed him for details but
he picked up his keys and backed towards the door. I let
him go. Angry as I was, I believed him. He'd blocked
her from his mind. He looked as appalled as I was.[48]

Gail realises that Vic's lost sister is the crucial answer to 'the
psychological puzzle'[49] of Vic's life. Her own sister, she recalls, has
a fixation that helps her to be more 'forgiving about Vic and the
weight of his past': a doll that lies 'like a child in a cardboard and
cellophane coffin', and stands 'between her and other people, a
kind of solace, really, but also a barrier to human intimacy'.[50] Vic's
memory of his sister, as it is gradually revealed, functions in the
same way. Throughout *The Turning* she is mentioned recurrently,
albeit briefly and peripherally, and in 'Long, Clear View', the
extent of Vic's devotion to her is made clear. The story hints, in
brief descriptions, that as his parents become increasingly preoccupied with their disintegrating marriage, Vic takes over the
care of his sister: 'Before they return the baby has taken her first
unaided steps and only you're there to see it';[51] '[y]ou walk down
by the river until your baby sister nestles into your shoulder and
sleeps';[52] '[y]ou bathe your sister and put her down and eat your
dinner cold and wipe out the high chair';[53] 'you come home to
mind your sister';[54] '[y]ou take the baby to your parents' room
and bounce her on the bed for a while to calm your nerves'.[55] By
the time the reader reaches 'Immunity', however peripheral Vic's
sister may have been in the overall narrative, the story's closing

description, in its double finality, is devastating. Bob's police car, lights flashing, pulls up beside the train station where the female narrator has been conversing with Vic. She explains his father's urgency: 'It was his little sister in hospital with meningitis. I heard all about it later. She died'.[56]

Gail is mistaken in thinking Vic has forgotten his sister. When, in 'Commission', he makes the excruciating visit to fetch his estranged father at the bequest of his dying mother, he notes the photographs of his family Bob has pinned to the wall – Vic at age fourteen, captured in time, and his mother similarly frozen in her thirties:

> And Kerry? I asked, despite myself.
> The old man pointed back to the doorway where, above the lintel, a faded shot of my dead sister hung like an icon. A chubby toddler in a red jumpsuit.[57]

This is the first and only time the baby is named in the collection, and the only time Vic speaks of her directly. Indeed, her presence hangs suspended in the collection, ever memorialised, an icon of love and loss.

Winton's paratextual reference to loss, an epigraph from T. S. Eliot's 'Ash-Wednesday',[58] informs *The Turning*'s overall themes and title:

> *And I pray that I may forget*
> *These matters that with myself I too much discuss*
> *Too much explain*
> *Because I do not hope to turn again*
> *Let these words answer*
> *For what is done, not to be done again.*[59]

The invocation of these lines is, of course, ironic, because Winton's collection repeatedly emphasises the return of the past. 'What is done' is relived repetitively in its melancholic incorporation in the memory and existence of the collection's characters. While the epigraph suggests the will to turn away from the past, this will is ultimately defeated, just as it is in 'Ash-Wednesday'.

'Ash-Wednesday' was written shortly after Eliot converted to Anglicanism, and is widely regarded as his 'conversion' poem. (The title story of *The Turning* also explores the conversion of its protagonist, Raelene, who finds some alleviation of the violence and misery of her life in her pitiful discovery of Jesus. In 'Defender', moreover, Gail tells Vic of her return to religion: 'I thought I'd try the Anglicans'.)[60] Eliot's poem consists of six numbered sections described by Ronald Tamplin as a 'succession of prayers and supplications'.[61] These sections come together, as Winton's stories do, to form a unified whole.

Eliot, writes Tamplin in a description equally applicable to Vic Lang and his desire not to fall into the trap of memory, has 'battled to conversion, against a troubled life and a troubled temperament, and the poem resignedly hopes not "to turn again"'.[62] At first, 'Ash-Wednesday' appears paradoxically to reject poetry itself in its striving for religious transcendence and Christian detachment. Yet its dominant mood is uncertainty and hesitation, revealed in the halting rhythm and paradoxically hesitant repetition of the opening lines:

> *Because I do not hope to turn again*
> *Because I do not hope*
> *Because I do not hope to turn*
> *Desiring this man's gift and that man's scope*
> *I no longer strive to strive towards such things* [...][63]

These lines immediately deal with the theme of renunciation and the loss of secular human ambition, perhaps even poetic ambition, inherent in religious detachment. The need to renounce the desire for 'this man's gift and that man's scope' is also the relinquishment of poetry, as this line is taken from Shakespeare's Sonnet 29, wherein the speaker attests to 'desiring this man's art and that man's scope'.[64] Like *The Turning*, then, 'Ash-Wednesday' explores loss; a sense of bereavement – strangely figured as a paradoxically melancholic joy – enters the poem when the poet considers the religious relinquishment of an attachment to the physical world:

> *Because I know that time is always time*
> *And place is always and only place*
> *And what is actual is actual only for one time*
> *And only for one place*
> *I rejoice that things are as they are and*
> *I renounce the blessèd face*
> *And renounce the voice*
> *Because I cannot hope to turn again*
> *Consequently I rejoice, having to construct something*
> *Upon which to rejoice [...]*[65]

Religious joy, therefore, is figured here as melancholic; it is premised upon the loss of the temporal world and the 'blessèd face' of its mortal inhabitant (and it is therefore paradoxically premised upon the loss of loss itself, loss being an inescapable dimension of the temporal world). The speaker hopes not 'to turn' to this world again.

In its very title, *The Turning* suggests that the hope not 'to turn again' is, in fact, futile. And indeed, 'Ash-Wednesday' itself constitutes a movement from the fear of turning to this very turning.

By the last section of the poem, the opening line ('Because I do not hope to turn again')[66] has been transmuted to the less definitive statement 'Although I do not hope to turn again';[67] turning has become increasingly inevitable. Caught in 'the dreamcrossed twilight between birth and dying',[68] the poet remains in the temporal world of specific place. Submitting to this world, previously interpreted as lost, or at least to the language that describes it, the poet yields to a genuine joy. As Julia Kristeva argues, 'a triumph over sorrow is made possible by the...capacity to identify now no longer with the lost object but with a third instance'[69] – the language that stands in for it:

> And the lost heart stiffens and rejoices
> In the lost lilac and the lost sea voices
> And the weak spirit quickens to rebel
> For the bent golden-rod and the lost sea smell
> Quickens to recover
> The cry of quail and the whirling plover [...]
> And smell renews the salt savour of the sandy earth [...][70]

Ultimately, the poet's cry is a request for the recognition of the temporal world within the vision of the spiritual. It is also a request for permission to sublimate loss through language. Moreover, it is a reminder that the lost world will return if it is ignored:

> Suffer us not to mock ourselves with falsehood
> Teach us to care and not to care
> Teach us to sit still
> Even among these rocks [...]
> And even among these rocks
> Sister, mother

And spirit of the river, spirit of the sea,
Suffer me not to be separated
And let my cry come unto Thee.[71]

In *The Turning*, Winton creates an elegiac collection of stories pivoting on love and loss, narrative and silence, presence and absence, and prosody and affect. As it is in 'Ash-Wednesday', the spirit of place, and particularly the 'spirit of the sea', is richly evoked, suggesting the incantatory power of language to alleviate loss. In *The Turning*, time itself is oceanic: 'It comes and goes in waves and folds like water; it flutters and sifts like dust, rises, billows, falls back on itself'.[72] Winton's deployment of the short story cycle mirrors this sense of oceanic and chronological circularity. Moreover, it enacts the dialectic of self and other – if not the merging of self and other – evident in the experiences of grief and love, the 'tension between the one and the many'[73] that Ingram regards as central to the story cycle:

> When do the many cease being merely many and congeal into one? Conversely, when does a 'one' become so discrete and differentiated that it dissolves into a 'many'? Every story cycle displays a double tendency of asserting the individuality of its components on the one hand and of highlighting, on the other, the bonds of unity which make the many into a single whole.[74]

Winton's emphasis upon the fragmentation of loss also foregrounds the 'bonds of unity' in love. Unable to turn from their memories, Winton's characters submit to the past, and also to the present that will eventually constitute it; this encompasses their 'turning', an experience linked via the reference to

'Ash-Wednesday' to a sense of religious transcendence that blurs the division between self and other. Like the narrator of 'Big World', at their most complete and tender Winton's men embrace transience and the inevitable loss this entails; simultaneously, they acknowledge the wide beauty of the temporal world and the love of and for others that is both impermanent and yet eternal: 'I don't care what happens beyond this moment. In the hot northern dusk, the world suddenly gets big around us, so big we just give in and watch'.[75]

Notes

1   R. Almeida, *The Politics of Mourning: Grief Management in Cross-Cultural Fiction*, Rosemont, Cranbury, New Jersey, 2004, p. 15.

2   C. J. Hallett, 'Minimalism and the short story', *Studies in Short Fiction*, vol. 33, no. 4, 1996, p. 487.

3   F. L. Ingram, *Representative Short Story Cycles of the Twentieth Century*, Mouton, The Hague, 1971, p. 13.

4   Ibid.

5   T. Winton, *The Turning*, Picador, London, 2006.

6   T. Winton, *Scission*, Picador, London, 2003.

7   T. Winton, *Minimum of Two*, Picador, London, 2003.

8   J. Butler, 'Violence, mourning, politics', *Studies in Gender and Sexuality*, vol. 4, no. 1, 2003, p. 13.

9   Winton, 'Abbreviation', *The Turning*, pp. 17–36.

10 Winton, 'Damaged Goods', *The Turning*, pp. 55–65.

11 Winton, 'On Her Knees', *The Turning*, pp. 101–12.

12 Winton, 'Long, Clear View', *The Turning*, pp. 189–204.

13 Winton, 'Reunion', *The Turning*, pp. 205–15.

14 Winton, 'Commission', *The Turning*, pp. 217–33.

15 Winton, 'Fog', *The Turning*, pp. 235–49.

16 Winton, 'Boner McPharlin's Moll', *The Turning*, pp. 251–92.

17 Winton, 'Immunity', *The Turning*, pp. 293–8.

18 Winton, 'Defender', *The Turning*, pp. 299–317.

19 Winton, 'Damaged Goods', p. 55.

20 Winton, 'The Turning', *The Turning*, pp. 133–61.

21 Winton, 'Sand', *The Turning*, pp. 163–9.

22 Winton, 'Family', *The Turning*, pp. 171–87.

23 Winton, 'Big World', *The Turning*, pp. 1–15.

24 Winton, 'Aquifer', *The Turning*, pp. 37–53.

25 Winton, 'Small Mercies', *The Turning*, pp. 67–99.

26 Winton, 'Cockleshell', *The Turning*, pp. 113–32.

27 Winton, 'Aquifer', p. 53.

28 S. Freud, 'Mourning and melancholia', *The Standard Edition of the Complete Psychological Works of Sigmund Freud*, vol. XIV, edited by J. Strachey, The Hogarth Press, London, 1955, p. 245.

29 Winton, 'Aquifer', p. 37.

30 Freud, 'Mourning and melancholia', p. 246.

31 Winton, 'Defender', p. 313.

32 Ibid., p. 299.

33 Ibid., p. 301.

34 Ibid., p. 302.

35 M. Klein, 'Mourning and its relation to manic-depressive states', in R.V. Frankiel (ed.), *Essential Papers on Object Loss*, New York University Press, New York, 1994, p. 96.

36 Butler, 'Violence, mourning, politics', p. 11.

37 Winton, 'Defender', p. 317.

38 Winton, 'Damaged Goods', p. 60.

39 Ibid., p. 58.

40 Winton, 'Abbreviation', p. 26.

41 Ibid., p. 36.

42 Winton, 'Damaged Goods', p. 58.

43 Ibid., p. 59.

44 Ibid., pp. 55–6.

45 M. Gatens, 'Privacy and the body: the publicity of affect', in B. Roessler (ed.), *Privacies: Philosophical Evaluations*, Stanford University Press, Stanford, California, 2004, p. 115.

46 Winton, 'Damaged Goods', p. 65.

47 Winton, 'On Her Knees', p. 112.

48 Winton, 'Damaged Goods', p. 59.

49 Ibid., p. 55.

50 Ibid., p. 56.

51 Winton, 'Long, Clear View', p. 193.

52 Ibid., p. 198.

53 Ibid.

54 Ibid., p. 200.

55 Ibid., p. 202.

56 Winton, 'Immunity', p. 298.

57 Winton, 'Commission', p. 223.

58 T. S. Eliot, 'Ash-Wednesday', *The Waste Land and Other Poems*, Faber & Faber, London, 1990, pp. 53–62.

59 Winton, epigraph, *The Turning*, p. vii.

60 Winton, 'Defender', p. 302.

61 R. Tamplin, *A Preface to T. S. Eliot*, Longman, London, 1988, p. 51.

62 Ibid.

63 Eliot, 'Ash-Wednesday', p. 53.

64 W. Shakespeare, Sonnet 29, *Shakespeare's Sonnets*, Methuen, London, 2010, p. 169.

65 Eliot, 'Ash-Wednesday', pp. 53–4.

66 Ibid., p. 53.

67 Ibid., p. 61.

68 Ibid.

69 J. Kristeva, 'On the melancholic imaginary', *New Formations*, vol. 3, 1987, p. 9.

70 Eliot, 'Ash-Wednesday', p. 61.

71 Ibid., p. 62.

72 Winton, 'Aquifer', p. 52.

73 Ingram, *Representative Short Story Cycles of the Twentieth Century*, p. 19.

74 Ibid.

75 Winton, 'Big World', p. 15.

Bibliography

Almeida, R., *The Politics of Mourning: Grief Management in Cross-Cultural Fiction*, Rosemont, Cranbury, New Jersey, 2004.

Butler, J., 'Violence, mourning, politics', *Studies in Gender and Sexuality*, vol. 4, no. 1, 2003, pp. 9–37.

Eliot, T. S., *The Waste Land and Other Poems*, Faber & Faber, London, 1990.

Freud, S., *The Standard Edition of the Complete Psychological Works of Sigmund Freud*, vol. XIV, edited by J. Strachey, The Hogarth Press, London, 1955.

Gatens, M., 'Privacy and the body: the publicity of affect', in B. Roessler (ed.), *Privacies: Philosophical Evaluations*, Stanford University Press, Stanford, California, 2004, pp. 113–32.

Hallett, C. J., 'Minimalism and the short story', *Studies in Short Fiction*, vol. 33, no. 4, 1996, pp. 487–95.

Ingram, F. L., *Representative Short Story Cycles of the Twentieth Century*, Mouton, The Hague, 1971.

Klein, M., 'Mourning and its relation to manic-depressive states', in R. V.

Frankiel (ed.), *Essential Papers on Object Loss*, New York University Press, New York, 1994, pp. 95–122.

Kristeva, J., 'On the melancholic imaginary', *New Formations*, vol. 3, 1987, pp. 5–18.

Shakespeare, W., *Shakespeare's Sonnets*, Methuen, London, 2010.

Tamplin, R., *A Preface to T. S. Eliot*, Longman, London, 1988.

Winton, T., *The Turning*, Picador, London, 2006.

—— *Minimum of Two*, Picador, London, 2003.

—— *Scission*, Picador, London, 2003.

9

TRANSCULTURAL WINTON: MNEMONIC LANDSCAPES OF AUSTRALIA

Sissy Helff

It had become her personal memory.[1]

In an essay now almost twenty years old, Paul Ricoeur ponders the difficulties of living together in a post–Cold War world marked not only by inequality and discrimination but also by severe crimes against humanity including genocides. In his remarks about possible future orders and new imaginaries of a better world, Ricoeur emphasises the importance of memory-work. He states that,

> [T]he first difference which calls for transference and hospitality is a difference of memory, precisely at the level of customs, rules, norms, beliefs and convictions which constitute the identity of a culture.[2]

He therefore proposes a careful combination of three dimensions – namely translation, exchange of memories and forgiveness – in order to generate a discursive foundation for an interaction between the identity and alterity of a country and its 'strangers'. Ricoeur believes that '[e]ven at the individual level it is through stories revolving around others and around ourselves that we articulate and shape our own temporality'.[3] Although Ricoeur developed this model in the aftermath of the dissolution of the Soviet Union and in light of the Balkan crisis in order to come to terms with the then extremely disparate European situation (one that may even have outlived the philosopher), his idea conveys a universal meaning that, as yet, has not lost its momentum.

In his writing, Tim Winton time and again emphasises the importance of such memory-work, especially when he confronts the reader with his fictional characters' handling of history and their individual acts of remembering the past. In this chapter I therefore argue that Winton's writing should be reread in the light of Ricoeur's idea in general and of a crucial second dimension, the exchange of memories, in particular. I seek to show that Winton's rich mnemonic narrative landscapes in his novel *Shallows* and the short story collection *The Turning*[4] imagine a multicultural Australia by applying diegetic modes of exchanging memories as well as using reciprocal interactions between the reader and the texts. In doing so Winton's narratives invest in fresh perspectives on Australian history and its *lieux de mémoire*[5] while paying close attention to the intergenerational, multicultural, transnational and transcultural dimensions of memory. Given that Winton's emerging mnemonic landscapes connect communities in Australia and beyond through memory practices that work not only on a local and global level but also on a mimetic and diegetic one, it can be said that Winton's narratives create memories of transnational or even transcultural quality.[6] The fact that Winton's narratives generate transcultural memories is often overlooked by critics. My essay sets out to argue that approaching Winton's narratives with a focus on the exchange of memories and the generation of transcultural memories opens fresh avenues in reading and understanding the author's literary oeuvre in general and his envisaged narrative project in particular.

Transcultural Winton

As a programmatic writer and poster boy of Australian literature, Tim Winton is both loved and hated by his critics. Much of the expressed mutual scepticism is related to his appealing style and the vivid utilisation of popular, often Australian iconic patterns such as the beach, the surf, the surfer, the whale and the sacred.[7] It's true that Winton's bestselling books convey a Zeitgeist that strikes not only a nostalgic Australian chord but also meets the sensibility of many international readers who take a piece of Australia home when purchasing a new Winton text. Yet there is more to Winton's narratives than meets the eye. In addition to his recurring motifs of rural working-class life, youth culture and environmental activism, Winton negotiates conditions and circumstances past and present that have influenced the fates of people living in modern Australia. This interest also explains why his narratives frequently oscillate between various temporalities connecting distinct local histories and cross-cultural memories.[8]

The epigraph to *The Turning*, taken from T. S. Eliot's poem 'Ash-Wednesday', adequately sets the tone for Winton's short story collection. Besides this, however, the cited lines cogently introduce the greater Wintonian story universe, a world that negotiates selfhood, transcultural memory and the idea of an interconnected Australian history concerned with just and moral decision-making.

> *And I pray that I may forget*
> *These matters that with myself I too much discuss*
> *Too much explain*
> *Because I do not hope to turn again.*

Let these words answer
For what is done, not to be done again[9]

In his article on *The Turning*, Stephen Torre states that,

> Winton's stories – like Eliot's 'words' – centralize the
> experience of turning as a fact of life. The stories…pre-
> sent characters in situations where identity and behaviour
> are subject to potential change as a result of identifiable
> factors…and ineluctable fate.[10]

Winton's ostensibly Romantic and apparently iconic Australian
story world and its places, landscapes and inhabitants are
punctuated with marks of industrialisation and modernisation,
developments integral to creating a global modernity that, in turn,
also had great impact on the history-making of rural communities
in Australia and beyond. Winton's writing thus weaves mnemonic
landscapes of Australia that include – in addition to histories
of settler-colonialism – processes of modernisation, accounts of
immigration and the politics of decolonising identity.

Focusing on memory exchange and Winton's usage of
transcultural memories suggests a research perspective in line with
the timely and more general discussion of Australian literature's
international, transnational, multicultural and transcultural quality.
The debate, however, is not new but started to gain momentum
in Australia in 1999, when a special issue of *Australian Literary
Studies* and essays by Gillian Whitlock and others[11] challenged
the significance of national schemata for approaching Australian
literature. The argument back then already pointed to a perspective that advocates reading antipodean literature through the lens
of transnational connections and transcultural trajectories.[12] The

field of memory studies flourished in Australia at about the same time, a fact to which Kate Darian-Smith and Paula Hamilton's essay collection *Memory and History in Twentieth-century Australia*[13] bears witness. Australian memory studies, as Jacqueline Lo states, has in the meantime undergone great developments.[14] In a recent article on Australian history and cosmopolitan memory, the critic writes that while memory studies as a field initially emerged within nation-specific paradigms, since then it has formulated an increasingly cosmopolitan research agenda 'for addressing memory cultures that exceed their national frame'.[15]

In the light of these observations it becomes clear that any analysis of an ostensibly local situation illuminates globalisation effects,[16] meaning that any study exploring local modernity and individual memory in fiction to some extent always traces and examines global developments, too. Interested in such local–global connections and entangled developments – and whether these manifest as a distinctively Australian modernity in Winton's work – critics started to explore representations of local contexts, especially with respect to Australia's declining whaling industry on the one hand,[17] and the writer's fictional realisation of white working-class gender relations on the other.[18] While critical readings of gendered identities are tremendously relevant to a better understanding of the memory-work at play in Winton's oeuvre,[19] this essay touches on this discussion only when arguing that Winton's narratives and the displayed models of identification are grounded in a self-reflexive negotiation of a transcultural Australian recollection. Winton's perception of how to deal with the inherited Australian memory and the country's disputed history finds expression in a sensitive literary project through which the author seeks to offer his personal memory-work, presenting the reader an intimate form of reconciliation.

Mnemonic *Shallows*

'It was the whalers that made this country!'[20] With this ostensibly simple sentence, the embittered German immigrant Hassa Staats summarises the dilemma that not only dictates his life but that describes in a nutshell the story world of Winton's novel *Shallows*. In short, the ecocritical novel sets out to negotiate the idea of lifeworld in the light of colonial history and the post-industrial developments of the country. Hassa Staats, as a representative of an early wave of migration, addresses the effects of globalisation without touching on the morally reprehensible annexation of terra nullius, thus this sentence presses a finger on the wound of Australian history-making and the hitherto erratically con-ducted Australian memory-work. The artist-cum-critic Ross Gibson is certainly right when he states that 'memory can recreate the gone world',[21] and this is exactly what Winton's *Shallows* achieves so successfully without flirting with the historical novel genre. The narrative illustrates the choices fictional characters have when engaging in acts of redemption and reconciliation by means of exchanging memories.

Having said this, it becomes clear that the story world of *Shallows* is concerned with fictionalising precisely such personal embodied experiences of remembering while trying to come to terms with its deep-rootedness in an emotional premise Judith Wright once claimed to be a particularly white Australian experience, namely love for one's country and 'the guilt of the invasion'.[22] Accordingly Wright coined the description of Australia as a 'haunted country',[23] a formulation Winton's novel fictionalises on three interrelated story levels: first by retelling the intergenera-tional colonial family history of the 'local' Coupar clan, second by introducing the industrial change in the rural community of

Angelus in the second half of the twentieth century, and third by depicting an internationally organised, militant ecological organisation that manifests itself in the fictional anti-whaling protest group Cachalot and Company. In his article on *Shallows* and the end of whaling in Australia, John P. Turner states that huge chunks of the plot are in fact 'based on real incidents which occurred at Cheynes Beach in 1977', and that 'one of the chief activists of the Canadian Greenpeace Movement, Robert Hunter, has given a first-hand account of these events in *Warriors of the Rainbow: a Chronicle of the Greenpeace Movement*'.[24] Winton, too, depicts the group of activists as an international and multicultural crowd who 'came to join some Australians to close down Paris Bay'[25] and who now join hands with the last of the Coupar offspring, young Queenie. Queenie, the heroine, connects various social and cultural realms; in fact, she embodies the very idea of cultural encounter, since she is a direct descendant of an Australian woman and the American whaler Nathaniel, who himself, having been marooned on Australian shores, penned his bleak memories of his arrival, and his experiences of colonialism and violence in a private journal. Nathaniel's gruesome account reconstructs a tragic, transnational family history that keeps haunting the Coupar clan, as Queenie's granddad Daniel resentfully remarks:

> People were driven off land, shot and beaten, and now we have land, we have Angelus – roads, cars, houses, parks, beaches – and there's nothing we can do about it. In dreams I go back into the past – it's like a well – and change it all back around, make the past right again and then I wake up and I don't exist any more [...] Yes, I'm ashamed of my father [...]

You have to inherit lots, Queenie, and I don't want
you to. You are the last real Coupar. Funny how it ends
up being a woman. A woman.[26]

Yet the journal is not rediscovered by the heroine herself but
by her husband, Cleveland Cookson (whose name, like many
others in the novel, speaks for itself), who eagerly reads the personal testimony, realising that

Other people's experiences had often seemed more
exciting, closer to the truth, than his own: but never
before had he felt so close to owning the experience of
another as he had with Nathaniel Coupar.[27]

Although Nathanial's testimony portrays the bleakest aspects
of colonialism, it is through his transnational and transcultural
memories as well as the intergenerational family memories that
Cleve feels connected to his partner and future wife, Queenie.
While Queenie flatly refuses to accept the journal as a resource
portraying her history and hence her legacy, she nonetheless shares
Cleve's interest in memory. The epigraph to this chapter, '[i]t had
become her personal memory',[28] is a case in point, illustrating
the personal embodied experiences of remembrance as well as
the intergenerational exchange of memories. The short sentence
expresses the omniscient narrator's point of view and summarises
the memory-work of Queenie Coupar as she recalls the tragic
death of her grandmother. Interestingly enough, the narrative
does not reveal whether Queenie's memories are first- or second-
hand. This strategic narrative manoeuvre, which incidentally
opens a gateway for sincere criticism, allows the novel to bypass

discussions of veracity, suggesting that the reliability of memories and their overall validity rank behind experiences of empathy.

In contrast to the overtly 'masculine' lineage of the Coupar clan, Queenie, the last descendant, is a woman with amphibian attributes. As a mediator between different worlds she feels as much at ease in water as on shore; she loves the sea as much as she understands the lifeworld of the people in Angelus. Additionally, she invests in a solidarity of interests with the foreign marine conservationists. Queenie's watery world thus represents a utopian transcultural realm, a space that incorporates, in addition to a rural Australian community and the international anti-whaling activists, an underwater world occupied by a multitude of creatures. In fact, Queenie and her being in the world represent an eternal humanitarian hope for a more just and sustainable future, a Romantic sublimation that represents the spiritual element of the story. It is she who reminds us of the sacred, an eternal circle of life connecting all time and tides. And she is the only one, too, who moves with ease between different worlds. Thus young Queenie embodies, as the queen, the key to a transcultural solidarity that reaches far beyond any given notion of multiculturalism, for Queenie embraces all species. While some critics may label such imagery ecocritical trash, the novel seeks to mitigate sentimentality by reminding the reader that a mutual understanding between different people, or even dissimilar 'creatures', cannot be taken for granted.

I believe we need to understand the ending of *Shallows* in this particular vein. When Queenie and her husband Cleve eventually witness the stranding of the whales, the reader shares a poignant moment of helplessness. Neither the reader nor Queenie leave the beach once the big cetaceans start digging their sandy graves. We endure pain together, and the reader shares yet another horrifying moment in the fictional history of this haunted place:

> Over the smacking rain, Cleve and Queenie Cookson heard the cries of the whales and were suddenly awake. They lay still for some time, paralysed by joy and disbelief, hearing the sounds come closer every moment as though nearly with them.
>
> 'They've come,' Queenie whispered.
>
> 'Yes.' Cleve hugged her [...]
>
> Queenie screamed. Surf thundered and the night was images in torch beams. Masses of flesh and barnacles covered the sand, creeping up, floundering, suffocating under their own weight. A pink vapour from spiracles descended upon Cleve and Queenie Cookson as they moved between the heaving monuments.[29]

Turning to transcultural memorialising

Set in Angelus and White Point, the same fictional, rural places in which *Shallows* unfolds, the short story cycle *The Turning* condenses and interconnects individual and collective memories by means of a fragmented storytelling and a colliding narrative style.[30] The combination of various individual acts of remembrance is central to this short story project, which consists of seventeen short stories; it is through this rich framework of polyphonic narrative voices and the combination of many story fragments that the individual stories as well as the story collection gain momentum. The compiled stories generate chains of memory whose literary repercussions reach far beyond *The Turning*. 'Turning' therefore is much more than the title of a book and a motif within the stories.

It refers to a reading practice that, as Stephen Torre has stated, is itself 'characterized by turning, returning, revision, re-seeing'[31] and, I believe, acts of remembering. It is in this way that the reader actively accompanies the characters in their daily attempts to make sense of their being in the world. This also explains why the author chooses to work with some characters over a greater period of time. Vic and Max pop up in several stories. In this way the characters of the short story collection create a network of associations and overlapping memories in which the reader plays a decisive role – because it is through reading and remembering that connections may be drawn between individual stories and memory fragments, and within Winton's greater story universe.

We meet Vic Lang, for example, as one of these recurring characters, in several of the seventeen short stories. The first encounter, if the reader follows the story sequence provided in the book, takes place in 'Abbreviation',[32] a juvenile story of a brittle first love, which is followed by a second tale of unrequited love, 'Damaged Goods',[33] before we learn more about Vic's relationship to his mother in 'On Her Knees'.[34] The three stories work with different narrative frameworks, namely through a heterodiegetic first- and third-person narrative in 'Damaged Goods' and 'Abbreviation', and a homodiegetic point of view in 'On Her Knees'. This approach is particularly important with regard to narrative reliability on the one hand and the representation of memories on the other. Whereas the first story is told in present tense, both the second and third are told in past tense, a narrative move that invites the reader to travel back in time. This journey into the past is also supported through the narrative point of view, since the stories are told by either Vic himself ('On Her Knees') or his much younger wife Gail ('Damaged Goods') – who appropriates episodes of her husband's youth to better understand Vic's present life and his inability to let go and be fully absorbed by love. He, as well as his former love interest Strawberry Alison, is damaged goods. Accordingly Gail states:

> So much of his youth seems to have taken place in an altogether different country [...] the soundtrack of his youth is different from mine, but we do share a sense of having lived under siege.[35]

It is through remembering, reimagining and retelling – all acts ingrained in the exchange of memories – that Gail hopes to get in touch with her partner emotionally. Whereas the first two stories describe Vic's first, hesitant attempt to find love outside his nuclear family, it is in 'On Her Knees' that Vic finally narrates his conscious turning towards maternal love. Being both narrator and protagonist of the story, Vic fully controls his storytelling and the pictures he draws. It is through this own memory-work that the now grown-up man assesses his former juvenile relationship to his mother. In pursuing his memories the autodiegetic narrator evokes an image of his ultimate love:

> My mother stood silhouetted in the open doorway. It seemed that the very light of the day was pouring out through her limbs. I had my breath back. I followed her into the hot afternoon.[36]

The story's closing sentences thus not only stress a son's love for his mother but render her the idealised parent with an almost god-like appearance.

By interconnecting Vic's stories and the individual memory-work of the three distinct narrators, *The Turning* generates a vivid polyphonic panorama and an impressively transcultural mnemonic landscape. Winton's memory-work therefore relies as much on fragmentation and association as on a homing in on Western Australian *lieux de mémoire* (Angelus and White Point). Moreover, the reader encounters an almost excessive yearning and imperative need for a utopian maternal love – as if such love could remedy and even overwrite an overtly male national history. In contrast to *Shallows*, *The Turning* pieces together a memory jigsaw that comes alive only in the mind of the reader. Here the very act of exchanging memories may be compared to what Cleve Cookson experiences while reading Queenie's family history. Transcultural memories in *The Turning* can thus probably be best understood in terms of a reading process that echoes the diegetic mnemonic landscapes of *Shallows*.

Transcultural mnemonic landscapes of Australia

I return, then, to my initial observation – that Winton's memory-work has a transnational or even transcultural quality. This reading of selected texts by Tim Winton in the light of transcultural memory aims at providing an insight into the author's memory-work, its creative application in general and the exchange of memories in particular. While the novel *Shallows* invests a great deal in exploring and depicting the various levels upon which memories can be exchanged and a transcultural mnemonic landscape evoked in diegetic mode, the short story collection *The Turning*, by contrast, illuminates the idea of exchanging of memories on a more abstract level, namely by suggesting a reading practice that interconnects fictional memories across several short stories.

Such creative assertions echo contemporary perspectives on the narration of fictional Australian history. By drawing this intergenerational and transnational picture of fictive Western Australian *lieux de mémoire*, Winton suggests that places are as much part of a local modernity as they are imperative in generating transcultural memories. While other texts by Winton, such as his prize-winning novel *Cloudstreet*[37] and his later *Dirt Music*,[38] invest little in mnemonic narrative landscapes, *Shallows* and *The Turning* successfully present a Wintonian story universe that imagines an increasingly internationalised and transnational Australia. Given that Winton's narratives and their emerging mnemonic landscapes oscillate between various temporalities, connecting distinct local histories and cross-cultural memories in Australia and beyond, they can be said to create transnational or even transcultural memories by employing the 'transcultural imaginary'. The emerging transcultural mnemonic landscapes eventually suggest that both the author's literary oeuvre and his overall narrative project work towards cultural engagement and reconciliation.

Notes

1   T. Winton, *Shallows*, Graywolf Press, Saint Paul, Minnesota, 1993, p. 125.
2   P. Ricoeur, 'Reflecting on a new ethos for Europe', *Philosophy & Social Criticism*, vol. 21, nos 5–6, 1995, pp. 5–6.
3   Ibid., p. 6.
4   T. Winton, *The Turning*, Picador, Sydney, 2005.
5   P. Nora, 'Between memory and history: *les lieux de mémoire*', *Representations*, vol. 26, 1989, pp. 7–24.
6   The transcultural quality of texts is particularly clear when writers employ the 'transcultural imaginary' as a vital tool to imagine story worlds. The term 'transcultural imaginary' draws from both Wolfgang Iser's concept of the imaginary (W. Iser, *The Fictive and the Imaginary*, Johns Hopkins University Press, Baltimore, Maryland, 1993) and Arjun Appadurai's concept of imagination (A. Appadurai, 'Global ethnoscapes: notes and queries for a transnational anthropology', in R. G. Fox (ed.), *Recapturing Anthropology: Working in the Present*, School of American Research, Santa Fe, New Mexico, 1991, pp. 191–210). While the latter term defines a cultural practice, the former denotes the crossing of the imagination into the realm

of literature. The 'transcultural imaginary' hence describes the process of amalgamation of different cross-cultural social realities with manifold styles, writing traditions and literary imaginaries into unique transcultural aesthetics, a transcultural imaginary (S. Helff, *Unreliable Truths: Transcultural Homeworlds in Indian Women's Fiction of the Diaspora*, Rodopi, Amsterdam, 2013, p. xiv).

7   The almost mythical connotation of the beach is commonly expanded to the surf and might serve as an explanation of why the Australian beachscape has become a kind of national institution within Australian popular culture, thus Fiske, Hodge and Turner write:

> The beach's increasing centrality to Australian myths coincides…with an increasing urbanisation. As the free, natural, and tough bush existence became more obviously an anachronistic version of national identity, the figure of the bronzed lifesaver filled the gap. (J. Fiske, B. Hodge and G. Turner, *Myths of Oz: Reading Australian Popular Culture*, Allen & Unwin, Sydney, 1987, p. 54.)

For an analysis of the sacred in Winton's work see V. Brady, 'The sacred and the social extreme: Tim Winton's *Breath*', Negotiating the Sacred V: Governing the Family, conference, Monash University, 14–15 August 2008, arts.monash.edu.au/ecps/conferences/negotiating-the-sacred/2008/brady-paper.pdf; S. Torre, '"Turning" as theme and structure in Tim Winton's short stories', in M. R. Dolce and A. R. Natalee (eds), *Bernard Hickey, a Roving Cultural Ambassador: Essays in His Memory*, Forum, Udine, Italy, 2009, pp. 281–92; and A. Taylor, 'What can be read, and what can only be seen in Tim Winton's fiction', *Australian Literary Studies*, vol. 7, no. 4, 1996, pp. 323–31.

8   In his essay 'National hauntings: the architecture of Australian ghost stories' (*JASAL Special Issue: Spectres, Screens, Shadows, Mirrors*, 2007, pp. 94–105), David Crouch seeks to excavate the textual remains of Australian history and its ghostly figures. He moreover asks how and to what extent history inscribes itself in the architecture of houses. Thus he writes:

> The ghosts in these stories are not alien to the architecture; indeed, while their human occupants may settle in these spaces and draw a sense of identity from them, the ghost itself is incorporated into the very economy of the dwelling, its otherness determining the identity of these spaces. In this way both texts raise the spectre of indigeneity in Australia. (pp. 95–6)

9   Winton, epigraph, *The Turning*, p. vii.

10 S. Torre, '"Turning" as theme and structure in Tim Winton's short stories', p. 281.

11 See G. Whitlock, 'Australian literature: points of departure', *Australian Literary Studies*, vol. 19, no. 2, 1999, pp. 152–62; M. Jacklin, 'The transnational turn in Australian literary studies', *JASAL Special Issue: Australian Literature in a Global World*, 2008, pp. 1–14, www.nla.gov.au/openpublish/index.php/jasal/article/viewArticle/1421; G. Huggan, *Australian Literature: Postcolonialism, Racism, Transnationalism Literature*, Oxford University Press, Oxford, 2007; and W. Ommundsen, 'The quest for Chineseness in Australian literature', *Cultural Studies and Literary Theory*, vol. 16, 2008, pp. 90–109.

12 The field of global memory studies started to emerge in Europe and around the world at about the same time, the turn of the millennium. This development was triggered by such publications as D. Levy and N. Szneider, 'Memory unbound: the Holocaust and the formation of cosmopolitan memory', *European Journal of Social Theory*, vol. 5, no. 1, 2002, pp. 87–106. Levy and Szneider's article marked a turning point in memory studies, since the field was until then mainly concerned with national memory-work. The change of approach in Australian literary studies is evident in a number of publications: S. Mycak and A. Sarwal (eds), *Australian Made: A Multicultural Reader*, Sydney University Press, Sydney, 2010; R. Dixon, 'Australian literature – international contexts' *Southerly*, vol. 67, nos 1–2, 2007, pp. 15–27; K. Gelder, 'Proximate reading: Australian literature in transnational reading frameworks', *JASAL Special Issue: Common Readers and Cultural Critics*, 2009, pp. 1–12; N. Birns, '"So close and yet so far": reading Australia across the Pacific', *Australian Book Review*, vol. 309, 2009, pp. 50–2; D. Carter, 'After post-colonialism', *Meanjin*, vol. 66, no. 2, 2007, pp. 114–19; R. Dixon, 'Australian fiction and the world republic of letters 1890–1950', in P. Pierce (ed.), *The Cambridge History of Australian Literature*, Cambridge University Press, Melbourne, 2009, pp. 223–53; and P. Mead, 'Nation, literature, location', in Pierce (ed.), *The Cambridge History of Australian Literature*.

13 K. Darian-Smith and P. Hamilton (eds), *Memory and History in Twentieth-century Australia*, Oxford University Press, Melbourne, 1994; see also K. Darian-Smith and P. Hamilton, 'Memory and history in twenty-first century Australia: a survey of the field', *Memory Studies*, vol. 6, no. 3, 2013, pp. 370–83.

14 J. Lo, '"Why should we care?" Some thoughts on cosmopolitan hauntings', *Memory Studies*, vol. 6, no. 3, 2013, pp. 345–7.

15 Ibid., p. 345.

16 Appadurai, 'Global ethnoscapes', p. 199.

17 See J. Turner, 'Tim Winton's *Shallows* and the end of whaling in Australia', *Westerly*, no. 1, 1993, pp. 79–85; and S. Helff, 'Sea of transformation: re-writing Australianness in the light of whaling', in L. Volkmann, N. Grimm, I. Detmers, and K. Thomson (eds), *Local Natures, Global Responsibilities: Ecocritical Perspectives on the New English Literatures*, Rodopi, Amsterdam, 2010, pp. 90–104.

18 See, for example, S. Zapata, 'Rethinking masculinity: changing men and the decline of patriarchy in Tim Winton's short stories', *ATENEA*, vol. XXVIII, no. 2, 2008, pp. 93–106; and B. Arizti Martín, 'Fathercare in Tim Winton's fiction', *Hungarian Journal of English and American Studies*, vol. 2, nos 1–2, 2006, pp. 276–86.

19 In this context, critics have observed that Winton's narratives often lack any maternal spaces of refuge. See C. McGloin, 'Reviving Eva in Tim Winton's *Breath*', *Journal of Commonwealth Literature*, vol. 47, no. 1, 2013, pp. 1–20; and S. Helff, 'Gendered gateways: Australian surfing and the construction of masculinities in Tim Winton's *Breath*', in J. Wilson and D. Tunca (eds), *Conference Proceedings: EACLALS Triennial Conference (Istanbul 2011)*, in press.

20 Winton, *Shallows*, p. 33.

21 R. Gibson, 'The flood of associations', *Memory Studies*, vol. 6, no. 3, 2013, p. 250.

22 J. Wright, *The Cry for the Dead*, Oxford University Press, Melbourne, 1981, p. 12.

23 Ibid., p. 12.

24 J. P. Turner, 'Tim Winton's *Shallows* and the end of whaling in Australia', *Westerly*, no. 1, 1993, p. 80.

25 Winton, *Shallows*, p. 36.

26 Ibid., pp. 78–9.

27 Ibid., p. 114.

28 Ibid., p. 125.

29 Ibid., p. 235.

30 For a study of the narrative style in *The Turning* through the lens of Wolfgang Iser's reader response theory, see Torre, '"Turning" as theme and structure in Tim Winton's short stories'.

31 Ibid., p. 289.

32 Winton, 'Abbreviation', *The Turning*, pp. 17–36.

33 Winton, 'Damaged Goods', *The Turning*, pp. 55–66.

34 Winton, 'On Her Knees', *The Turning*, pp. 101–12.

35 Winton, 'Damaged Goods', p. 62.

36 Winton, 'On Her Knees', p. 112.

37 T. Winton, *Cloudstreet*, Simon & Schuster, New York, 2002.

38 T. Winton, *Dirt Music*, Picador, Sydney, 2001.

Bibliography

Appadurai, A., *Modernity at Large: Cultural Dimensions of Globalization*, University of Minnesota Press, Minneapolis, 1996.

—— 'Global ethnoscapes: notes and queries for a transnational anthropology', in R. G. Fox (ed.), *Recapturing Anthropology: Working in the Present*, School of American Research, Santa Fe, New Mexico, 1991, pp. 191–210.

Arizti Martín, B., 'Fathercare in Tim Winton's fiction', *Hungarian Journal of English and American Studies*, vol. 2, nos 1–2, 2006, pp. 276–86.

Birns, N., '"So close and yet so far": reading Australia across the Pacific', *Australian Book Review*, vol. 309, 2009, pp. 50–2.

Brady, V., 'The sacred and the social extreme: Tim Winton's *Breath*', paper presented at Negotiating the Sacred V: Governing the Family, conference, Monash University, 14–15 August 2008, arts.monash.edu.au/ecps/conferences/negotiating-the-sacred/2008/brady-paper.pdf.

Carter, D., 'After post-colonialism', *Meanjin*, vol. 66, no. 2, 2007, pp. 114–19.

Crouch, D., 'National hauntings: the architecture of Australian ghost stories', *JASAL Special Issue: Spectres, Screens, Shadows, Mirrors*, 2007, pp. 94–105.

Darian-Smith, K. and Hamilton, P., 'Memory and history in twenty-first century Australia: a survey of the field', *Memory Studies*, vol. 6, no. 3, 2013, pp. 370–83.

—— *Memory and History in Twentieth-century Australia*, Oxford University Press, Melbourne, 1994.

Dixon, R., 'Australian fiction and the world republic of letters 1890–1950', in P. Pierce (ed.), *The Cambridge History of Australian Literature*, Cambridge University Press, Melbourne, 2009, pp. 223–53.

—— 'Australian literature – international contexts', *Southerly*, vol. 67, nos 1–2, 2007, pp. 15–27.

Fiske, J., Hodge, B. and Turner, G., *Myths of Oz: Reading Australian Popular Culture*, Allen & Unwin, Sydney, 1987.

Gelder, K., 'Proximate reading: Australian literature in transnational reading frameworks', *JASAL Special Issue: Common Readers and Cultural Critics*, 2009, pp. 1–12.

Gibson, R. 'The flood of associations', *Memory Studies*, vol. 6, no. 3, 2013, pp. 245–52.

Helff, S., 'Gendered gateways: Australian surfing and the construction of masculinities in Tim Winton's *Breath*', in J. Wilson and D. Tunca (eds), *Conference Proceedings: EACLALS Triennial Conference (Istanbul 2011)*, in press.

—— *Unreliable Truths: Transcultural Homeworlds in Indian Women's Fiction of the Diaspora*, Rodopi, Amsterdam, 2013.

—— 'Sea of transformation: re-writing Australianness in the light of whaling', in L. Volkmann, N. Grimm, I. Detmers, and K. Thomson (eds), *Local Natures, Global Responsibilities: Ecocritical Perspectives on the New English Literatures*, Rodopi, Amsterdam, 2010, pp. 90–104.

Huggan, G., *Australian Literature: Postcolonialism, Racism, Transnationalism*, Oxford University Press, Oxford, 2007.

Iser, W., *The Fictive and the Imaginary*, Johns Hopkins University Press, Baltimore, Maryland, 1993.

Jacklin, M., 'The transnational turn in Australian literary studies', *JASAL Special Issue: Australian Literature in a Global World*, 2008, pp. 1–14, see www.nla.gov. au/openpublish/index.php/jasal/article/viewArticle/1421.

Levy, D. and Szneider, N., 'Memory unbound: the Holocaust and the formation of cosmopolitan memory', *European Journal of Social Theory*, vol. 5, no. 1, 2002, pp. 87–106.

Lo, J. '"Why should we care?" Some thoughts on cosmopolitan hauntings', *Memory Studies*, vol. 6, no. 3, 2013, pp. 345–58.

McGloin, C., 'Reviving Eva in Tim Winton's *Breath*', *Journal of Commonwealth Literature*, vol. 47, no. 1, 2013, pp. 1–20.

Mead, P., 'Nation, literature, location', in P. Pierce (ed.), *The Cambridge History of Australian Literature*, Cambridge University Press, Melbourne, 2009, pp. 549–67.

Mycak, S. and Sarwal, A. (eds), *Australian Made: A Multicultural Reader*, Sydney University Press, Sydney, 2010.

Nora, P., 'Between memory and history: *les lieux de mémoire*', *Representations*, vol. 26, 1989, pp. 7–24.

Ommundsen, W., 'The quest for Chineseness in Australian literature', *Cultural Studies and Literary Theory*, vol. 16, 2008, pp. 90–109.

Ricoeur, P., 'Reflecting on a new ethos for Europe', *Philosophy & Social Criticism*, vol. 21, nos 5–6, 1995, pp. 1–13.

Schürholz, H., 'Gendered spaces: the poetics of domesticity in Tim Winton's fiction', *Journal of the European Association for Studies on Australia*, vol. 3, no. 2, 2012, pp. 59–79.

Taylor, A., 'What can be read, and what can only be seen in Tim Winton's fiction', *Australian Literary Studies*, vol. 7, no. 4, 1996, pp. 323–31.

Torre, S., '"Turning" as theme and structure in Tim Winton's short stories', in M. R. Dolce and A. R. Natalee (eds), *Bernard Hickey, a Roving Cultural Ambassador: Essays in His Memory*, Forum, Udine, Italy, 2009, pp. 281–92.

Turner, J. P., 'Tim Winton's *Shallows* and the end of whaling in Australia', *Westerly*, no. 1, 1993, pp. 79–85.

Whitlock, G., 'Australian literature: points of departure', *Australian Literary Studies*, vol. 19, no. 2, 1999, pp. 152–62.

Winton, T., *The Turning*, Picador, Sydney, 2005.

—— *Cloudstreet*, Simon & Schuster, New York, 2002.

—— *Dirt Music*, Picador, Sydney, 2001.

—— *Shallows*, Graywolf Press, Saint Paul, Minnesota, 1993.

Wright, J., *The Cry for the Dead*, Oxford University Press, Melbourne, 1981.

Zapata, S., 'Rethinking masculinity: changing men and the decline of patriarchy in Tim Winton's short stories', *ATENEA*, vol. XXVIII, no. 2, 2008, pp. 93–106.

10

FROM THE SUBLIME TO THE UNCANNY IN TIM WINTON'S *BREATH*

Brigid Rooney

Set in a small community on the southern coastline of Western Australia, *Breath*[1] revisits a world familiar to readers of Tim Winton's fiction. Narrated by fifty-year-old paramedic Bruce Pike, the novel recounts events from Pike's past that have rendered him a wary isolate even as, from the wreckage, he salvages a modicum of self-knowledge and grace. Pike's isolation and loneliness condition his retrospective narration of early adolescence in the 1970s working-class mill town of Sawyer, an outpost of Angelus – the fictional version of Albany in a number of Winton's books. Known in those days as 'Pikelet', the narrator tells how he drifted away from his fond but conventional parents into wild company, first with his friend Ivan Loon, or 'Loonie', and then with the ageing, thirty-something hippie and ex-surfing champion Bill Sanderson, or Sando.

A self-appointed guru, Sando inducts the boys (for reasons that are veiled but verge on the sinister) into the plane of the extraordinary. Sando grooms his disciples for elect status, for heroic masculinity, by taking them on surfing expeditions in increasingly wild, remote and risky locations. *Breath*'s hyperbolic, male-centric surfing adventures occur in vividly evoked, sublime and elemental seascapes. Eventually, however, the surfing plot is subsumed by an even wilder interior of sexual adventurism, as Sando's maimed and embittered wife Eva draws adolescent Pikelet into her game of erotic asphyxiation. Here Winton's novel traverses difficult moral terrain in which hubris, existential terror and abuse of the other threaten to unravel the self.

Response to *Breath* echoes established patterns in Winton's Australian reception to date.[2] Winner of the Miles Franklin Literary Award, *Breath* is widely regarded as a mature, powerfully achieved work, its nuanced temporal design belying its apparently straightforward narrative. Yet for some readers, *Breath* produces troubling ambiguities. Carmen Lawrence, for example, baulks at Winton's strain of 'puritanism'.[3] Childhood contact with Christian evangelism underpins the recurring moral struggle in Winton's fictional universe between spirit and flesh, sin and salvation, an influence he has himself acknowledged. Winton has spoken of growing up in a 'house full of Bibles' with parents who converted to the Church of Christ: as 'converts their flame burned bright' and 'the heat of their conversion has carried beyond them'.[4] It is not hard to see how Winton's fictional worlds reflect these polarities. His favourite gospel writers, Luke and John, doctor and mystic respectively, correspond to the 'two halves of my upbringing'.[5] Seeking to 'balance' physical and spiritual planes, inner and outer worlds, Winton's fiction is marked by the ebb and flow of emotional intensities, apprehending the spiritual through the sensory realm of body, landscape and natural elements.[6]

Along with this emotional terrain, the novels seem to evoke a sense of unresolved underlying disturbance or anxiety, the sources of which may be multiple. One minor but critical strand of academic commentary on Winton's fiction examines its expression of anxiety about contemporary masculinity and sees the gendering of his characters as conservative. For Linzie Murrie, Winton's fiction on the one hand challenges 'dominant masculinity by positing the "feminine" as constituent of male subjectivities',[7] but on the other hand marginalises its strong female (often maternal) figures, reflecting anxiety in response to late-twentieth-century pathologisation of masculinity. In an extended critical reading of *Breath*, Colleen McGloin argues that desire to reconfigure hegemonic masculinity is routed through the biblically named Eva. For McGloin, Eva's masculine power and erotic agency make her a threatening phallic figure who must ultimately be excised from the narrative so that equilibrium and its (white-settler) male perspective may be restored.[8]

Recognising with these critics that Winton's fictional investment in feminised men frequently entails the marginalisation of powerful women, I want to understand this pattern by situating it within the larger system of binary opposition produced in his writings. One of the hallmarks of Winton's fiction is its series of polarities between elemental forces of sea and land, male and female, wilderness and urban blight, public world and private life, literal reality and spiritual plane. His narratives profit from the libidinal energy of these oppositions, inciting the desire to read on even as his characters negotiate their way through and beyond what is often some kind of wreckage. The epigraph to his third novel, *That Eye, the Sky*, from Les Murray's 1981 poem 'Equanimity',[9] defines Winton's project as one of reimagining the divided world as an 'interleaved continuing plane'.[10] Winton is by no means the only novelist interested in overcoming binaries, but so pronounced and powerful are they in his work that a flattening of affect can follow in their wake, a point made by Lawrence about the ending of *Breath*.[11]

Winton's characters often find themselves unable to resolve or banish the oppositions that divide their world; they can only ward them off or simply survive. This recurring sense of polar oppositions in Winton's fictional world arguably resonates with his discourse of the littoral, which serves as a space of withdrawal from those metropolitan literary values that seem inimical to his project. The sense of between-ness in his fiction, together with the ambivalence produced by its unresolved polarities, is generative of his writing. The ambivalence of Winton's fiction seems sourced not only in childhood experience of extreme Christianity, but in the rootlessness of settler-colonial modernity, notwithstanding desires for belonging to place that his body of work otherwise implies or performs.

In *Breath*, the metaphoric interleaving of polarised scenarios of surfing and sexual adventure is achieved through the mutating trope of breath. At the level of the plot, the movement from one scenario to the other amplifies Winton's major examination of risk-taking as a practice at once generative of and damaging to the self. While surfing is positively coded in *Breath* as a potential avenue for the configuration of a non-imperial masculinity, the surfing adventurism advocated by Sando presents the rhetoric of the sublime in its most dangerously imperial form. In what follows, I begin with *Breath*'s unravelling of the hyper-masculinist quest for sublimity – where the sublime is a vehicle for subject formation – and then consider the terms in which sublime surfing landscapes are interleaved with domestic interiors and overtaken by the uncanny.

Both forms of encounter – sublime and uncanny – draw attention to the limits of the self, leading in one case to the self's triumph over its limitations, and in the other to the unsettling recognition of the self's inconsequentiality, its lack of authenticity and autonomy, and the threat of its extinction. The movement from the sublime to the uncanny in *Breath* inducts readers into the psychological terrain of repetitive drives, doublings and absent presences, destabilising hegemonic systems of meaning and value. Raw polarities enter the very texture of Winton's prose, as its rhythms of immersion in the elements are broken by cold, unsettling exterior views. What is in the foreground can suddenly recede and what is in the background swell, momentarily, into consciousness. The impact of these uncanny doublings and reversals in narrative perspective rehearse, without fully admitting or resolving, the polarities that drive settler subjectivity in a desiring but anxious relationship to the land. As Gelder and Jacobs argue, the settler-Australian experience is contingent on perpetually changing modernity, and in this context, forces of unsettlement inherent to settler fantasies of belonging to place yield the uncanny.[12]

Surfing and sublimity

In a distant echo of Edmund Burke's famous treatise on the sublime,[13] surfing in *Breath* is not just about the experience of sublimity; it is also about beauty. Beauty in Winton's novel attaches not only to the sight of men unselfconsciously open to embodied, sensual delight – 'death was hard to imagine when you had these blokes dancing themselves across the bay with smiles on their faces and sun in their hair'[14] – but also to pointlessness: 'later I understood what seized my imagination that day. How strange it was to see men do something beautiful. Something pointless and elegant, as though nobody saw or cared'.[15]

Bringing escape from the mundane, workaday world of the globalised economy, surfing's pointlessness, its lack of utilitarian value, aligns closely with artistic disinterest. Surfing is pointless in the way that writing or reading a novel is pointless. As an ideal upon which the narrative finally comes to rest, beauty is ultimately accorded the higher value in *Breath*. But beauty's pointlessness, its freedom from use value, from the economy, is uncertain and unsettled from the outset. That the ideal of beauty is touched by the illusory is suggested almost imperceptibly in the phrase 'as though', which shadows Pike's disavowal of desire to be recognised, making its status ambiguous. Likewise, the notion of beach or shoreline as an innocent, natural zone for the free expression of self is a fantasy. Though for Clifton Evers surfing should be understood as an embodied practice with potential to reconfigure masculinity,[16] beaches have long been socially stratified places within which (white) masculine assertions of power have been implicated – as Evers also acknowledges.[17] Australian beaches and shorelines have been primal scenes of invasion and colonisation; they have been repeatedly deployed in popular nationalism as sites of re-enactment of settler claims to possession.

In *Breath*, the conflict between two versions of surfing – on the one hand linked to the sublime and on the other to the beautiful – marks the narrative's desire to reconfigure hegemonic masculinity. This tension is amplified by a whole series of pairings: of exteriors with interiors and past with present. Bruce Pike's present life has him hurtling in his ambulance through dark suburban streets towards scenes of domestic trauma, then repairing alone to his flat overlooking a degraded urban landscape of 'brutalist condos that stand between me and the beach [...and] gulls eating pizza down in the carpark'.[18] Against these degraded vistas are held the beauty of the natural world, and the sublime power of the sea encountered through an experience of surfing that for Pikelet gives men, burdened by the ugly tedium of daily life, access to another world.

These oppositions are mediated by Winton's dynamic, immersive prose that moves beyond the visual aspect of seascapes and plunges into the ocean's restless kinetic element. Much narrative space is allotted to Pikelet's underwater experiences. He is propelled breathless between depth and surface, hammered or 'poleaxed'[19] by churning waves, with lungs, body and consciousness strained to the limit. These passages perform a literary counterpoint to the exercise known as 'bathymetry',[20] the measuring of oceanic contours and depths. *Breath*'s fictional topographies are primarily aquatic, but its terrestrial topographies can also suddenly loom in the foreground. These include the forest outside Sawyer, Camp Quarantine, the Sanderson house, and the space of the body itself.

The visceral, elemental and immersive quality of Winton's prose exerts a degree of tension with the rhetoric of the sublime that it otherwise invokes. The natural sublime – as theorised by Western philosophers from Longinus to Burke and Kant – is defined in the encounter of the spectating subject who stands at an implied distance and gazes upon, for example,

> [T]hreatening cliffs, thunder clouds towering up into the heavens, bringing with them flashes of lightning and crashes of thunder, volcanoes with their all-destroying violence, hurricanes with the devastation they leave behind, the boundless ocean set into a rage, a lofty waterfall on a mighty river...[21]

and is filled with wonder and terror. Temporarily awed by the infinite power of nature – and by the threatened nullification of human purpose and meaning – the spectator compensates by internalising and appropriating the grandeur of the spectacle in an aestheticising manoeuvre that ennobles the self. The symbolic conquest of nature's external otherness serves to restore and augment the self. Ubiquitous in Western culture, the sublime is an ideology that normalises the domestication of wild nature and the appropriation of otherness for self-definition and mastery, for spiritual replenishment, for touristic pleasure, and for the repair of the alienated modern self.[22]

Winton's *Breath* both evokes and critiques the sublime as a dominant mode of elite masculine subject formation via practices of extreme risk and self-mastery. Recollecting the sense of control over his life that his surfing adventurism provided, Pike explains that:

> [F]or a brief period I had something special that afforded me a private sense of power. It let me feel bigger, more vivid than I'd been before [...] I belonged to an exclusive club, drove around with a full-grown man and a mate who spooked people. Even among surfers we had an enigmatic status.[23]

Under Sando's tuition, Pikelet and Loonie engage in superhuman exploits that separate them from the herd. Winton's earlier phrase – 'as though nobody saw or cared' – contrasts with the boys' situation: they bask in the awed gaze of more ordinary others. According to Sando, their exclusive status is warranted by their pursuit of a self-mastery in which mind learns to triumph over matter. After conquering Old Smoky, Sando says: 'You'll be out there, thinkin: am I gunna die? Am I fit enough for his? Do I know what I'm doin? Am I solid? Or am I just...ordinary?'[24] Sando's description of the inner transformation precipitated by these adventures accords fully with the rhetoric of sublimity:

> [T]he weird, reptilian thing that happened to you: the cold, supercharged certainty which overtook your

usually dithering mind, the rest of the world in a slow-
motion blur around you, the tunnel vision, the surrender
that confidence finally became [...]

It's like you come pouring back into yourself, said
Sando one afternoon. Like you've exploded and all the
pieces of you are reassembling themselves. You're new.
Shimmering. Alive.[25]

As in the encounter with the sublime, the surrender to the power
of nature is superseded by the return of a self that is ennobled,
shiny and reassembled in a more blissfully alive configuration.
Doubts press home, however, as the danger of these adventures
escalates: is Sando a visionary or is he just a self-congratulatory
guru arrested in adolescent patterns of thrill-seeking? Eva
accuses him, at one point, of refusing to grow up, alleging he
requires the adulation of disciples to perpetuate his fantasies.[26]
Sando's cultivation of the boys verges, as Ronan McDonald
remarks in his review of *Breath*,[27] on the kind of sadomaso-
chism Susan Sontag links to fascism's aesthetic: 'the seduction is
beauty, the justification is honesty, the aim is ecstasy, the fantasy
is death'.[28]

Indeed, as the story unfolds from Pikelet's perspective – a
perspective always imbued with the monitory retrospection of
the adult Pike – Sando becomes increasingly menacing. As Sando
courts death in his quest to forge a more powerful self, his exploi-
tation of the sublime tips beyond ethical limits and threatens to
subjugate the other. Just at the tipping point, however, Sando is
relegated to the background, and the uncanny – registered in the
deathliness of repetition – becomes increasingly palpable.

Breath and death: repetition compulsion

The rationale Pike offers for the attraction of high-adrenaline surfing is his need to escape the tedium of the 'ordinary' in a 'rebellion against the monotony of drawing breath'.[29] The link between 'breath' and 'monotony' is both obvious and multivalent. 'Breath' is habitual and routine but also vital, the continuous thread upon which life hangs. The 'monotony of drawing breath' is the result of its 'repetition'; rebellion against that monotony therefore entails interruption, the stretching of lung capacity to heighten experience. Breath-holding is thus the narrative's recurring trope, one that binds together the two spheres of wild exteriors and domestic interiors: Pikelet listens at night, on edge, to his father's snoring in dangerous sleep apnoea; as young boys Pikelet and Loonie play at holding their breath underwater; episodes of near drowning are recounted; and Pikelet becomes Eva's reluctant collaborator in the high-risk game of erotic asphyxiation.

Like 'breath', furthermore, 'monotony' yields a paradox. The adult Pike plays the didjeridu to channel pent-up feelings. This establishes a connection between the 'monotony of breath' and the spiritual state of being attuned – that is, in tune with life. This appropriation of the didjeridu for settler purposes, as I discuss shortly, is one of the ways the uncanny of an otherwise suppressed frontier history is summoned. For now, the salient point is that the didjeridu is a monotone instrument. Its single droning note is sounded in a rhythmic repetition that in fact becomes a continuity. Playing the didjeridu requires the unbroken circulation of breath. As the focus of Pike's rebellion, monotony is therefore paradoxical. It refers both to compulsive repetition – to the death drive – and to its opposite: the thread of continuity, survival and return.

Sando, Loonie and Pikelet are captive to the compulsive urge to repeat. In Freud's terms, 'repetition of the same thing' is a phenomenon that 'does undoubtedly, subject to certain conditions and combined with certain circumstances, arouse an uncanny feeling, which, furthermore, recalls the sense of helplessness experienced in some dream-states'.[30] In the unconscious mind, he asserts, there lurks,

> '[A] compulsion to repeat'…powerful enough to over-rule the pleasure principle, lending to certain aspects of the mind their daemonic character, [...so that] whatever reminds us of this inner 'compulsion to repeat' is perceived as uncanny.[31]

The trio's surfing adventures acquire the mechanical quality of an automated process or drive, an emptying of individual agency that evokes the uncanny. Freud stipulates, moreover, that arousal of the uncanny is only possible in the type of fiction in which the writer engages in the pretence that we are moving in 'the world of common reality'[32] rather than in the realm of fantasy or fairy tale. Winton's fictional mode is realist – that is, faithful in its verisimilitude to the 'world of common reality' upon which it draws: with its recognisable times and places, psychologically rounded characters and causally arrayed plot, *Breath* is conducive to the uncanny.

Uncanny repetition, signifying deathliness, is conveyed by the image of kangaroo roadkill that Sando – for perfectly rational reasons – prepares to butcher. The image of the upside-down animal prompts Pikelet's meditation on mortality:

> With its forepaws outstretched, the animal looked as though it was caught in a perpetual earthward dive [...]
> The roo aimed and aimed and never arrived. Only its

blood made the journey. I thought of it at the road-
side, in the heavy thicket, gathering itself to leap across
the bitumen.[33]

In its urgent futility, the striving self is an automaton monoto-
nously caught in its mortal body, repetitively aiming but never
arriving. Likewise, surfing becomes a process of perpetually
aiming but never arriving, in a deathliness figured in the massive
white pointer shark, for example, that patrols Barney's beach.
Loonie, who glimpses the shark, observes poetically: 'That eye
[…] was like a fuckin hole in the universe'.[34]

The repetitive drive to conquer impossible waves culminates
in the trio's assault on a remote bombora located three miles
offshore, called the Nautilus:

> It came in at an angle, just a hard ridge of swell, but
> within a few seconds, as it found shallow water, it
> became so engorged as to triple in volume. And there
> at its feet lay the great hump of rock that gave the place
> its name […]
>
> [T]here were times when the water broke over no
> water at all […] It was a sight I had never imagined, the
> most dangerous wave I'd ever seen.[35]

Devoid of beauty, the Nautilus also defies reason. As Sando enters
the wave, it takes on the qualities of a devouring monster, a thing
of extreme otherness:

> Sando […] was gone in a moment, like a bone in the
> thing's throat. And then a squall of spume belched him

free and it was over. He skidded out into the deep, dead water ahead of me and let the board flutter away.[36]

Disenchanted with Sando's menacing nihilism, Pikelet makes a pivotal decision and refuses to surf the Nautilus. The refusal takes courage but he is left with a feeling of emptiness, having refused to belong to the elect:

What would success there really mean – perhaps three or four or even five seconds of upright travel on a wave as ugly as a civic monument? You could barely call such a mad scramble *surfing*. Surely there were better and bigger waves to ride than that deformity. Yet nothing could assuage the lingering sense of failure I was left with.[37]

Here there is a shift from the language of sublimity towards ugliness, deformity and nothingness. The wave acquires its name from the normally submerged, 'great hump of rock'[38] from which it rises. Perhaps alluding to the submarine in Jules Verne's *Twenty Thousand Leagues Under the Sea*, the name 'Nautilus' also holds a submerged paradox. A nautilus is a marine creature that makes a spiralling shell. The cross-section of a nautilus shell reveals inner chambers arrayed in a repetitive series. Each new chamber repeats and enlarges the previous chamber, and the overall pattern forms a spiral. The nautilus is said to exemplify the golden spiral, a pattern popularly (though not necessarily scientifically) associated with patterns of growth in nature – as observed in shells, flowers, pine cones, the branching habit of trees and even in the shape of galaxies. Nature's golden spiral is often analysed using Fibonacci numbers, a mathematical progression most routinely illustrated by diagrams of the nautilus shell. From outer to inner curl, the nautilus is divisible into successively diminishing squares in proportions that match the Fibonacci progression. The golden spiral is allied to the golden mean associated with classically proportioned architecture. In other words, through its name, the deformity that is the Nautilus in *Breath* turns out to be affiliated with what, for the Western mind at least, is the opposite of deformity: the well-proportioned and the beautiful.[39]

With its chambers iterated into a spiral, the Nautilus reflects the uncanny logic of repetition played out in the narrative's succession of ever bigger and more dangerous waves to be conquered. The 'deformity' of the Nautilus also evokes Eva's ruined knee, a physical deformation that is the literal consequence of her own pursuit of extreme freestyle skiing. In a curious description, understood by McGloin as the textual stripping of Eva's femininity to allow Pikelet's feminised position,[40] Eva's body is pictured as:

> [A] sequence of squares and cubes. Her teeth were square, so were her ears. Her breasts and buttocks were block-like. Even her calf muscles, which squirmed beneath my fingers, had corners. She had wide, blunt hands with square nails and deep ruts at the joints and her feet were the same.[41]

Eva may well be a 'decoy' for masculinity, but she is also its uncanny double. Further, her cubist image evokes an architectural proportionality, reminiscent of the golden spiral and thus also the paradoxical Nautilus, with its kinetic power, deformity and beauty.

The Nautilus is both the culmination of the surfing plot and the precise point at which sublimity sheers off into the terrain of the uncanny, as surfing is overtaken by dark sexual adventure.

The Nautilus uncannily repeats itself in Eva's bedroom, a place far more dangerous for Pikelet than any preceding seascape. The Sandersons' Malibu-style beach house is a dwelling that roots itself familiarly onsite, since it appears to have grown on the property like a tree. Yet by virtue of its familiarity, the house is *unheimlich* or uncanny, especially because it bears an indeterminate relation to the present. Always out of its time, or untimely, the house points towards a future that will not come since, in the present of Pike's narration, it no longer exists, the property having been subdivided for the 'ostentatious weekenders'[42] of lawyers and architects from the city. Simultaneously, the eco-modernist design of the house makes it proleptic, anticipating the gentrification of Sawyer beyond the 1970s.

At the same time, the house bears an uncanny relation to the colonial history of the place. Its huge old-growth timber supports suggest the sawmilling town's earliest era: like an 'elevated safari tent, a tent whose every pole was an old-growth log that three men could barely link arms around'.[43] In her discussion of the uncanny Sanderson house, Hannah Schürholz notes how its dark undercroft suggests unconscious desire and finds its 'reflection in the "shivering darkness" of Eva's sexuality'.[44] Pikelet's encounter with Eva – whose deathliness is only amplified by her pregnancy – conjures Freud's remark about the female genital organs as *unheimlich*, as the gateway to the place 'where each one of us lived once upon a time and in the beginning'.[45]

From foreground to background: *Breath*'s absent presences
The Sando–Eva–Pikelet drama is uncanny because it both displaces and repeats the structure of Pikelet's own oedipal family triangle. Pikelet's parents stay mostly in the background, though he becomes increasingly guarded around them lest they learn of

his dangerous secret life: 'I was anxious to make myself inconspicuous', he states, adding:

> I believed I was alert to their moods, but really my concentration was elsewhere. My mother and father became figures in the background. They'd always been quiet and solicitous but throughout my adolescence and especially during this period they became so insubstantial that I hardly knew them anymore. I didn't know what they thought, what they suspected, what their lives had become. I could only think about Eva.[46]

The phrase 'figures in the background' is telling. When Pikelet's father is fatally injured in a freak mill accident, the narrative's dominant rhythms are unexpectedly arrested, enacting the interruption of breath. The background switches to the foreground as the event hits 'with a force that felt targeted and personal', bringing the realisation that '[d]eath was everywhere – waiting, welling, undiminished'.[47] As the narrative unfolds, hidden undercurrents swell and strengthen, overtaking that which otherwise monopolises Pikelet's, and the reader's, attention.

The movement between foreground and background, generating the uncanny, refers readers obliquely to the settler history that conditions Winton's own writing of place and mobilises its absent presences. The deeper colonial past, otherwise unspoken except for the trace left by Pike's ambiguously appropriated didjeridu, swells into the present, though it is never openly articulated. The past also looms at Camp Quarantine, the site of a school excursion during which Pikelet and his ex-girlfriend Queenie spend a chaste night together on a cold mortuary slab. It is significant that *Breath*'s Queenie is a younger version of the Queenie who appears in Winton's early novel *Shallows*,[48] where she is an independent young woman drawn into anti-whaling activism. The return of Queenie, like that of other returning characters and settings in Winton's fictional universe, effects a kind of literary uncanny, interleaving the present with the past of his own writing.

Located on a peninsula, the site of Camp Quarantine looks across the bay to Angelus:

> The decommissioned buildings seemed hunkered down, besieged by sky and sea and landscape. The steep isthmus behind them was choked with thickets of coastal heath from which granite tors stood up at mad angles. Every human element, from the slumping rooftops to the sad little graveyard, seemed older and more forlorn than the ancient country beyond. The scrub might have been low and wizened and the stones badly weathered, but after every shower of rain they all shone; they stood up new and fresh, as though they'd only moments ago heaved themselves from the skin of the earth […]
>
> From there I could gaze across to the distant wharf at Angelus whose cranes and silos looked too small to be real. It was like seeing the familiar world at a twofold remove, from another time as much as from another direction, for it felt that I was in an outpost of a different era. It wasn't only the colonial buildings that gave me such a sense, but also the land they were built on. Each headstone and every gnarled grasstree spoke of a past forever present, ever-pressing, and for the first time in my life I began to feel, plain as gravity, not only was life short, but there had been so much of it.[49]

Here the frontier past intrudes into the present. Figures are diminished and life is foreshortened as the past enlarges and grows heavy. The uncanny is less associated with the colonial buildings or the ghosts of settlers than with reanimated nature, the gnarled grasstrees and the upright gravestones renewed after rain. Camp Quarantine interrupts *Breath's* intensely polarised settings of surf and bedroom, implicating Pike's story in a pervasive melancholy based on settler-colonial un-belonging. This collective history is buried beneath – and profoundly conditions – the present, interpenetrating the personal history that weighs on and exhausts Pike, who never quite recovers from past trauma. Old patterns replicate themselves, but this time emptied of the driving energy of youth:

> I didn't exactly pull myself together – I got past such notions – but bits of me did come around again, as flies or memories or subatomic particles will for reasons of their own. Bit by bit I congregated, I suppose you could say, and then somehow I cohered. I went on and had another life. Or went ahead and made the best of the old one.[50]

Bruce Pike's lingering diffidence, registered in the fatigue that attends his effort to congregate himself after the trauma of adolescence, suggests the hollowing-out of the present, even as it points to the ambivalence of settlement in ways that necessarily implicate Winton's literary project. Marshalling himself in the end, Pike cannot shake off the feeling that he is 'creepy'[51] – a term synonymous with the uncanny and indicative of contamination by hidden perversions produced by a past that cannot be entirely superseded or relinquished.

Breath unravels the hegemonic masculinity implicated in Australia's history of frontier imperialism, salvaging only the damaged settler–survivor. Returning Pike to the scene of white men dancing in the surf, the narrative seeks to retrieve for him, and for readers, that modicum of grace and equanimity won through hard work and humble service to what is left of family. Qualities of grace, endurance and survival are, in the end, what remain. These limited consolations express Winton's literary vision in its maturity. Even so, they cannot contain a troubling sense of fatalism that may be a gauge of literary limits, of the difficulty for the settler–writer, of the search for belonging, of reconciling incommensurable weights, and of redressing the legacy of the past in the present.

Notes

1   T. Winton, *Breath*, Hamish Hamilton, Melbourne, 2008.

2   See R. Dixon, 'Tim Winton, *Cloudstreet* and the field of Australian literature' (*Westerly*, vol. 50, pp. 245–60) for a full appraisal of factors shaping the academic avoidance, to date, of Winton's fiction, despite his success and significance in the Australian literary field and his popularity with readers beyond the academy.

3   C. Lawrence, 'Life as a wave not caught', review of *Breath*, *Australian*, 7 May 2008, www.theaustralian.com.au/news/arts/life-as-a-wave-not-caught/story-e6frg8px-1111116200446.

4   T. Winton, cited in H. A. Willis, 'According to Winton', interview with Tim Winton, *Eureka Street*, vol. 4, no. 7, 1994, p. 20.

5   Ibid., p. 21.

6   Ibid.

7   L. Murrie, 'Changing masculinities: disruption and anxiety in contemporary Australian writing', *Journal of Australian Studies*, vol. 56, 1998, p. 174ff.

8   C. McGloin, 'Reviving Eva in Tim Winton's *Breath*', *Journal of Commonwealth Literature*, vol. 47, no. 1, 2012, p. 111.

9   L. A. Murray, 'Equanimity', *The Vernacular Republic: Poems 1961–1981*, Angus & Robertson, Sydney, 1982, pp. 208–10.

10 T. Winton, epigraph, *That Eye, the Sky*, McPhee Gribble, Melbourne, 1986, p. v.

11 Lawrence, 'Life as a wave not caught'.

12 K. Gelder and J. M. Jacobs, *Uncanny Australia: Sacredness and Identity in a Postcolonial Nation*, Melbourne University Press, Melbourne, 1998, pp. 24–5.

13 E. Burke, *A Philosophical Inquiry into the Origin of Our Ideas of the Sublime and the Beautiful with an Introductory Discourse Concerning Taste, and Several Other Additions* (first published 1756), eBooks@Adelaide, Adelaide University, ebooks.adelaide.edu.au/b/burke/edmund/sublime.

14 Winton, *Breath*, p. 23.

15 Ibid.

16 C. Evers, 'He'enalu: bodies that surf', *Notes for a Young Surfer*, Melbourne University Publishing, Melbourne, 2010, pp. 41–68.

17 C. Evers, 'The Cronulla race riots: safety maps on an Australian beach', *South Atlantic Quarterly*, vol. 107, no. 2, 2008, pp. 411–29.

18 Winton, *Breath*, p. 7.

19 Ibid., p. 49.

20 Ibid., p. 82.

21 I. Kant, *The Critique of Judgment*, trans. P. Guyer and E. Matthews, Cambridge University Press, Cambridge, 2000 (first published 1790), pp. 144–5.

22 See W. Cronon, 'The trouble with wilderness; or, getting back to the wrong nature', in W. Cronon (ed.), *Uncommon Ground: Rethinking the Human Place in Nature*, W. W. Norton, New York, 1995, pp. 69–90; C. Hitt, 'Towards an ecological sublime', *New Literary History*, vol. 30, no. 3, 1999, pp. 603–23; and B. Rooney, 'Pathological geomorphology and the ecological sublime: Andrew McGahan's *Wonders of a Godless World*', *Southerly*, vol. 72, no. 3, 2012, pp. 55–77.

23 Winton, *Breath*, pp. 147–8.

24 Ibid., p. 75.

25 Ibid., p. 111.

26 Ibid., p. 64.

27 R. McDonald, 'Grace and surrender', review of *Breath*, *Times Literary Supplement*, no. 5485, 16 May 2008, p. 19.

28 S. Sontag, 'Fascinating fascism', *New York Review of Books*, 6 February 1975, see www.history.ucsb.edu/faculty/marcuse/classes/33d/33dTexts/SontagFascinFascism75.htm.

29 Winton, *Breath*, p. 41.

30 S. Freud, 'The uncanny', *The Standard Edition of the Complete Psychological Works of Sigmund Freud*, vol. XVII, *An Infantile Neurosis and Other Works*,

edited by J. Strachey, Hogarth Press, London, 1955, p. 238.

31   Ibid.
32   Ibid., p. 250.
33   Winton, *Breath*, pp. 60–1.
34   Ibid., p. 74.
35   Ibid., pp. 142–3.
36   Ibid., p. 144.
37   Ibid., p. 146.
38   Ibid., p. 142.
39   The application of the golden mean, ratio or spiral to the natural world is the product of popular discourses, as currently suggested by numerous internet sites (e.g. goldenratiomyth.weebly.com/the-logarithmic-spiral. html). It is not within the purpose or scope of this essay to assess the validity or applicability of these constructs.
40   McGloin, 'Reviving Eva in Tim Winton's *Breath*', p. 113.
41   Winton, *Breath*, p. 175.
42   Ibid., p. 215.
43   Ibid., p. 38.
44   H. Schürholz, 'Gendered spaces: the poetics of domesticity in Tim Winton's fiction', *Journal of the European Association of Studies on Australia*, vol. 3, no. 2, 2012, p. 67.
45   Freud, 'The uncanny', p. 245.
46   Winton, *Breath*, pp. 173–4.
47   Ibid., p. 201.
48   T. Winton, *Shallows*, Allen & Unwin, Sydney, 1984.
49   Winton, *Breath*, p. 117.
50   Ibid., p. 211.
51   Ibid., p. 204.

Bibliography

Burke, E., *A Philosophical Inquiry into the Origin of Our Ideas of the Sublime and the Beautiful* (first published 1756), eBooks@Adelaide, Adelaide University, ebooks.adelaide.edu.au/b/burke/edmund/sublime.

Cronon, W., 'The trouble with wilderness; or, getting back to the wrong nature', in W. Cronon (ed.), *Uncommon Ground: Rethinking the Human Place in Nature*, W. W. Norton, New York, 1995, pp. 69–90.

Dixon, R., 'Tim Winton, *Cloudstreet* and the field of Australian literature', *Westerly*, vol. 50, pp. 245–60.

Evers, C., *Notes for a Young Surfer*, Melbourne University Publishing, Melbourne, 2010.

—— 'The Cronulla race riots: safety maps on an Australian beach', *South Atlantic Quarterly*, vol. 107, no. 2, 2008, pp. 411–29.

Freud, S., *The Standard Edition of the Complete Psychological Works of Sigmund Freud*, vol. XVII, *An Infantile Neurosis and Other Works*, Hogarth Press, London, 1955.

Gelder, K. and Jacobs, J. M., *Uncanny Australia: Sacredness and Identity in a Postcolonial Nation*, Melbourne University Press, Melbourne, 1998.

Hitt, C., 'Towards an ecological sublime', *New Literary History*, vol. 30, no. 3, Summer 1999, pp. 603–23.

Kant, I., *The Critique of Judgment*, trans. P. Guyer and E. Matthews, Cambridge University Press, Cambridge, 2000 (first published 1790), pp. 144–5.

Lawrence, C., 'Life as a wave not caught', review of *Breath*, *Australian*, 7 May 2008, www.theaustralian.com.au/arts/life-as-a-wave-not-caught/story-e6frg8px-1111116200446.

McDonald, R., 'Grace and surrender', review of *Breath*, *Times Literary Supplement*, no. 5485, 16 May 2008, p. 19.

McGloin, C., 'Reviving Eva in Tim Winton's *Breath*', *Journal of Commonwealth Literature*, vol. 47, no. 1, 2012, pp. 109–20.

Murray, L., *The Vernacular Republic Poems 1961–1981*, Angus & Robertson, Sydney, 1982.

Murrie, L., 'Changing masculinities: disruption and anxiety in contemporary Australian writing', *Journal of Australian Studies*, vol. 56, 1998, pp. 169–79.

Rooney, B., 'Pathological geomorphology and the ecological sublime: Andrew McGahan's *Wonders of a Godless World*', *Southerly*, vol. 72, no. 3, 2012, pp. 55–77.

—— *Literary Activism: Writer Intellectuals and Australian Public Life*, University of Queensland Press, Brisbane, 2009.

Schürholz, H., 'Gendered spaces: the poetics of domesticity in Tim Winton's fiction', *Journal of the European Association of Studies on Australia*, vol. 3, no. 2, 2012, pp. 59–79.

Sontag, S., 'Fascinating fascism', *New York Review of Books*, 6 February 1975, see www.history.ucsb.edu/faculty/marcuse/classes/33d/33dTexts/SontagFascinFascism75.htm.

Willis, H. A., 'According to Winton', interview with Tim Winton, *Eureka Street*, vol. 4, no. 7, 1994, pp. 20–5.

Winton, T., *Breath*, Hamish Hamilton, Melbourne, 2008.

—— *That Eye, the Sky*, McPhee Gribble, Melbourne, 1986.

—— *Shallows*, Allen & Unwin, Sydney, 1984.

11

A NOT COMPLETELY POINTLESS BEAUTY: *BREATH*, EXCEPTIONALITY AND NEOLIBERALISM

Nicholas Birns

Bruce Pike, known as 'Pikelet', the protagonist of Tim Winton's 2008 novel *Breath*,[1] starts out as a daredevil surfer and as an adult becomes a paramedic. It is in this latter capacity that readers first see him, doing his job, responding to an emergency. This shift from extreme athlete to first responder counterpoints a continuity that pertains to risk. Ulrich Beck, in books such as *World Risk Society*, has postulated risk as a signal provocateur of neoliberal behaviour, in that the threat of risk makes modern society reorganise from traditional class hierarchies to new risk hierarchies, which privilege those who secure themselves risk-averse positions and leave the risk to others in their society, or export the risk to other societies.[2] Thus, in both youth and maturity, Pikelet is someone deputed to deal with risk, with 'the outlaw feeling of doing something graceful',[3] from which the rest of society wants to insulate itself, to experience only as metaphor.

Discussion of Winton's novels has tended to centre around classic Australian themes – masculinity, landscape, working-class identity – that have *seemingly* not been changed or impacted by neoliberalism, that are, as Robert Dixon puts it, 'resistant to post-modern or metropolitan trends'.[4] Even when Wintonian themes show up in the work of other writers, such as Nam Le's 'Halflead

Bay' (in *The Boat*,[5] published the same year as *Breath*, 2008 – also the year when the world risk society began to implode), the diasporic writer is praised for inhabiting so seamlessly a tale of seaside coming of age that it might as well, as it were, have been done by a white Australian of a different generation. The transnational valence of Le's story is viewed as a bravura feat by a writer keyed in to more contemporary themes and agile enough to tap into Winton territory – a territory evaluated as more timeless. There is no doubt, however, that *Breath* speaks to our own time; in several cases when risk is described, it does so in the business as well as the physical sense.

The role of modernity and change in *Breath*'s deployment of risk is signalled by the presence of Eva, who is not simply the femme fatale who breaks up both the boyhood friendship between Pikelet and Loonie and the mentorial relationship between Sando and Pikelet, but whose American origin signifies the intimate relationship of risk and globalisation. Sando is an 'investment guru'[6] who talks of 'risk in the financial sense'.[7] Winton makes clear the linkage between financial risk and athletic risk when Loonie is described as 'greedy about risk',[8] and later on when the adult Pikelet muses, 'thriving on risk is perverse – unless you are in business'.[9] To put it another way, risk in business is risk for the risk-averse, risk that can be aesthetically enjoyed. Risk in the external reaches of risk society is too genuinely risky – as Pikelet realises – to be thrived upon.

In this respect, the empirically enacted risk of risky behaviour, the visible risk, serves as an allegorical figure for the invisible risk of neoliberalism. And, it might be said, Beck's theories themselves can be read allegorically, risk standing for something close to what Zygmunt Bauman describes as 'liquid modernity'.[10] In other works by Winton, this allegorised sense of risk is palpable, as in the smuggling theme in *Dirt Music*[11] and the themes of the local and the global in *The Turning*,[12] in which what might seem a frustrating provincialism can be examined as the provincial reverberations of global neoliberalism, the global masking itself as the local.

If Winton's fiction of the 1980s through to the 2000s has been analysed in the light of contemporary political economy, it has been largely on the material level of his publishing success and, as Robert Dixon has stressed, his quick canonicity in Australian secondary schools.[13] Just as Pikelet knowingly — avowedly, not just as a passive subject of neoliberal aptitudes — takes on the role of risk warrior as an adult, Winton's fiction knowingly engages a neoliberalism that would dehumanise humankind by dividing it between the privileged who do not have to worry about risk, and the rest who do.

Breath begins as the paramedic team is answering a call that will lead to finding the corpse of a young man who has erotically asphyxiated himself. In the first sentence, we are told, 'the GPS urges us to make the next left'.[14] Unobtrusively, in the grain of the emergency response, we have a reference to the global, to the all-pervasiveness of technology, and to the methodical accessibility patently part of the neoliberal outlook, an outlook that sees information as a way of managing risk and trying to control outcomes. It would appear, at first, that the accidental death of the thrill-seeking young man is the precise obverse of the omniscient classification present in the idea of a global positioning system, but in the course of *Breath* Winton makes us recognise them as different branches of the search for individual distinction, of a refusal to be merely ordinary.

Surfing is positioned in *Breath* as very much a step beyond the normal, beyond the association of Pikelet's family of origin with what Malcolm Knox calls the 'practical and plain'.[15] Pikelet takes up surfing, becoming friends with Loonie and then the older, charismatic Sando, an expert surfer who has excelled professionally in the sport, and finally with Sando's mysterious wife, Eva. Surfing in *Breath* is no ordinary male pastime; it is a metaphor for staving off the suffocation of the normal, the desperate, 'barely getting by' life Pikelet sees his working-class father endure. For the stereotypically laconic and inarticulate Anglo-Celtic Australian male, surfing is as close as he might get to the aesthetic. Thus it is indicative of their philistinism and low aims for themselves that Pikelet's parents never learned to swim. Surfing becomes for Pikelet his access to the exceptional and the rarefied, a place where he can excel beyond his parents' narrow scope.

The honest, blue-collar georgic idyll of Pikelet's youth in Sawyer is contrasted to his soaring yet problematic adolescence at school in Angelus. Angelus is a name Winton has used in his previous fiction and is widely accepted as a fictionalisation of Albany. This raises several issues: why use such a spiritual-sounding name, connoting exaltation and rarefied states, for a rather ordinary regional town? What is the message of 'Angelus' meaning 'message'? Does Angelus convey a menacing perfection, the opposite of the imperfection sought, for instance, by the narrator of Winton's short story 'Damaged Goods',[17] when he falls in love with a girl named Strawberry Alison because of the birthmark everyone thinks mars her? Does the name (given the cult-like allure of Sando) connote a false spirituality, the seeds of which have already been implanted by Angelus's weirdly spiritual name for a middle-sized town?

Angelus is figured in the novel as a place of sophistication, the 'global' pole of the novel's binaries, opposed to the more local and secure Sawyer, whose evocation of manual labour is a far cry from the sublimity evoked by a name such as Angelus. One of the consequences of Winton's naming practices might be to suggest that sophistication is subjective, transposable: a teenage boy going from Perth to London, or from Albany to Perth, might feel the same sense of dislocation, the same feeling of arriving in a place where things matter more and people care less. In other words, Winton encourages his readers to see the provincial and cosmopolitan in relative and not absolute terms, to understand that, while most readers of *Breath* might see Albany/Angelus and think it provincial, for Pikelet it is not only cosmopolitan but excessively, even malevolently, so. On the other hand, Winton is informing the reader that provincial Australian cities – Albany, Geraldton, Toowoomba, Wagga Wagga – can in their own way be surprisingly, given stereotypes of Australian provinciality, cosmopolitan. It is as if the provincial–cosmopolitan dialogue is not between specific places but between standpoints. This is true even of the waves the boys surf – the ultra-challenging Nautilus is much riskier and more sublime than the earlier Old Smoky, whereas of course for most people the benign Old Smoky would in fact be 'Nautilus' enough.

In the greater scheme, however, even Angelus is provincial, and certainly the spectacular way the worldly, Americanised Sando and Eva stand out is proof of this. Though it might seem an affirmation of transparent embodiment, of the here and now, the physicality of surfing is a substitute for the transposability of diaspora. Going back to Nam Le's 'Halflead Bay', in a sense what is happening there is swimming, and the male-gendered physicality it represents is deployed not as something authentically local or national but, instead, what happens when there is no outlet for diaspora. Both swimming and diaspora represent different outlets of the search for distinction, for the extraordinary.

Breath pivots, as do so many coming-of-age narratives, on betrayal and life illusions. It is tempting to see something timeless about this or, if there is a temporal–historical dimension to the book, it is easy enough to see it as a story of bluff, country-honest Aussie mates betrayed by city-slicker Americans. The association of surfing with an easygoing, non-labour-intensive lifestyle, as suggested by its association with Beach Boys songs and the standard image of the cultural lassitude of, say, southern California's surfer culture, lends credence to the pursuit of surfing excellence as an abstention from the bourgeois pursuit of wealth and status that an earlier nature-lover, William Wordsworth, memorably castigated as 'getting and spending'.[18]

It is more complicated than this, though. First, we cannot see the two boys, Pikelet and Loonie, as simple surrogates for Winton; they are perhaps of the same generation, or slightly younger, as is signalled by the references to AC/DC and Sherbet – bands that first became popular in Australia in the mid-1970s – but they are not portrayed as people who are in any way creative or incipient writers. Indeed, surfing for both boys is the acme of their creativity, and their immersion in it is a form not just of recreation but, as the novel's repeated motif of 'something beautiful. Something pointless and elegant'[19] demonstrates, aesthesis. Surfing is thus a correlate of the affective properties of sublimity that Angelus as a name carries with it, and indeed Malcolm Knox, in his review of *Breath* in *The Monthly*, sees surfing as 'an experience of the sublime'.[20]

As such, Sando's appeal for the boys is not just as a hero, someone who does something they value in a way they would like to emulate, but as someone who presides over '[a] select and peculiar club, a tiny circle of friends, a cult, no less. Sando and his maniacal apprentices'.[21] Elsewhere Sando is described as a 'guru',[22] and it is mentioned that the boys' involvement with Sando occurs at a time when cults are all the rage, in presumably the mid- to late 1970s. Sando's careful cultivation of his own charisma in order to control a small circle of people who will be emotionally in thrall to him is redolent of the practices of the cult leaders of this era, who did not so much want to be popular on a wide scale as to have a strong emotional hold over those who were drawn to them.

Ironically, after he and Eva go back to the States, Sando becomes an investment guru: the entire surfing-with-the-boys episode in Angelus has served only as a training ground for neoliberalism. It all ends up for/with money: Sando's seeming spiritual search ends up too literalised, too centred in the ego, for him to carry it off. He can be a leader if those led are small boys, but ultimately, in the larger world – what David Malouf might call 'the great world',[23] or Winton himself the 'big world'[24] – all he can be is a follower of a neoliberal consensus. In the end, despite the rhetoric of charisma, it all boiled down to money. All the thrill-seeking, the daredevil excitement, the risking of breath itself that surfing entails, was a roundabout way to pursue making money, divested of the odious aura of bourgeois mediocrity with which making money had become associated in the era of the welfare state and, later on, of the counterculture. As Philip Larkin famously put it at the beginning of this counter-bourgeois turn, which ended up re-privileging the bourgeoisie, '[a]ll we can hope to leave them now is money'.[25]

Long before Sando leaves to pursue wealth and the exceptional in a more standard way, though, the idyllic unity of Sando, Loonie, and Pikelet – a triadic and almost entirely homosocial unit – has been broken up. The first link to fall is Loonie, the seemingly sophisticated teenager who has stolen an early march on finding out the secrets of life. Yet the still-naive Loonie is the first victim of unscrupulous adults who can see a bit further around the bend than he can. As a migrant – his full name is Ivan Loon, denoting eastern European descent – Loonie is also particularly eager to assimilate into an Aussie, matey machismo that in fact is a phantom engineered by Sando, and more broadly by the forces of privilege and what Pierre Bourdieu has termed 'distinction' and 'cultural capital'[26] behind Sando. It is when Pikelet feels at once slighted and relieved that Loonie, and not he himself, has accompanied Sando to Indonesia – ostensibly for more challenging surfing but inferentially for a shady drug transaction – that readers see both that Pikelet is a far more peripheral disciple of Sando than Loonie, and also that Pikelet is grateful for that.

The growing maturity of the boys also no doubt brings sexual feelings to their consciousness: and Pikelet transposes risk to his relationship with Eva, not with Sando. On the other hand, even if Pikelet will, to some degree, always be maimed and foiled by his adolescent experiences, he has salvaged a constructive and honorable life from them. Paramedics, as a vocation, offers the potential for both healing and excitement, both risk and morality. It is, if not in itself, something completely pointless and beautiful in a way that the surfing was not – the surfing was somehow a search for cultural capital but the emergency work offers at least the possibility of seeing a Platonic pointless and beautiful thing in the distance, uncompromised: something other than work or even surfing, something held at a radical distance, perhaps only as part of what Bill Ashcroft has termed 'the horizonal sublime'.[27]

Thus it is a mistake to see the high Sando years, the high Loonie years, in Pikelet's life as an Edenic, prelapsarian idyll, even though Eva's name and some of the imagery would seem to suggest this. The fall into experience occurred at the same moment, and beneath, the ascension into the sublime: Pikelet's moving between Sawyer and Angelus. Surfing with Sando, for all its emphasis on pleasure and intrinsic accomplishment, is a search for competition and excellence that anticipates the search for competition and excellence within neoliberal economics, which Sando later pursues.

For all its thrilling adventurousness, all its embodiment of 'the extraordinary',[28] Sando's surfing is a closed system, something that those who are not in his world cannot understand or convincingly simulate. The aura of secrecy perhaps explains why Sando doesn't show the boys the box of magazines that feature him surfing around the world, and why Eva, subtly undermining him, wants to expose them; the manifest reason for this is Sando's vanity about his age, but it is also a sense of strengthening his cult carapace by shrouding himself in secrets. When he becomes a financial guru in the States, this seems a move from a closed counterculture to an open system; and indeed this is how neoliberalism tries to style its relation to the 1960s–70s counterculture and to other phenomena that preceded it. If this were true, neoliberalism would not be a total loss, but more often than not the rhetoric of openness has replaced real openness, and what Beck calls a state of 'risk society'.[29] Here, threats to the norm are carefully contained and kept out. This is precisely because the neoliberal individual, as Beck argues, is encouraged to assume an abnormal risk. They are compelled to live within a 'liquid modernity' in which everything is valued so that everything can be devalued – deregulated and thus devalued, discounted. Pike's adult work – to save life, to restore breath – is service-centred, not neoliberal and marketised.

Indeed, Winton is so straightforward in adopting a working-class subject position in his writing that it almost makes him seem oppositional. As critic Robert Dixon notes, despite Winton's prominent role in Australian literary studies, he does not try to be scholarly or academic himself.[30] Why, then, is he studied so frequently in academia, even if more so in secondary school than at the undergraduate level? One could say the same of a writer such as Christos Tsiolkas: not at all academic, not placing himself in a tradition of Australian (white, Anglo–Celtic, settler) literature, yet consummately adopted by the Australian literary establishment, even if more so at the tertiary level than the secondary-school icon Winton. Winton is a subaltern writer not merely in his regionalism but, far more consequentially, in his writing about a set of people traditionally excluded from the Australian literary imaginary: Australian working-class males who are not politically or socially organised. (The sense of empathy with the Joneses, the Indigenous family portrayed in Winton's short story 'Aquifer',[31] is emblematic here.) Indeed, it is only stretching the point to see Winton's realism, instead of insufficiently avant-garde and self-reflexive, as an instance of what a 2012 special issue of *Modern Language Quarterly* called 'peripheral realism', described as 'a vital and variegated critical realism' pertinent to 'the problems of a post–Cold War world'.[32]

Winton's identity as an outsider, his disdain for an Anglophile literary tradition, is demonstrated in his 2004 comment to an Indian blogger that '[m]uch of Australian writing…including the kind I do myself, has an animus that comes from years of being condescended to';[33] it would not sound surprising if a migrant writer of his generation had said this. His working-class origins serve not only as a redress to the quest for status and perfection critiqued in *Breath*, but as a redress to the emphatically upper- or middle-class origins of some of Australia's canonical writers (Patrick White, Judith Wright, and so on). Although, as Nathanael O'Reilly has pointed out, Winton himself has, with the exception of *Cloudstreet*,[34] avoided representing his own suburban origins in favour of more obviously rural and working-class ones such as Pike's, it cannot be denied that his upbringing was not at all an elite one.[35] As a white working-class man, Winton is, in a sense, an outsider to all this: something especially true given that many working-class Australian novelists who are canonical – such as Frank Hardy or Judah Waten – express their class origins in terms of labour unions or other forms of class solidarity. Winton does not. Indeed, his subject is the working-class Australian male who is not, because of the eclipse of unionised workers in a neoliberal era, a part of organised labour.

Another vector of comparison for Winton, one both regional and generational, would be John Kinsella. Kinsella, born in Western Australia three years after Winton, has similarly achieved a world readership, largely for his poetry, but also for his fiction and essays. Although Kinsella's avant-garde and experimental associations are very different from Winton's tight-lipped, unassuming concision, just as Winton is far more complex than his conventional image, so Kinsella has a local and demotic side that his international admirers do not always perceive. In this poem, written about Albany – Winton's Angelus – Kinsella associates breath, sublimity and peril in a way quite analogous to Winton's approach in his novel:

Breath, an icy pocket,
opens ultramarine,
a dry sea
tracking its glacial
course beyond
Eclipse Island
and beyond
the course,
cancelling
as the tide
rip back and forth
covering all earth [...][36]

And Kinsella has also written what are, in effect, elegies for the rise of neoliberalism and the decline of everything else, analogous to the tea/coffee switch on page 54 of *Breath*, as exemplified in these tercets from perhaps Kinsella's greatest work, *Divine Comedy*:

[W]eekend hideaways, decline of birds
rise of BMWs and four-wheel drives; so bereft
So emotionless and impersonal
Like a car on blocks, revved to shithouse
Or the brand spanking new plasma TV,
They want satellite, they want foxes
Through the living room they can shoot
With a flick of the joystick [...][37]

Kinsella's poem presents a clear image of the neoliberal 'turning', of the great change Sando at first appears to buck but upon which he ultimately thrives. Winton may exist on a sea-side verge compared to other Australian writers, especially his

274

contemporaries, but he is not islanded away from them. *Breath* is very much a book about (early) generation X experiences; listening to AC/DC makes the boys indubitably generation X, and a comparison with other Australian writers born in the 1960s might be probative, even if their reputation would tend to be edgier.

Breath, though, has its own edginess: the portrayal of asphyxiation as a sexual practice, which is shown in the corpse at the beginning and also in Eva's conduct with Pikelet and, later on, her American tragedy. Is there a sociology of erotic asphyxiation, especially the autoerotic asphyxiation of which the victim at the beginning and Eva both die? Autoerotic asphyxiation received its first major media coverage in the *New York Times* in 1984, in a 27 March article by Jane Brody on autoerotic deaths of teenage boys in the wealthy suburbs of New York's Westchester County.[38] *Newsweek* declared the same year, 1984, 'The Year of the Yuppie'. It is therefore a neoliberal, not a countercultural, thrill that Winton is referencing in narrating this search for extreme erotic ecstasy. The mature Bruce Pike's response to the initial incident illustrates this: he is familiar with it as a syndrome. Pike understands that the mother has dressed up her child, removed the signs of the erotic obsession that drove him to an early and undesired death to avoid opprobrium, but he himself recognises the autoerotic asphyxiation as what one might call the 'next wave'.

Why autoerotic asphyxiation 'now' – in other words, after the 1980s? On the one hand, autoerotic asphyxiation was the further extension of the ethics of 1960s–70s sexual liberation, the same sense of erotic openness that made Eva's affair with Pikelet more fashionable, if not necessarily any more likely, than in the decades in which Pikelet's parents had raised him in Sawyer, or the era in which Pikelet's mother had endured the Blitz in England. On the other hand, autoerotic asphyxiation added to general sexual liberation, a search for special status, a quest for more rarefied ground after more usual sexual transgressions had become normalised and sanctioned by the bourgeoisie. It also, however, partook of the thrill associated with neoliberalism, with deregulation, with rules lifted, with people autonomously assuming risk (rather than simply and inevitably enduring it, as with Pike's father who is killed in a sawmill accident after a lifetime of deliberate prudence), with financial flotation and opportunism previously deemed uncongenial to the social compact. That Eva meets her end through a practice Pikelet recognises from his own experimentation with her decades earlier is a melancholy coda; by the time she does it, it is no longer novel or shocking, simply a known, if horrifying, practice that trained professionals like Pike know to recognise and cope with; it is likely, in other words, that if Pikelet had not had his specific experiences with Eva as a youth, he would nevertheless have recognised the condition of autoerotic asphyxiation merely through his work as a paramedic.

Winton is addressing an ongoing social problem he knows to have occurred in Australia as well as the United States, as evidenced most famously in the allegations concerning the death of Michael Hutchence, lead singer of the band INXS. Eva is perhaps an early adopter of this practice, but it is one that long before her demise has become routine, an aspiration for exceptionality that becomes, ironically, generic. Sando and Eva are also early adopters of extreme sports, a mode of athletics that became a genre and entertainment category in the 1990s and after. Jonathan Simon links neoliberalism and extreme sports in their shared 'embrace of risk'.[39] Neoliberalism, extreme sports, and erotic asphyxiation are all manifestations of the quests for 'a rebellion against the monotony of drawing breath',[40] of the desire to always be exceptional or interesting.

As 'free agents',[41] Sando and Eva represent heedless individualism; as people who 'rise to a challenge and set a course',[42] they seem to embody an idea of Americans as 'driven by ambition'.[43] This phrase is associated with an image of false spirituality uncannily reminiscent of the implications of Angelus as a name: 'God was in everything'.[44] Eva is from Mormon-dominated Utah, quintessential avatar of a discernibly American hybrid of Christianity and nationalist mythology. Even though her aerial skiing and erotic thrill-seeking take her far away from Mormon precepts, her lifestyle and Sando's – which try to make the divine immanent through their worldly deeds – is clearly seeking the sacred in some way. If one is to read the book through the prism of neoliberalism, one can see the transformation of the divine into a narcissistic market-god as no longer a national trait but an anthropology – what all men and women are like, are supposed to be like, under the mantle of neoliberal ideology: bearers of risk, self-motivated gods. Pikelet's transition from tea- to coffee-drinker is, for example, not an instance of Americanisation but of neoliberalisation. The identity he relinquishes thereby is not that of a fair-dinkum Australian, but one redolent of the support, solidarity and, it must be said, mediocrity associated with his parents and Sawyer, and an egalitarian mid-century consensus associated with the Second World War.

The mature Bruce Pike is married to and then divorced from the only barely present Grace. Her name – which can be compared with the earlier quoted line about the outlaw feeling of grace – and her fleeting role in his life, signify an only limited recovery from trauma. The grown-up Pike is father to daughters (not sons; there will be no next-generation Pikelet and Loonie). These daughters find him baffling and rather disappointing. That he is not in a high-status job – not a high wage-earner or a daredevil – may seem limited. It is certainly an anticlimax, filled not with risk but with 'watchful rectitude'.[45] But at the very least he does not have an image of himself as a self-motivated deity, an image that, readers may infer, Eva died still embracing. On the other hand, while the adult Pike seems consoled by the 'priestly authority'[46] of his uniform, he also feels happier having embraced the idea that 'maybe ordinary's not so bad'.[47] Pikelet's continued affirmation of a completely pointless and beautiful ideal signifies aesthetic, not cultural capital. The book holds out hope that art – and the 'art', not the competitive 'sport' of surfing – can be different, that it can take risks without hurting anybody, that with its unselfish pointlessness it can protect the integrity of the truly beautiful.

Even though Eva exploits Pikelet, and even though prima facie she should not be having sex with underage boys, Pikelet is not totally an object in the relationship; he uses it to disenthrall himself from his cultic subservience to Sando. Although it has often been said, most recently by Hannah Schürholz, that Winton objectifies women as figures of allurement and entrapment,[48] Eva, although not representing these qualities, also half-liberates Pikelet from a paralysing attachment to the more minatory Sando. As much as the Eva relationship was the catastrophe that traumatised Pike, in another sense if he had cast his lot fully with Sando, never broken with him, he would have been in even worse shape.

That Pikelet manages to survive in a position where he is socially respected and cares for others – even if it is not, as a job, particularly high-status or glamorous – may not be due to the affair with Sando's wife, or indeed may have occurred in spite of it. But had Pikelet not in some way freed himself from Sando, and distanced himself from the merely material idols Sando constitutes and pursues, he would not have survived to achieve the moral integrity of his mature years. The mature Bruce Pike is not meant to have achieved perfection. But he has carved out a life free of the desperate search for distinction, liquidity and risk that consumed the lives of his one-time role models Eva and Sando. Pike has found a respite from the jaws of neoliberalism; he continues to breathe.

Notes

1   T. Winton, *Breath*, Farrar, Straus and Giroux, New York, 2008.
2   U. Beck, *World Risk Society*, Wiley, New York, 1999.
3   Winton, *Breath*, p. 26.
4   R. Dixon, 'Tim Winton, *Cloudstreet* and the field of Australian literature', *Westerly*, vol. 50, 2005, p. 241.
5   N. Le, 'Halflead Bay', *The Boat*, Vintage, New York, 2009 (first published 2008), pp. 94–162.
6   Winton, *Breath*, p. 208.
7   Ibid., p. 208.
8   Ibid., p. 33.
9   Ibid., p. 215.
10 Z. Bauman, *Liquid Modernity*, Polity, London, 2000.
11 T. Winton, *Dirt Music*, Picador, Sydney, 2001.
12 T. Winton, *The Turning*, Scribner, New York, 2004.
13 Dixon, 'Tim Winton, *Cloudstreet* and the field of Australian literature', p. 41.
14 Winton, *Breath*, p. 3.
15 M. Knox, 'In the giant green cathedral', *Monthly*, no. 34, May 2008, pp. 60–1, www.themonthly.com.au/issue/2008/may/1215670870/malcolm-knox/giant-green-cathedral.
16 Winton, *Breath*, p. 38.
17 T. Winton, 'Damaged Goods', *The Turning*, pp. 55–63.
18 W. Wordsworth, 'The World is too Much with Us' (1807), in D. Wu (ed.), *Romanticism: An Anthology*, 3rd edn, Blackwell Publishing, Oxford, 2006, p. 534.
19 Winton, *Breath*, p. 25.
20 Knox, 'In the giant green cathedral'.

21 Winton, *Breath*, p. 102.

22 Ibid., p. 167.

23 D. Malouf, *The Great World*, Random House, New York, 1991 (first published 1990).

24 T. Winton, 'Big World', *The Turning*, pp. 1–16.

25 P. Larkin, 'Homage to a Government' (1969), *High Windows*, Faber & Faber, London, 1974.

26 P. Bourdieu, *Distinction: A Social Critique of Judgement and Taste*, trans. R. Nice, Routledge, London, 1984.

27 B. Ashcroft, 'The horizonal sublime', *Antipodes*, vol. 19, 2005, pp. 141–51.

28 Winton, *Breath*, p. 102.

29 Beck, *World Risk Society*.

30 Dixon, 'Tim Winton, *Cloudstreet* and the field of Australian literature', p. 244ff.

31 T. Winton, 'Aquifer', *The Turning*, pp. 37–54.

32 *Modern Language Quarterly Special Issue: Peripheral Realisms*, vol. 73, no. 3, 2012.

33 T. Winton, cited in J. A. Singh, 'Meeting Kate Grenville and Tim Winton', Jabberwock (blog), 30 November 2004, jaiarjun.blogspot.com.au/2004/11/meeting-kate-grenville-and-tim-winton.html.

34 T. Winton, *Cloudstreet*, Simon & Schuster, New York, 2002.

35 N. O'Reilly, *Exploring Suburbia: The Suburbs in the Contemporary Australian Novel*, Teneo, Amherst, New York, 2012, p. 119.

36 J. Kinsella, 'The Phenomena that Surround a Sighting of Eclipse Island' (1992), *Full Fathom Five*, Fremantle Arts Centre Press, Fremantle, 1993.

37 J. Kinsella, *Divine Comedy: Journeys through a Regional Geography*, Norton, New York, 2008, p. 88.

38 J. Brody, 'Autoerotic death of youths causes widening concern', *New York Times*, 27 March 1984, p. C1.

39 J. Simon, 'Taking risks: extreme sports and the embrace of risk in advanced liberal societies', in T. Baker and J. Simon (eds), *Embracing Risk: The Changing Culture of Insurance and Responsibility*, University of Chicago Press, Chicago, 2002, p. 179.

40 Winton, *Breath*, p. 43.

41 Ibid., p. 112.

42 Ibid., p. 116.

43 Ibid., p. 138.

44 Ibid.

45 Ibid., p. 207.

46 Ibid., p. 216.

47 Ibid., p. 200.
48 H. Schürholz, 'Shadows of the dead: stories of transience in Tim Winton's fiction', *Westerly*, vol. 57, no. 1, 2012, pp. 1561–81.

Bibliography

Ashcroft, B., 'The horizonal sublime', *Antipodes*, vol. 19, 2005, pp. 141–51.

Bauman, Z., *Liquid Modernity*, Polity, London, 2000.

Beck, U., *World Risk Society*, Wiley, New York, 1999.

Bourdieu, P., *Distinction: A Social Critique of Judgment and Taste*, trans. R. Nice, Routledge, London, 1984.

Brody, J., 'Autoerotic death of youths causes widening concern', *New York Times*, 27 March 1984, p. C1.

Dixon, R., 'Tim Winton, *Cloudstreet* and the field of Australian literature', *Westerly*, vol. 50, 2005, pp. 240–60.

Kinsella, J., *Divine Comedy: Journeys through a Regional Geography*, Norton, New York, 2008.

—— 'The Phenomena that Surround a Sighting of Eclipse Island' (1992), *Full Fathom Five*, Fremantle Arts Centre Press, Fremantle, 1993.

Knox, M., 'In the giant green cathedral', *Monthly*, May 2008, no. 34, pp. 60–1, www.themonthly.com.au/issue/2008/may/1215670870/malcolm-knox/giant-green-cathedral.

Larkin, P., 'Homage to a Government' (1969), *High Windows*, Faber & Faber, London, 1974.

Le, N., *The Boat*, Vintage, New York, 2009.

Malouf, D., *The Great World*, Random House, New York, 1991.

Modern Language Quarterly Special Issue: Peripheral Realisms, vol. 73, no. 3, 2012.

O'Reilly, N., *Exploring Suburbia: The Suburbs in the Contemporary Australian Novel*, Teneo, Amherst, New York, 2012.

Schürholz, H., 'Shadows of the dead: stories of transience in Tim Winton's fiction', *Westerly*, vol. 57, no. 1, 2012, pp. 1561–81.

Simon, J., 'Taking risks: extreme sports and the embrace of risk in liberal societies', in T. Baker and J. Simon (eds), *Embracing Risk: The Changing Culture of Insurance and Responsibility*, University of Chicago Press, Chicago, 2002, pp. 177–208.

Singh, J. A., 'Meeting Kate Grenville and Tim Winton', Jabberwock (blog), 30 November 2004, jaiarjun.blogspot.com.au/2004/11/meeting-kate-grenville-and-tim-winton.html.

Winton, T., *Breath*, Farrar, Straus and Giroux, New York, 2008.

—— *The Turning*, Scribner, New York, 2004.

—— *Cloudstreet*, Simon & Schuster, New York, 2002.

—— *Dirt Music*, Picador, Sydney, 2001.

Wordsworth, W., 'The World is too Much with Us' (1807), in D. Wu (ed.), *Romanticism: An Anthology*, 3rd edn, Blackwell Publishing, Oxford, 2006.

12

EXTREME GAMES, HEGEMONY AND NARRATION: AN INTERPRETATION OF TIM WINTON'S *BREATH*

Hou Fei

*B*reath[1] won Tim Winton his fourth Miles Franklin Award. It is a unique novel in the Winton oeuvre because, unlike his previous works *An Open Swimmer*,[2] *Cloudstreet*[3] and *Dirt Music*,[4] Indigenous and religious motifs are noticeably absent from its pages. The novel follows Winton's tradition of writing geographically specific texts, locating itself in the south-western region of Western Australia. As a writer, Tim Winton trawls the ocean of his imagination and, as Martin Flanagan puts it, 'his other life… spent in almost daily communication with the sea, discussing tides and weather, surfing, fishing, diving'.[5] *Breath* unfolds as an exhilarating surfing story, with vivid descriptions of surfing itself, as well as depictions of the waves, the sand and lovers of the beach. In Malcolm Knox's review of *Breath*, entitled 'In the giant green cathedral', he claims:

> Winton brings the experience of surfing to life with far more subtle and effective means than stream-of-consciousness or breathless hyperbole…[I] suspect…this book will have two kinds of readers: those who see the surfing as the prelude to the love affair, and those see the love affair as a painful diversion from the surfing.[6]

Indeed, there are many critical approaches to the novel, focusing on: its surfing narrative; an exploration within a surfing-novel framework; or risk-taking, extreme excitement, fear and intoxication. McGloin explores Eva in *Breath* by providing a feminist reading of the novel:

> [I]t is the text's phallocentric re/presentation that draws attention to the absence of colonial history and the reproduction of a nation as white. Eva's eventual excision from the narrative, the absence of colonial history or indigenous presence contributes significantly to the difficulties this text faces in its attempts to reconfigure white surfing masculinities.[7]

Peter Kelly reads *Breath* as an

> [A]llegorical tale about the terror of being ordinary: and of the teenage years as being a time in a life in which the fear of being ordinary compels Winton's key characters to seek out...that which promises to make their's [sic] *a life less ordinary*.[8]

McGloin seems to have overlooked the novel's multicultural Australia, with its characters being Australian-born, English or American, and with Asia not far away. I would argue further, however, that Winton has produced a novel that aims for more than these contextual themes alone. The narration concerning Australia and its involvement in the Vietnam War, Americanisation, and banal Australian small-town lives do connect with each other historically and in relation to the probing of the characters' fates. This essay attempts to argue that interpretation of the novel needs to take into account the context of the Vietnam War, which is not used by Winton merely as a historical event for background colour within a surfing novel.

Breath begins and ends with the middle-aged paramedic Bruce 'Pikelet' Pike and his life and work, the plot centring on Pike recalling his childhood and adolescent days. In a purely narrative sense, *Breath* is a story about the rites-of-passage surfing experiences of its main character, Pikelet, and those of his childhood pal, Ivan 'Loonie' Loon. Alongside Loonie, the two characters of Bill 'Sando' Sanderson and Eva Sanderson are crucial to Pikelet's story. In the fictional coastal village of Sawyer, Sando and Eva's hippie lifestyle is entirely different from that of the locals, not only because they are newly arrived in town but, more importantly, because their activities, careers and former careers revolve entirely around extreme sports. McGloin describes Sando as 'ex-champion counter-cultural surfer'.[9]

Sando soon becomes a name in the town, his skills as a surfer showcased; Loonie and Pikelet are quickly hooked by this guru, honoured to become his chosen followers. The boys' lives change as Sando encourages them to challenge the unknown: shark-infested waters and dangerous, unsurfed beaches. A powerful manipulator, Sando seduces the two young men to compete for his favour, actively involving them in his plans when he feels it necessary, while keeping them ignorant of his business. In the end, Pike and Loonie each separate entirely from the other; their understandings of fear and awe are too different for them to remain friends. While Loonie continues to chase surf and excitement in a prolonged adolescence, Pike gradually begins to move away from the dangerous activities of his youth, and returns to his family and school life, finding it sometimes banal and ordinary.

Woven into the surfing narration, the novel also presents fragments of information about the Vietnam War, as well as the seemingly dull style of education found in small schools of the late 1960s. One section of the novel covers a situation that saw some young Australians with nothing else to do being enticed into army training for eventual deployment to the battlefields of Vietnam. Interpreting the novel through this historical context lends a deeper and more melancholy resonance to this book about adolescence and maturity. The relationships between Sando and Pikelet, and Sando and Loonie, produce an extended metaphor for those power relationships, found throughout history, between dominant gurus and their obedient disciples.

Although Sando is Australian-born, he has largely adopted a recognisably American lifestyle. Sando is married to Eva, an American woman who shares his passion for extreme sports, he is a well-known star within the American surfing culture, and he later conducts business and thrives in America. These aspects of the characterisation lead us to see that Sando has been deliberately given an Americanised life, and comes to stand for American values – physical, competitive prowess; entrepreneurship; individualism – that have so enchanted Australians. We see Sando's extraordinary surfing skills more than once, and learn that he and Loonie travel internationally together to ride bigger and bigger foreign waves. As readers, however, we gain this knowledge second-hand without seeing exactly what happens during these trips, and our suspicions as to their real purpose begin to grow once we learn that Loonie's eventual violent death is drug-related.

As for the Vietnam War, Australia did send troops, including conscripts, to the Vietnam battlefield, in part as a supportive gesture towards the United States. For many this was a meeting with disappointment and despair, including, along the way, drug-dependency. The war was long and frustrating, costing Australia a considerable number of lives and impacting on its international reputation. Maddox points out that,

> On 15 May 1962 the Australian Cabinet agreed to Rusk's request, setting in train a military involvement that would ultimately see 46,852 Australians serving in Vietnam, 494 of whom would die.[10]

The history of Australia's involvement in the Vietnam War continues to shape the nation's understanding of itself in various ways. The experience of the war in Vietnam has not been ignored in Australia, but offers continuing valuable lessons to light the future. In 2008, near the beginning of the twenty-first century, Winton, through the publication of *Breath*, invited his readers to think globally, conscientiously reassessing Australia's relationships and affiliations both internal and external.

In order to fully understand the significance of the Vietnam War subtext in *Breath*, we must analyse the character of Bill Sanderson, or Sando. The relationship between Sando and the novel's two young protagonists is more like that of guru/hegemon to disciple/follower. Analogously, it resembles the relationship between the United States and Australia during their involvement in the Vietnam War. In the later part of the novel, Pikelet gradually removes himself from the triangular relationship he shared with Sando and Loonie. Pikelet goes forward into his life by leaving behind the obsessiveness of the surfing culture, beginning to think independently, and taking on personal adult responsibility, his behaviour progressing from insanity to sanity.

So *Breath* touches upon the Vietnam War with skilful narration, indirectly and symbolically, in establishing the subservience of the boys to Sando.

Bill Sanderson takes on many functions – husband of a fractious wife, surfer extraordinaire, role model for adolescent boys and, later, successful businessman. It seems that Sando, however, has something to hide: he never reveals his surfing destinations or itineraries; he refuses to let Pikelet and Loonie know where he ships surfboards to or, conversely, who ships them to him; and he is noticeably secretive about his true motive for guiding Pikelet and Loonie, two novices, to surf on perilous untouched beaches. Ultimately, Sando exerts a near absolute power over the people and things he wishes to control.

Energetic children, Pikelet and Loonie rebel against the dull and tedious atmosphere of Sawyer, and so they seek danger, aiming to exceed the ordinary. In early scenes they compete with each other to stay under water for as long as possible, not just to determine who can hold their breath the longest but to see who can best convince passersby they are drowning. In living this way, the boys believe themselves somehow above the rest of the dull teenagers around town:

> In Sawyer, a town of millers and loggers and dairy farmers, with one butcher and a rep from the rural bank beside the BP, men did solid, practical things, mostly with their hands.[11]

In Pikelet's eyes, such 'practical things' are less than beautiful, elegant or admirable, but rather represent a routine of ordinariness he is eager to escape:

> Everything around me seemed so pointless and puny. The locals in the street looked cowed and weak and ordinary. Wherever I went I felt like the last person awake in a room of sleepers.[12]

Here, the sleeper represents a backward or closed and underdeveloped condition. Pikelet is in fact bored by the culture and longing for something new, exciting and thrilling. In this sense, the fictional Sawyer symbolises the underdeveloped Australia of the 1960s, while Sando and Eva's hippie lifestyle seems to represent modern, exotic America, and the world beyond Australia. As for Loonie, he is addicted to '[a]ny game [...] as long as it was dangerous [...] he was greedy about risk [...and] absolutely loved a dare'.[13] What Pikelet and Loonie want to do is something big, something extraordinary, beyond the town and its stagnation.

Only after Sando appears do they find their idol: a real surfing guru in the eyes of two young boys. Sando is noticed quickly on the surfing beach: 'One surfer seemed to show up on only the very biggest days [...] His skill was extraordinary'.[14] It is this surfer who changes the lives of Pikelet and his friend: 'That was how we got to know Sando, how our lives took such a turn'.[15] When Pikelet and Loonie finally meet their athletic hero, he permits them to store their surfboards at his place not far from the beach. Sando's 'friendly' gesture of inviting the two young men to his place is not, however, a simple gesture of hospitality. A person's living space bears many individual marks and reveals personal life stories, which metonymically constitute the person who lives in that space. Along with Pike and Loonie, readers discover Sando's achievements when they open the surfing magazines left beside their surfboards:

They were American magazines, lavish and confident in their production, with a welter of ads and products and images of famous riders at Hawaiian breaks like Sunset Beach and Pipeline and Makaha. Within a few minutes I began to recognize a familiar stance, a silhouette I knew very well [...]

We strewed the contents of the box across the bench and clawed through them to find other images of Sando. There he was, in Maui in 1970, in Morocco in the winter of '68, and at the Hollister Ranch in '71.[16]

Understandably, these glossy magazines hook the young men completely: 'Our admiration for him had enlarged; it had metastasized'.[17] Before this, Pikelet and Loonie are admiring fans of Sando. Afterwards, however, the two are determined to become obedient disciples of the older man. To the boys, Sando is extraordinary, open-minded, brave and strong, and as they recognise this, Sando builds his guru status easily. The images they find in the magazines, however, cement the boys' awe. Those glamorous magazines, one of the media carriers of American culture and values, are extremely attractive to these would-be escapees from rural Australian culture. Once popular American culture begins to permeate relatively conservative Australia, it becomes absolutely powerful and widespread.

A self-absorbed character, Sando's attraction to his young protégées is far from simply nurturing or pedagogical. He introduces the two young men to a series of challenging and risky beaches, often using force in the guise of encouragement. The first of these is a beach called Barney:

There were no huts or jetties here, nothing to suggest
that people came by at all, and it was obvious that none
of this country had ever been logged. The landscape
looked primeval [...]

There was still no sign of habitation, no footprints in
the sand, not even a vehicle track in the hills beyond.[18]

Old Smoky, Sando's next introduction, proves an even more
challenging and demanding surfing experience. Pikelet shows his
apprehension and anxiety immediately at the sight of it. Nautilus,
likewise, is among the most dangerous surfing sites, '[a] sharkpit
[...] On the charts it was marked as a navigation hazard with
multiple warnings'.[19] Later, Pike recalls of his time there:

I was gutted by that day at the Nautilus. A small,
cool part of me knew it was stupid to have been out
there trying to surf a wave so unlikely, so dangerous,
so perverse.[20]

Sando, ever the master, stirs his disciples to excel, which
often involves great risk-taking. Sando's seductions come one after
another: the beach will '[m]ake men of you, said Sando'.[21] His
manhood challenged, the twelve-year-old Pikelet has to go on: 'A
few moments later, hapless and terrified, I followed him'.[22] When
Pikelet hesitates to surf the wild wave, Sando expertly prompts
him, declaring, 'I think you're ready, Pikelet'.[23] Eventually, Pikelet
recognises he has failed Sando's masculinity test and confesses to
being a coward, but Sando refuses to surrender, taunting the child:
'I thought I brought surfers with me. Men above the ordinary'.[24]
According to Sando, then, arguably sane hesitations and fears

make men cowardly and ordinary. Terms and phrases like 'man', 'surfer' and 'men above the ordinary' are all highly provocative in terms of seduction. Sando takes the lead in his society of three, but once Pikelet retreats, Loonie seems more excited to have Sando for himself than he is sad to lose his boyhood friend. Once Pikelet refuses to be controlled, he is excluded from Sando's business:

> Sando was distant now, preoccupied. He seemed suddenly closed off from me. I began to sense that there were secrets between him and Loonie, things they kept from me with grins and furtive glances.[25]

McGloin notes that 'the normalizing of the relationships between the three male characters is ambivalent...Pikelet's refusal to surf the "Nautilus" with the other two introduces a shift in the friendship'.[26] It becomes obvious that Sando is less a guru than a hegemon, one whose will must be obeyed and carried out. In this way, the older surfer possesses insurmountable power over his followers. Like Loonie, other followers discern risk-taking as an excellent opportunity to ingratiate themselves with the 'guru'. Earlier, Pikelet confessed that '[w]hen [Sando] gave you his full attention you could feel yourself quicken, like a tree finding water'.[27] But increasingly Pikelet is excluded.

Contributing to his authority, Sando keeps secrets from Pikelet and Loonie from the beginning of their relationship. In his eyes, the two young men can only know what he allows them to know:

> He wouldn't tell us what the deal was or who sent them [the surfboards], and on more than one occasion I slipped behind the shed where he stacked the packaging before

he shredded it all for compost, and furtively scanned
the senders' address in Perth, Sydney, San Francisco
and Maui. There was one from Peru, another from
Mauritius. Boards came and boards went.[28]

Although full of suspicion, Pikelet dares not venture to know the
origins or whereabouts of the boards. Sando does not need to
work as the majority of Sawyer locals do, and it seems that money
comes easily to the Sanderson household. This mystery about
the source of the money causes Pikelet's suspicions to grow. At the
novel's end, Loonie has died during a drug deal turned violent,
and Eva later dies from sexual asphyxia, but Sando has forged a
successful career in the sporting goods business.

McGloin treats Eva 'as a victim of loneliness imposed by her
surfie husband's escapades'.[29] Sando's later success in life leads
the reader's mind back to the surfboards appearing at the beginning of the novel. Sando practises extreme sports not purely for
personal enjoyment, but also as a lucrative means of profit-making.
His business empire, however, is not built within one day; over
the course of the novel he makes several ambiguously motivated
foreign trips whose purpose we, as readers, do not know. But we
are provided with clues as to his business. Sando takes Loonie
with him during many of his foreign travels, and while this may
indicate closeness, he relays news of Loonie's death without signs
of guilt or regret. For Pikelet, Sando's guru status is shattered, and
ultimately the reader sees him as an utterly selfish hegemon whose
money-making prevails over anything else, such as responsibility
and morality. Sando is primarily motivated by money, which
strongly echoes the new religion of America, capital.

The subtext of the Vietnam War

Using figures slightly different from those of Maddox, Stuart Rintoul states,

> [A]lmost fifty thousand Australians went to the Vietnam War between 1962 and 1972. Five hundred and one died there, two thousand four hundred were wounded physically. Most of them were scarred.[30]

Vietnamese, American and Australian soldiers and civilians suffered much from this war, and these cultures have been painfully processing the aftermath for more than five decades. The war witnessed 'raping [of] women, mistreating or killing civilians and unarmed combatants such as prisoners of war, destroying entire villages, even mutilating the dead'.[31] Vietnam veterans were miserably haunted by nightmares from the dangerous and dirty war. According to Aphrodite Matsakis,

> [P]ermanently crippling or disabling wounds such as castration and amputation were sustained at a far greater rate in Vietnam than in previous wars; 300% higher than in WWII and 70% higher than in Korea.[32]

And while the veterans themselves endured psychological pain and physical torture, their families, too, suffered. Peter Pierce holds that 'in Australia, there is no extensive literature portraying returned servicemen from Vietnam as outlaw victims'.[33] Pierce argues that Vietnam War history in literature should not be ignored. Rather, he demonstrates how Australian writers have worked on it, both overtly and in more subtextual modes. Tim Winton is one of the latter. On the surface, his *Breath* seems to have little to do with the war, but this essay argues that his inconspicuous narration, set across the Vietnam War years and inflected with Australia's subservient attitude towards American hegemony, demands attention.

The opening of *Breath*, in introducing us to middle-aged paramedic Bruce Pike at a call-out, shows us that he is not easy to get along with. When his young colleague Jodie complains of his unfriendly behaviour, he responds by emphasising: 'I'm not a Vietnam vet',[34] presumably because he was not old enough to have been conscripted, but also because he didn't want to be described in this way. There are memorials all over Australia built to honour war veterans, but Vietnam veterans particularly were initially confronted with embarrassed and embarrassing treatment, not only in America, but also in Australia. Coates writes: 'Vietnam veterans were, then, the only ones labeled drug-abusing baby killers, the only ones not offered societal forgiveness, the only ones left to carry the burden of national shame'.[35] Herman notes that 'returning soldiers look for tangible evidence of public recognition',[36] but in America and Australia they often had to put up with coldness and even hostility.

Interestingly, in Vietnam the war is also referred to as the American War. Based on thorough analysis, Lloyd Cox and Brendon O'Connor write:

> Australia used war as a means of cultivating its relationship with the US, in the expectation that national benefits would outweigh costs. Australia's military involvement at the side of the US was…the manifestation of a broader strategic culture. Its essential feature was, and is, cultivating the support of, and intimacy with, a great and powerful friend – not as an end in itself, but with the aim of increasing Australian security and

attempting to ensure that friend's engagement in the Asian region.[37]

Arguably, the Menzies Australian government cared less about the reasons for the war itself, and the tragic consequences it generated, than about the status of its alliance with the United States. To the Vietnamese, the war was catastrophic and disastrous, while to the Australian government, it seems, it was a golden opportunity. The same may be said of the second Gulf War, of which Cox and O'Connor note that

> This pattern of behaviour and commentary provides strong evidence that [Prime Minister] Howard saw wars with no direct threat to Australia as opportunities to strengthen alliance relations with the US.[38]

As America's ally, Australia conducted a policy of conscription to enlist soldiers for the Vietnam War. In *Breath*, both Australia's conscription policy and its active support for America can be clearly seen through Pike's descriptions of his early education:

> We could have been staying back at school as army cadets, learning to fire mortars and machine-guns, to lay booby traps and to kill strangers in hand-to-hand combat like other boys we knew, in preparation for a manhood that could barely credit the end of the war in Vietnam [...] Eva was right – we were Sando's wide-eyed disciples – but in the sixties and seventies when we were kids there were plenty of other cults to join, cults abounding.[39]

As *Breath* reveals, there were various kinds of 'followings', or 'cults' as Winton labels them, during the Vietnam War period in Australia. Is this sense, the novel draws parallels between the 'cult-like' nature of army recruiting and Sando's position as master of his small sect. And much like Loonie and Pikelet worshipping Sando from afar, Australians found out the reality of the Vietnam War only after they threw themselves into it.

Like Australia following the United States blindly into battle, or unquestioningly living out national 'values', Pikelet and Loonie don't hesitate to follow Sando:

> [He] was good at portraying the moment you found yourself at your limit, when things multiplied around you like an hallucination. He could describe the weird, reptilian thing that happened to you: the cold, super-charged certainty which overtook your usually dithering mind […] Eva sometimes sank back with her eyes closed and her teeth bared, as though she understood only too well […]
>
> It's like you come pouring back into yourself, said Sando one afternoon. Like you've exploded and all the pieces of you are reassembling themselves. You're new. Shimmering. Alive.[40]

Sando takes the lead on the beach, tutoring Pikelet and Loonie in the mechanics and ideology of surfing, which translates into them feeling meaningful, alive and brand new.

Without surfing, Sando teaches the boys, life is routine and bleak. Eva shares the same attitude towards the extreme sports her husband loves, and Sando identifies with American surfing values.

For Eva, the extreme-sports spirit is the American spirit of competition and full-throttle selfhood: 'they were driven by ambition in a way that no Australian could possibly understand. They wanted fresh angles, better services, perfect mobility'.[41] Sando echoes Eva's sentiments when he interprets ambition:

> Every day, people face down their own fears. They make calculations, bargains with God, strategic manoeuvres. That's how we first crossed oceans and learnt to fly and split the atom [...] That's mankind for you, he said. Our higher side. We rise to a challenge and set a course. We take a decision. You put your mind to something. Just deciding to do it gets you halfway there. Daring to try [...]
>
> Husband and wife exchanged glances I couldn't interpret.[42]

The contrast here seems to be that while American values advocate ambition, typical Australian culture focuses on something else, something safe: 'Here in Sawyer people seemed settled – rusted on, in fact. They liked to be ordinary. They were uncomfortable with ambition and avoided any kind of unpredictability or risk'.[43] But the younger generation is seeking something unusual, even thrilling. Finding Loonie in this condition, Sando successfully changes him into a fervent follower of his 'extraordinary life' ideology. Pikelet is hesitant because eventually reason must prevail over insanity, in his terms. When he chooses to retreat from the crazy risk-taking of his youth, however, Pike is inflicted with a pain that disturbs his inner peace well into adulthood, which brings to mind the post-traumatic stress disorder suffered by Vietnam veterans. Metaphorically, Pikelet is a wounded 'veteran' from the 'society of three', Sando still taking the lead, Loonie dead. As the older Pike recalls,

> I have no doubt that in a later era he'd have been seen as reckless and foolhardy, yet when you consider the period and the sorts of activities that schools and governments sanctioned, Sando's excursions seem like small beer.[44]

Both at the government and the individual level, Australia seems to have experienced a period of blindness during the 1960s, which many times resulted in a lack of confidence, in unhesitant and enthusiastic following, and in a failure of self-identification. The Vietnam War narration in the novel helps readers better identify and further understand the relationship between the surfing guru and his disciples while inviting them to rethink Australia's involvement in Vietnam. At the same time, the vivid surfing story reminds readers to connect both national and international history to the novel's narration. The individual life becomes a metaphor for national history, and national history simultaneously provides footnotes to the individual's fate.

At the same time, individual lives are differentiated by Winton. In *Breath*, for example, Loonie symbolises impulse, excess and vigour, while Pikelet comes to represent reason and self-identification. Sando influences both boys deeply, but Pikelet survives Sando's projected superiority, seductiveness and hegemony, while Loonie does not. Though this survival comes at a price for Pikelet, it is justified by his regained independence and self-identification, whether as an individual or, symbolically, a nation.

Pikelet and Loonie: metaphorical Australian youth

As we have seen, *Breath* is highly metaphorical. There are parallel narratives within the novel: the 1960s context of the Vietnam War, and Bruce Pike's retelling of his surfing boyhood. Predominantly, the surfing story is clearly narrated to readers, while the history of the Vietnam War is treated partly as known fact but also partly as a submerged narrative. Readers need imagination to draw parallels.

At the beginning Pike and Loonie are almost equally devoted to their surfing master, but gradually Pike chooses to retreat from Sando's little club, while Loonie eagerly continues his journey. Years later, Bruce Pike deals with the news of Loonie's death with grief and with blame for Sando:

> Loonie died in Mexico, shot in a bar in Rosarito, not far from Tijuana. Some kind of drug deal gone bad [...] His reputation for fearlessness endured. He surfed hard and lived hard and seemed to finance it all with drug scams and smuggling [...] I wonder about his apprenticeship to Sando [...] – all those side-trips to Thailand, the long, unexplained absences, surfboards arriving from all over the globe – and whether Sando's family money had been augmented by his darker business interests.[45]

Bit by bit, Pike makes out the scope of Sando's business empire and concludes that his money-making methods may not be that aboveboard, while the fearless and naive Loonie turns into Sando's best money-making apprentice. The picture becomes clear: Sando the surfing guru uses his skills to recruit his young protégées to serve his 'darker' purposes. Sando preaches American values about ambition and the ecstasy of life at the limit, but conceals completely his real financial intentions. Sando is a complex, vivid metaphor of

Australia succumbing to American hegemonic culture, a culture that holds high the flag of peace and democracy in public but has other agendas – of capital and of extreme individual enterprise.

Pikelet and Loonie can be read as one, representing as they do the conflicting aspects of a single personality. This reading is best seen in the older Bruce Pike's reaction to Loonie's death:

> I felt a pang when I heard about Loonie. It hardly sent me into a spin the way Eva's death had, but I felt hollow, as though there was suddenly less of me.[46]

Although Pikelet ends his blind following when he detects obsessive and dangerous directions in Sando's company, he nevertheless suffers all his life from the memory of surfing those untouched beaches. In fact, what Pike suffers from is just what Loonie puts into extreme practice. Though he chooses to suppress them, the impulsiveness and risk-taking that characterise Loonie are arguably still a part of Pike's psyche. They never disappear from him completely. The middle-aged Pike is haunted by his early adolescent experiences with both Sando and, in a different way, with Eva:

> Nobody wants to be creepy. I was careful, always backing off. And somehow, somewhere along the track, I went numb. I couldn't say what it was and didn't dare try.[47]

As we learn, Eva and Sando know only too well about American versions of new religion and new money. It's this money logic that unveils Sando's real identity and intention. Despite staying away from Sando's substantial control, Pike can't enjoy a peaceful life, experiencing spiritual tortures and anxieties. Pike tries every possible means to seek an engaging and meaningful life, trying to be a tender husband, a helpful paramedic, a loving father and a good son, but feeling himself to be a failure in almost every category.

In their teens, Pike and Loonie were both hooked by a guru figure, falling into trouble in different ways. Metaphorically, the two young men stand for their young nation. If there is a lesson to be learned from this metaphor, it is surely that when power, glamour and influence come knocking, it is hard to resist and retain independence. Australia's relationship to American culture, and the part Australia played in the Vietnam War as America's junior ally, arguably evokes a similar lesson. To Australia, Vietnam was a lesson that stirred many in the country to rethink national and international identity and responsibility. The meaning of an independent country and the concept of a responsible nation were both enhanced through this lesson.

Breath's subtextual narration of the Vietnam War works to open up the context and reach of the novel, and to enlarge the scope for interpretation. Surfing, more than simply an extreme sport that combines challenge and risk-taking, has become an arena imbued with seductive hegemonic powers. While the overwhelming penetration of this awareness of hegemony informs the novel, the individual excitement and ecstasy in surfing are deliberately described as individual values, as a desire to escape otherwise dull and ordinary lives. Through the deadly, risky and extreme games the boys learn to play, *Breath* reveals the excitement, but also the trauma, generated by hegemonic relationships. The novel's context – the Vietnam War years – drives this awareness of trauma home at personal, national and global levels. In this sense, *Breath* is an epic novel that demands rereading, rethinking and re-discussion.

Notes

1   T. Winton, *Breath*, Picador, London, 2009.
2   T. Winton, *An Open Swimmer*, Allen & Unwin, Sydney, 1982.
3   T. Winton, *Cloudstreet*, McPhee Gribble, Melbourne, 1991.
4   T. Winton, *Dirt Music*, Picador, Sydney, 2001.
5   M. Flanagan, 'Tim Winton in conversation with Martin Flanagan', *Monthly*, 24 March 2013, www.themonthly.com.au/node/981, accessed 1 December 2013.
6   M. Knox, 'In the giant green cathedral', *Monthly*, no. 34, May 2008, pp. 60–1, www.themonthly.com.au/issue/2008/may/1215670870/malcolm-knox/giant-green-cathedral.
7   C. McGloin, 'Reviving Eva in Tim Winton's *Breath*', *Journal of Commonwealth Literature*, vol. 47, no. 1, 2012, p. 119.
8   P. Kelly, '*Breath* and the truths of youth at-risk: allegory and the social scientific imagination', *Journal of Youth Studies*, vol. 14, no. 4, 2011, p. 431 (original italics).
9   McGloin, 'Reviving Eva in Tim Winton's *Breath*', p. 111.
10 K. Maddox and B. Wright (eds), *War: Australia and Vietnam*, Harper & Row, Sydney, 1987, p. 15.
11 Winton, *Breath*, pp. 23–4.
12 Ibid., p. 135.
13 Ibid., p. 33.
14 Ibid., p. 29.
15 Ibid., p. 40.
16 Ibid., p. 71.
17 Ibid., p. 73.
18 Ibid., pp. 79–80.
19 Ibid., pp. 130–1.
20 Ibid., p. 168.
21 Ibid., p. 82.
22 Ibid., p. 83.
23 Ibid., p. 107.
24 Ibid., p. 166.
25 Ibid., p. 160.
26 McGloin, 'Reviving Eva in Tim Winton's *Breath*', p. 111.

27 Winton, *Breath*, p. 142.

28 Ibid., pp. 64–5.

29 McGloin, 'Reviving Eva in Tim Winton's *Breath*', p. 119.

30 S. Rintoul, *Ashes of Vietnam: Australian Voices*, Heinemann, Melbourne, 1987, p. ix.

31 D. Coates, 'Coming home: the return of the (Australian Vietnam War) soldier', *Southerly*, vol. 65, no. 2, 2005, p. 107.

32 A. Matsakis, *Vietnam Wives: Facing the Challenges of Life with Veterans Suffering Post-traumatic Stress*, Sidran, Baltimore, Maryland, 1996, p. 40.

33 P. Pierce, 'Australian and American literature of the Vietnam War', in J. Doyle, J. Grey and P. Pierce (eds), *Australia's Vietnam War*, Texas A&M University Press, College Station, 2002, p. 134.

34 Winton, *Breath*, p. 6.

35 Coates, 'Coming home', p. 109.

36 Herman, *Trauma and Recovery*, Basic Books, New York, 1992, p. 54.

37 L. Cox and B. O'Connor, 'Australia, the US, and the Vietnam and Iraq wars: "Hound Dog, not lapdog" ', *Australian Journal of Political Science*, vol. 47, no. 2, 2012, p. 185.

38 Ibid., p. 183.

39 Winton, *Breath*, pp. 98–9.

40 Ibid., pp. 128–9.

41 Ibid., p. 156.

42 Ibid., p. 133.

43 Ibid., p. 157.

44 Ibid., p. 98.

45 Ibid., p. 240.

46 Ibid.

47 Ibid., p. 234.

Bibliography

Coates, D., 'Coming home: the return of the (Australian Vietnam War) soldier', *Southerly*, vol. 65, no. 2, 2005, pp. 105–17.

Cox, L. and O'Connor, B., 'Australia, the US, and the Vietnam and Iraq wars: "Hound Dog, not lapdog" ', *Australian Journal of Political Science*, vol. 47, no. 2, 2012, pp. 173–87.

Flanagan, M., 'Tim Winton in conversation with Martin Flanagan', *Monthly*, 24 March 2013, www.themonthly.com.au/node/981, accessed 1 December 2013.

Herman, J., *Trauma and Recovery*, Basic Books, New York, 1992.

Kelly, P., '*Breath* and the truths of youth at-risk: allegory and the social scientific imagination', *Journal of Youth Studies*, vol. 14, no. 4, 2011, pp. 431–47.

Knox, M., 'In the giant green cathedral', *Monthly*, no. 34, May 2008, www.themonthly.com.au/issue/2008/may/1215670870/malcolm-knox/giant-green-cathedral.

McGloin, C., 'Reviving Eva in Tim Winton's *Breath*', *Journal of Commonwealth Literature*, vol. 47, no. 1, 2012, pp. 109–20.

McPhee, H. (ed.), *Tim Winton: A Celebration*, National Library of Australia, Canberra, 1999.

Maddox, K. and Wright, B. (eds), *War: Australia and Vietnam*, Harper & Row, Sydney, 1987.

Matsakis, A., *Vietnam Wives: Facing the Challenges of Life with Veterans Suffering Post-traumatic Stress*, Sidran, Baltimore, Maryland, 1996.

Pierce, P., 'Australian and American literature of the Vietnam War', in J. Doyle, J. Grey and P. Pierce (eds), *Australia's Vietnam War*, Texas A&M University Press, College Station, Texas, 2002, pp. 110–35.

Rintoul, S., *Ashes of Vietnam: Australian Voices*, Heinemann, Melbourne, 1987.

Winton, T., *Breath*, Picador, London, 2009.

—— *Dirt Music*, Picador, Sydney, 2001.

—— *Cloudstreet*, McPhee Gribble, Melbourne, 1991.

—— *An Open Swimmer*, Allen & Unwin, Sydney, 1982.

13

'INTOLERABLE SIGNIFICANCE':[1] TIM WINTON'S *EYRIE*

Lyn McCredden

It may seem perverse to many readers to examine Tim Winton in terms of dejection – Winton, iconic Australian author of boyhood, surf, beach, family sublimity and comic possibility. Primarily, Winton's popular reputation has accrued around a core of optimism or positivity, centring on his much-loved and often reprinted 1991 novel *Cloudstreet*,[2] with its comic promise of personal and national transformation after the barren war years of loss and melancholy. There are, however, many representations of human failure and grief in Winton's oeuvre: the empty centre of *The Riders*,[3] its narrative shaped around the bleak collapse of a relationship; *Dirt Music*[4] and its grappling with fate, accident and mortality; or *The Turning*[5] and *Breath*,[6] with their fragmented, compulsive and melancholic characters. While Fish, the wounded and diminished character in *Cloudstreet*, is given a holy innocence and a moral beauty, and while the postwar nation, along with the families at Cloudstreet, look to a future of fresh beginnings, a growing and deepening concern in Winton's writing is what theorist and novelist Julia Kristeva calls the weight of 'intolerable significance', a state aligned with dejection:

[A]n intrinsically corporeal and already signifying brand, symptom, and sign: repugnance, disgust, abjection. There is [in this state] an effervescence of object and sign – not of desire but of intolerable significance; [dejects] tumble over into non-sense or the impossible real, but they appear even so in spite of 'myself' (which is not) as abjection.[7]

When we come to Winton's most recent novel, *Eyrie*,[8] it seems that a critical vocabulary alert to the parameters of this state of dejection is necessary. For the central character Tom Keely, life has imploded in repugnance and disgust, but against what, and for what reasons, the novel refuses to clarify. From the beginning of the novel readers begin asking where a centre, or even a footing – psychological, moral, political or spiritual – might emerge in this novel. Is there in fact such a centre? Some reviewers have detected it in the novel's sharp political representation of modern-day, capital-obsessed Western Australia; others see it in the personal, psychological and material disintegration, and slow return to meaning, of the central character. *Eyrie* does indeed ravel up the darkness and loss of many earlier Winton novels. It also confronts readers with an antiphonally autobiographical character, Tom Keely, the fallen man. However, neither the plucky mother figure, Doris, nor the persistent memory of Nev, the good father, serve to transform this novel's multiple states of loss, its ontological vertigo. These loved parent figures also become ghosts of meaning, to be dealt with, in Keely's catastrophic state.

Ex-environmentalist Tom Keely – defeated and ineffectual, a pill-popping former idealist – has fallen out of his life. He is also, arguably and fascinatingly, a haunted version of 'Tim Winton', except that Tom has run out of (or refuses to acknowledge) ways to make meaning. But a novelist, too, can run beyond or out of meaning. In *Eyrie*, character and author are of an age, and share a similar first name. They have come from solid, caring, households with deep wells of Christian charity. Both author and character express themselves through a desire for justice that is political and personal, particularly expressed through environmentalism. And both, in different ways, are concerned with what it means to be fractured and displaced from within these moral and spiritual centres.

This warped mirroring of author and character – a kind of repetition or haunting that can in fact be read throughout Winton's oeuvre, and that is rarely commented on – can also be seen in *Scission*,[9] *Minimum of Two*,[10] *That Eye, the Sky*[11] (the title of which is another kind of echo of *Eyrie*), *Cloudstreet*, *The Riders*, *Dirt Music*, *The Turning* and *Breath*. Further, there is in all these novels the same preoccupying set of questions: about family as cradle of identity and of values; the redemptive or tragic possibilities of family; and family as the primary crucible of language formation and signification. In all these novels there is a preoccupation with the ability or failure of signs – that eye the sky, the riders, dirt music, the eyrie – to signify, to make meaning. Will language stand up or fall short? This of course is a necessary preoccupation for a novelist, but it is also a question that defines the ontological state of so many Winton characters. It is a counterintuitive question, perhaps, for a novelist, a maker with words, but the argument of this essay is that such an inquiry increasingly informs Winton's work, both aesthetically and ontologically.

During Winton's national tour to promote *Eyrie*, the Adelaide *Advertiser*'s books editor, Deborah Bogle, reported under the headline 'Winton…uses words to ponder change':

Novelists and art can't effect change, says West Australian
author Tim Winton. But in his new book, *Eyrie*, he
paints a powerful picture of what happens when a culture embraces the notion that we are an economy first
and a community second.[12]

While not convinced immediately by this media version of
'Winton', readers may be intrigued, or worried, by Winton's
further claims quoted in the article:

'I don't think I'd flatter myself to think I'd have any
impact,' said Winton. 'Just because Keely gets to vent
doesn't mean there's any use in me venting, I don't think
that would serve any purpose. Novels aren't a means
of persuasion. Fiction doesn't have answers. It's a means of
wondering, of imagining'.[13]

What then, readers might wonder, is the purpose of wondering,
or imagining, or of fiction, if it has no impact, no persuasive-
ness? And what might be the role of the reader of fiction beyond
simply wondering? This essay will argue that in reading *Eyrie*,
coloured by the author's public comment here, we are confronted
with Kristeva's notion of 'intolerable significance',[14] a psychic and
cultural state of being that, potentially, may reduce to intolerable
insignificance, the loss of faith in meaning-making and ontological
power, a symptomatic condition circling, in consideration of this
novel, between author, fictional character and reader.

The falling self

In Kristeva's *The Powers of Horror*, 'intolerable significance' is a state
in which self, other and language are entangled in a jagged battle

over signification that, for the deject, the abject, the symptomatic character – and possibly more universally – is a deep realisation of loss and failure to signify:

> Instead of sounding himself [sic] as to his 'being', he does so concerning his place: 'Where am I?' instead of 'Who am I?' For the space that engrosses the deject, the excluded, is never one, nor homogeneous, nor totalizable, but essentially divisible, foldable, and catastrophic. A deviser of territories, languages, works, the deject never stops demarcating his universe whose fluid confines – for they are constituted of a non-object, the abject – constantly question his solidity and impel him to start afresh.[15]

The deject is thus one who is displaced, disjointed, out of place, dealing in ambiguity and unceasing demarcation; the self is experienced as dissolving, or falling – the central metaphor of *Eyrie*. Tom Keely peers down at his world – Freo as capitalist dystopia – from the tenth storey of the seedy Mirador apartments, a clapped-out, distorted version of the house at Cloud Street, barely keeping at bay the world of drugs and prison, abusive sex, greed and political corruption. *Eyrie*'s 'good old Freo' is Winton's home territory (or one of them), 'gateway to the booming state of Western Australia. Which was, you could say, like Texas. Only it was big [...] The nation's quarry, China's swaggering enabler. A philistine giant'.[16] In this world the fallen person, the outsider, the loser, the naysayer, is nobody, and Keely has indeed fallen from his former sense of self and purpose as environmentalist, from his roles as husband and son.

Why should a reader be interested in this nauseous, self-pitying, unlovable failure of a man who is barely able to prop himself up, staunching his hunger and nursing painful hangovers? But the narrative of Tom Keely, from child, to man, to this next abject state, is compelling. We are drawn into the story of how an idealistic man has been brought to this place beyond his former solid ideals, beyond the codes of family and sociability. Keely has become one of those for whom,

> [T]he path of analysis, or scription, or of a painful or ecstatic ordeal has led to a tearing of the veil of com-munitarian mystery, on which love of self and others is set up, only to catch a glimpse of the abyss of abjection with which they are underlaid...abjection...the other facet of religious, moral, and ideological codes on which rest the sleep of individuals and the breathing spells of societies. Such codes are abjection's purification and repression. But the return of their repressed make up our 'apocalypse', and that is why we cannot escape the dramatic convulsions of religious crises...Who would want to be a prophet? For we have lost faith in One Master Signifier...[17]

While Kristeva slips perhaps precipitately into 'we' in her diagnosis of contemporary abject states, she certainly offers a breathtakingly resonant description of this individual character, Keely. Readers may understandably baulk at the notion of Keely as prophet, but along with Gemma, and in a different way the child Kai, he is bravely (of necessity) staring down his multiple fears and the world's corruptions. In the convulsive grip of abjection, Keely peers at his past and its shattered remains: a disappointed and worried mother and sister; the expectations exerted by a strong, dead father; his environmentalist ideals; his income and material wellbeing; his masculinity. Love of self is gone, utterly, and others seem little more than intruders. It is for Keely an all-consuming personal apocalypse, one that mirrors the whirling corruption of the world around him, and in which he seems stripped of any ability to think, or speak, or write himself free or solid. The place where Keely finds himself is rushing headlong,

> [T]o drill, strip, fill or blast [...] Oil, gas, iron, gold, lead, bauxite and nickel [...in] the boom of all booms [...] There was pentecostal ecstasy in the air, and to resist it was heresy.[18]

and Keely is the mad heretic, or 'just another flannel-tongued Jeremiah with neither mission nor prophecy, no tribe to claim him but family'.[19]

The novel traces the ways this character attempts to construct – or lurches away from – a new script for his life, both through strength of individual will and from sources beyond himself. Codes of moral, legal and familial expectation may have been available to buffer his poisoned being, but they only falteringly support him now. It is through the accidental, surprising and painful arrival of Gemma and Kai at his security door that Keely tentatively faces the remaking of meaning and being; but equally, the novel works with the realisation – the author's, the characters' or the readers'? – that meaning may never be stable, or beyond the abyss of abjection. The powerful insight of this novel is that an awareness of this abyss is an ontological imperative for both

312

the symptomatic sufferer and those on the edge of such a realisation – such as writers, readers, the compassionate.

Ghosts of meaning: Doris and Nev, Wal and Gemma and Kai
From beyond his own self-annihilating will, the world of others
keeps coming at Keely, insisting on offering him meaning:

> His mother was a brick, a saint. Which of course made
> everything so much worse, especially since she'd had
> ample time to form a view of his situation. Two years
> since the break-up. A whole year since his catastrophic
> brain-snap and all its rewards. Doris was a shrewd old
> bird. She didn't miss much. He did not want to suffer
> her thoughtful analysis a single moment but he was
> pretty certain he already understood it in all its loving,
> pitiless permutations.[20]

The people of his past are both loving and pitiless interpreters
of Keely, who seems to be seeking not to signify at all. The novel
repeatedly expresses relationships in terms of signification: Doris
reads him shrewdly and impales him on her 'thoughtful analysis',
Doris who could 'read him in five languages and scan him in
Braille. Since his cataclysmic truth-telling, he'd felt the eloquence
of her every withheld judgement and longsuffering stare'.[21] Doris
as plucky mother love is admirable and realistically drawn, so
readers may decide not to accept Kristeva's more abstract psychoanalytic version of 'the maternal' in its connection to abjection:

> If 'something maternal' happens to bear upon the uncer-
> tainty that I call abjection, it illuminates the literary

scription of the essential struggle that a writer (man or woman) has to engage in with what he calls demonic only to call attention to it as the inseparable obverse of his very being, of the other (sex) that torments and possesses him...[22]

Eyrie edges around this double state of mother and maternal. The maternal is a force, sometimes monstrous, sometimes indifferent, alternatingly oppositional and comforting in Keely's psychic battles. *Eyrie* presents a motley crew of mothers: plucky Doris; Gemma, the dogged grandmother and mother, whose own daughter betrays her; Kai's mother, whose drug dependency comes before her young son's wellbeing; Keely's wife, who had become pregnant by another man, has had an abortion and separated from Keely. Indeed, 'something maternal' does write itself upon Keely; it 'torments and possesses him' in equal parts, and he is bound to it. In Hannah Schürholz's essay in this volume, she argues that there are many dead or missing mothers in Winton and that there is

> [A] constant 'othering' and stigmatisation of the women in the stories that seem to condition the ability of the men to speak but, at the same time, suffocate the same ability for the women.[23]

But it is worth registering that 'the maternal' as a concept, and mothers as characters in a narrative, are distinct categories.

Kristeva sees the maternal not primarily in terms of individual mothers, but as a universal force, and as connected to the birth of language and ontological significance for the child, a force compounded in the deject, or person caught in the thrall of abjection:

For he is not mad, he through whom the abject exists. Out of the daze that has petrified him before the untouchable, impossible, absent body of the mother, a daze that has cut off his impulses from their objects, that is, from their representations, out of such daze he causes, along with loathing, one word to crop up – fear…But that word, 'fear' – a fluid haze, an elusive clamminess – no sooner has it cropped up than it shades off like a mirage and permeates all words of the language with nonexistence, with a hallucinatory, ghostly glimmer. Thus, fear having been bracketed, discourse will seem tenable only if it ceaselessly confronts that otherness, a burden both repellent and repelled, a deep well of memory that is unapproachable and intimate: the abject.[24]

For Keely, this maternal force is repelled but also sought out, confronted in Doris, Gemma Buck, ex-wife Harriet, and all the 'yummy mummies [...and] Über-matrons'[25] swarming on the strip below his window. The maternal represents home, belonging and intimacy, and simultaneously it overpowers Keely with fear, drawing him back towards a world of signification beyond his own semi-existence, his state illuminated by 'hallucinatory, ghostly glimmer'.[26] The mysterious, unexplained stain on the carpet acts as a metonym for this 'intolerable signification': 'It was there again [...] a dirty great blotch [...] he didn't need this [...] staggering bright-eyed and bushy-tailed into the frigging Shroud of Turin [...] scratching his head and reading entrails'.[27] The suggestion that the stain may be urine or vomit, a sign or symptom left by Keely of which he has no memory in his hung-over, disintegrating state, adds to this overwhelming sense of vertigo, this 'daze that has cut off his impulses from their objects'.[28]

And then there is the father Nev, Keely's big-hearted, born-again preacher dad, whose sudden death also signifies too much or not enough. When the son half-consciously seeks out his Dad's old friend Wally – 'a short, fat man, bald and speckled with sun lesions [...and sporting] a glass eye'[29] – Wal impresses on him that Keely is the image of his dad:

> Just think of it, but. Last time I saw him he was younger'n you.
>
> Yeah, I do think about it. Too much, these days [...] He's a hard one to live up to, Wal.
>
> But you're a chip off the old block, son.
>
> No.
>
> Any mug can see it. Out there savin the world from itself. Callin it as ya see it. And getting ya tit in the wringer for ya trouble. He'd be proud, the mad sod.[30]

Meeting Wal is for Keely a confrontation with a ghostly father figure – intimate, uncomfortable, nostalgic, disorientating – presenting the son yet again with the memory of his father, that 'gigantic presence':[31] 'His father. Once more. Forever. The father'.[32] Keely does not want to be the man his father was – sitting defeated 'in a cane chair beneath the almond tree, praying, weeping, his beard full of crumbs',[33] but at the same time '[a]ny mug can see it', the son reiterating the father, bearded prophet of justice, repudiated and defeated. Keely can experience himself as only a pale shadow of the 'courageous Bonhoeffer'[34] his father was, and this brings relief, guilt, amusement, disorientation. In his dejected state the past offers Keely both a paternal version of himself and prohibits him from 'model[ling] himself upon a memory'.[35]

The past will not let Keely go, will not stop imprinting itself on him, offering him meaning that terrifies and fascinates him. Standing just behind the loving and pitiless parents, Gemma appears, the forlorn ghost of his childhood. In his fear he desires only to be '[s]afe. All he wanted. Was to be safe. In his flat. In himself'.[36] The staccato lines given to Keely, again and again, indicate a mind and a self that are clenched and impotent. And into his closed space there is a knocking at his door:

> The rapping continued. The fridge kicked in so hard he felt it in the neck. And a voice, like something through water. Burbling. Ramping up the pain [...]
>
> Tommy Keely, she said.
>
> He blinked. It was nasty, hearing his name uttered [...]
>
> It took a while, she said. But I knew it was you.
>
> Well, he croaked, congratulations. I guess.
>
> It's you, though, isn't it? I'm right, aren't I?
>
> Maybe. Who cares?
>
> Sorta bloody question's that?
>
> I dunno. I'm sorry. I'm. I dunno.[37]

Keely's ontological vertigo – assisted by red wine, Mersyndol, loss of status, loss of marriage, loss of face – is converting him into a nameless, mumbling, self-pitying figure stripped of past and present. But confronted with Gemma he is blasted with memory: 'Blackboy Crescent. The swamp, corrugated-iron canoes, tuart trees, yellow dirt, the engine-oil smell of his father'.[38] Again, Keely's mind works in staccato rhythm, each memory a separate symbol armed with significance beyond itself but equally experienced as frightening, engulfing, ghostly. Of the deject, Kristeva writes:

The one by whom the abject exists is thus a deject who places (himself), separates (himself), situates (himself), and therefore strays instead of getting his bearings, desiring, belonging, or refusing. Situationist in a sense, and not without laughter – since laughing is a way of placing or displacing abjection. Necessarily dichotomous, somewhat Manichaean, he divides, excludes, and without, properly speaking, wishing to know his abjections is not at all unaware of them. Often, moreover, he includes himself among them, thus casting within himself the scalpel that carries out his separations.[39]

Keely's first meeting with the adult Gemma is written on the edge of farce. Keely is self-indulgent, in the grip of a monstrous hangover. The conversation is conducted against wavering boundaries and interspersed with slapstick: Keely slamming his hip against the bench as he moves reluctantly to answer the door, Gemma and the boy 'still there, backlit into fuzzy silhouettes on the other side of the insect screen',[40] the conversation peppered with swearing and disjuncture:

It's Gemma, by the way, in case you were actually wondering.
Gemma? Gemma Buck? Are you serious?
No, I'm bloody makin it up, what d'you think?
I'm, I —
And then she was gone.
The bed came halfway across the flat to meet him.[41]

The scene is slapstick and humorous in its dance of incongruities: past and present collide, as do class differences, genders, the obliterated, self-dissolving Keely and the Keely who worries for the safety of the little boy 'scampering somewhere along the open gallery'.[42] As readers we cannot know whether Keely's moral responses towards the boy, his growing tenderness throughout the novel at the child's vulnerability, his (sometimes reticent) acceptance of caring for the child, come from a habitual moral centre, sign of a residual, learned ability to care, a compassion that has almost dried up, or whether it is another form of abject over-reading, seeing himself in the child – fatherless, abandoned, endangered. As Keely confronts the trauma of the child's life and takes some form of responsibility for both Gemma and the boy, are we to understand that the novel is offering a kind of redemptive possibility, a return to significance? At a thematic level this seems to be true, haltingly, but if we turn to the sustained linguistic undercurrents of the novel, its probing of signification and the modes in which humans make meaning, we find a more layered, puzzling sense of these processes. These undercurrents question any easy return to significance, let alone redemption.

Syllables emerging from chaos

Keely buys Kai a second-hand game of Scrabble. The boy, often reticent, silent, non-answering, is also fascinated by letters, words, images and symbols, and their potential for meaning:

> [F]rom the outset Kai seemed less interested in scores than in the words themselves. Games might begin in a spirit of boyish competition, but Kai seemed to fall into a trance, rousing now and then in a momentary shiver of recognition. Keely imagined the syllables emerging from chaos. He recalled his own childhood, how words hid as if aching to be found, transformed by his gaze,

reaching out to meet him. He was fascinated by the way the boy handled the tiles, how he turned them over in his hands, running the tips of his thumbs across their faces as if tempted to slip them into his mouth like milky chocolates. His fingers twitched, tantalized, over the board, as he breathed upon his row of letters on their little pine plinth.[43]

There is poignancy in the way the subjectivities of man and boy waver and intersect in Winton's prose. Winton skilfully entwines the trance of Kai with Keely, who 'imagined the syllables emerging from chaos', recalling an awkward childhood intimacy with words. Words, for boy and man, seem to take on a maternal aspect, as if the boy, but also the man, were 'tempted to slip them into his mouth like milky chocolates'. Winton also creates a more slippery interplay between words themselves and the child Keely, as he imputes words with agency – 'how words hid as if aching to be found' – projecting his own desires onto the words in the game.

This intimate, even sensuous interplay between language and self, self and other, is related to Keely's dangerous, ludicrous game with signs in response to Stewie and the thugs who threaten Gemma and Kai. At stake now are Keely's manhood, his ability to be an agent who can make sense in and of a world of crude actions and injustices. Finding a tattered old postcard from Rio in his mother's glove box, Keely writes a threatening note to Stewie, but first he registers the faded image on the card: 'Cristo Redentor',

Photographed from above, across the figure's shoulder. And beyond the great head and the Redeemer's outstretched arms, the teeming city below. Roiling chaos

320

at his feet. The watchful Saviour. It was perfect. Christ the Redeemer, why not? Enough Nev in that to make you smile.

The ballpoint was dry and the ink a little lumpy at first but with the notepad as backing, he got his message written quickly enough.

> *Jesus loves you, Stewie.*
> *Which is just as well.*
> *Because we are watching you.*
> *All day. All night.*
> *All eyes.*[44]

Even Keely recognises the ludicrousness of this note, with its message of threatening justice. He recognises too that he is like and unlike his father – courageous and afraid ('trembling as he was, suppressing the spasms of laughter that welled up in his neck')[45] as he embellishes his twisted little hymn with a sign: two threatening eyes. He delivers 'Jesus on the doorstep'[46] for Stewie, signs shuddering and warping, carrying both too much meaning and not enough. Can Keely's words stand in for legal or manly actions? Does his twisted religious message suffice? What is his message, this shambling prophet who posts his card at Stewie's front door, stabbing himself on a stray verandah-post nail, impaling the sign of a gun and shoving another of the cross, 'bloodied into the letterbox', and then running away 'like a maniac'?[47] The message reduces to something like: please don't hurt us, or we'll hurt you back. A child's frightened gesture.

The novel circles around the figure of a child, Kai – so like Keely, but six years old, deeply traumatised, haunted and watchful:

Even before things for him *are* – hence before they are signifiable – he drives them out...and constitutes his own territory, edged by the abject. A sacred configuration. Fear cements his compound, conjoined to another world, thrown up, driven out, forfeited. What he has swallowed up instead of maternal love is an emptiness, or rather a maternal hatred without a word for the words of the father; that is what he tries to cleanse himself of, tirelessly.[48]

This is Kristeva's portrait of the deject, constituting 'his own territory', fearful of signification and fascinated by it. And so, because both fearful and fascinated, the deject – and by analogy in this novel, the child and possibly the writer – rounds on emptiness, rounds on the mother, who must be faced (whether a good or bad mother, present or absent), and on the father (powerful or weak, violent or a gentle Scrabble player). Another essay could concentrate on the figure of Kai, poring entranced over the Scrabble board 'as he breathed upon his row of letters on their little pine plinth'. Opposite him, Keely, mirroring the boy, is caught 'in a momentary shiver of recognition […] imagining the syllables emerging from chaos'.

So *Eyrie* is about signification out of chaos. How far does the novel go in its sense of the futility always there in the seeking or construction of meaning? Of the abyss that is meaning's other, and being's other? The novel confronts the possibility that words form and make meaning, that they conjoin with human desire in a world that is irretrievably fallen. But are they potent against such loss? In his review of *Eyrie*, Michael McGirr writes that:

> *Eyrie* makes reference to figures as diverse and passionate
> in their views as Calvin, Bonhoeffer, Stanley Spencer
> and even Billy Graham. The lexicon of the book
> embraces words and phrases such as shriven, redeemed,
> salvation, mercy, prayer, deliverance, fierce saviour,
> Great Defender and so on.[49]

Making reference and making meaning are not the same, of
course. McGirr's review focuses mainly on the politics of the novel,
its opposition to the rabid capitalism of the Western Australian
mining boom and its attendant desecration of land. But McGirr
turns with satisfaction to the novel's stream of religious signs,
arguing of the 'theological vocabulary':

> None of this is to imply that *Eyrie* is a religious tract.
> But it is enthralling to see a writer blunting the sharp
> edge of contemporary culture with such a hard stone as
> intelligent theology, which is a very different beast from
> the self-righteous mush that generally gets passed off as
> the religious contribution to public debate.[50]

The theological language of the novel is not necessarily read,
however, as the triumphant, hard instrument suggested here.
Rather, Keely's words and actions remain embroiled in abjection.
And that is perhaps where the novel's theology – one kind of
meaning-making – needs to be placed: not as triumphalist or as
solving the riddle of the self, but rather as impossibly, farcically, even
humbly scrabbling for meaning when what is solid is out of reach.

As the novel draws to its close, Keely pursues Clapper, the
violent little thug sent to harm him, Gemma and Kai. He tears

down the Mirador's stairs in pursuit of Clapper, and into the startling afternoon light, into the embrace of

> So many people. Coming. Surging in, a gathering flock of heads and legs. Whatever it was out there on the road, whatever had happened at the kerb, it was waiting for him, just within reach. He swam the hot air, reaching, clawing the breeze towards the flare of turning faces, open mouths, buffeting against the empty space of morning, puzzled, happy, still reaching.[51]

We can draw a line of connection between the characterisation of Keely and that of Bruce Pike in *Breath*. There are similarities in the characters' experience of loss, but the novels carry different conclusions. The older Bruce – melancholic, reticent, still a surfer – reaches out with (Winton's) words, in an internal monologue:

> I'm not there to prove anything – I'm nearly fifty years old. I've got arthritis and a dud shoulder. But I can still maintain a bit of style. I slide down the long green walls into the bay to feel what I started out with, what I lost so quickly and for so long: the sweet momentum, the turning force underfoot, and those brief, rare moments of grace.[52]

There is a certain joy and regained poise in this ending, found by Pike from amidst the loss and self-doubt, even if momentary. There has been a fall, but there is also grace.

What do readers make, however, of the ending of *Eyrie*? Rather than finding grace, corporeal or theological, Keely falls again, or is knocked down, as the faces of the crowd discombobulate, turn into open mouths, 'pieces of face though the letterbox slits of cloth'[53] in 'an effervescence of object and sign'.[54] Significance, sought in the bodies and presence of others, and in the language that should ferry meaning between self and other, warps and falls. And yet the reader is left with an image of the stranded Keely, 'still reaching'.[55] Confronted here and throughout the novel by Keely's abjection – farcical, bloodied and addled – we ask whether he belongs with the living or the dead, whether he will ever make sense. For Kristeva,

> On close inspection, all literature is probably a version of the apocalypse that seems to me rooted...on the fragile border...where identities (subject/object, etc.) do not exist or only barely so – double, fuzzy, heterogeneous, animal, metamorphosed, altered, abject.[56]

And here Keely lies, as humans become a flock, faces and mouths and eyes disengaging from whole selves, '[t]he world flash[ing] outside him'.[57] What is it that Keely is reaching for? And Winton, in his language of suffering and in/significance?

In her discussion of the relationship between psychoanalysis and literature, Dominique Hecq offers a number of ways of approaching the deeply influential Lacanian notion of language, and literary language in particular, in terms of '[t]he letter... evoked *en souffrance*, in the wings, in suffering, leaving a trace of the fundamental discordance between knowledge and being'.[58] *Eyrie* as autobiographical antiphon can only ever be a hypothesis, but novelist Marguerite Duras might assist: she describes the 'discordance'[59] of writing and the apocalyptic relationship between author and fiction. She writes in startling, autobiographical terms of 'authors who are able to avow through their writing the consequence of language for the speaking being – [and] the litter or waste that the author's being becomes'.[60] Duras writes:

> I write to replace myself with the book...relieve myself of my own importance. So that the book can take my place. To destroy myself, spoil, ruin myself in the book. To become vulgar, public, to lie down in the street.[61]

This present essay has not sought to veer very far into psycho-biography. We can speculate further about Winton's 'relationships' to the characters of Tom or Bruce or Luther or Scully – or Doris or Georgie or Jennifer – but the elaboration of that aspect is for another time. What this essay has worked with is the struggle over signification in the novel itself, and in the character of Tom Keely.

The novel *Eyrie* cannot conclude. For critic or author finally to place or redeem or stabilise Keely would be to betray the conceptual proposition of the novel: that signification and meaning-making – writing, autobiography, plotting, characterisation, ideology, theology, moral declaration, communication with others – are intimately, even irretrievably, entwined with what is – humanly, culturally – intolerable. Winton's writing increasingly recognises and finds ways of confronting this 'fragile border'.[62]

Notes

1 J. Kristeva, *The Powers of Horror: An Essay on Abjection*, trans. L. S. Roudiez, Columbia University Press, New York, 1982, p. 11.

2 T. Winton, *Cloudstreet*, McPhee Gribble, Melbourne, 1991.

3 T. Winton, *The Riders*, Macmillan, Sydney, 1994.

4 T. Winton, *Dirt Music*, Picador, Sydney, 2001.

5 T. Winton, *The Turning*, Picador, Sydney, 2004.

6 T. Winton, *Breath*, Hamish Hamilton, Melbourne, 2008.

7 Kristeva, *The Powers of Horror*, p. 11.

8 T. Winton, *Eyrie*, Hamish Hamilton, Melbourne, 2013.

9   T. Winton, *Scission*, McPhee Gribble, Melbourne, 1985.

10 T. Winton, *Minimum of Two*, McPhee Gribble, Melbourne, 1987.

11 T. Winton, *That Eye, the Sky*, McPhee Gribble, Melbourne, 1986.

12 D. Bogle, 'Australian novelist Tim Winton, author of *Cloud Street*, *Dirt Music* and new book *Eyrie* uses words to ponder change', *Advertiser* (Adelaide), 20 October 2013, p. 15, www.adelaidenow.com.au/ lifestyle/australian-novelist-tim-winton-author-of-cloud-street- dirt-music-and-new-book-eyrie-uses-words-to-ponder-change/ story-fnizi7vf-1226743412355.

13 Ibid.

14 Kristeva, *The Powers of Horror*, p. 11.

15 Ibid., p. 8.

16 Winton, *Eyrie*, p. 5.

17 Kristeva, *The Powers of Horror*, p. 209.

18 Winton, *Eyrie*, p. 6.

19 Ibid.

20 Ibid., pp. 40–1.

21 Ibid., p. 41.

22 Kristeva, *The Powers of Horror*, p. 208.

23 H. Schürholz, '"Over the cliff and into the water": love, death and confession in Tim Winton's fiction', in L. McCredden and N. O'Reilly (eds), *Tim Winton: Critical Essays*, University of Western Australia Publishing, Perth, 2014, pp. 96–121.

24 Kristeva, *The Powers of Horror*, p. 6.

25 Winton, *Eyrie*, p. 20.

26 Kristeva, *The Powers of Horror*, p. 8.

27 Winton, *Eyrie*, p. 111.

28 Kristeva, *The Powers of Horror*, p. 232.

29 Winton, *Eyrie*, p. 124.

30 Ibid.

31 Ibid., p. 128.

32 Ibid., p. 127.

33 Ibid., p. 130.

34 Ibid., p. 128.

35 Ibid.

36 Ibid., p. 11.

37 Ibid., p. 27.

38 Ibid., p. 29.

39 Kristeva, *The Powers of Horror*, p. 8.

40 Winton, *Eyrie*, p. 27.

41   Ibid., p. 29.
42   Ibid., p. 28.
43   Ibid., p. 232.
44   Ibid., p. 328.
45   Ibid., p. 329.
46   Ibid.
47   Ibid., p. 330.
48   Kristeva, *The Powers of Horror*, p. 6.
49   M. McGirr, 'The room at the top', review of Tim Winton's *Eyrie*, *Sydney Morning Herald*, 2 November 2013, www.smh.com.au/entertainment/books/the-room-at-the-top-20131031-2wjpk.html.
50   Ibid.
51   Winton, *Eyrie*, p. 423.
52   Winton, *Breath*, p. 215–16.
53   Winton, *Eyrie*, p. 424.
54   Kristeva, *The Powers of Horror*, p. 11.
55   Winton, *Eyrie*, p. 423.
56   Kristeva, *The Powers of Horror*, p. 207.
57   Winton, *Eyrie*, p. 423.
58   D. Hecq, 'Writing the unconscious: psychoanalysis for the creative writer', *Text*, vol. 12, no. 2, 2008, www.textjournal.com.au/oct08/hecq.htm.
59   M. Duras, cited in ibid.
60   Duras, cited in ibid.
61   M. Duras and M. Porte, *Les lieux de Marguerite Duras*, Seghers, Paris, 1977, p. 102 (Dominique Hecq's translation).
62   Kristeva, *The Powers of Horror*, p. 207.

Bibliography

Bogle, D., 'Australian novelist Tim Winton, author of *Cloud Street*, *Dirt Music* and new book *Eyrie* uses words to ponder change', *Advertiser* (Adelaide), 20 October 2013, p. 15, www.adelaidenow.com.au/lifestyle/australian-novelist-tim-winton-author-of-cloud-street-dirt-music-and-new-book-eyrie-uses-words-to-ponder-change/story-fnizi7vf-1226743412355.

Duras, M. and Porte, M., *Les lieux de Marguerite Duras*, Seghers, Paris, 1977.

Hecq, D., 'Writing the unconscious: psychoanalysis for the creative writer', *Text*, vol. 12, no. 2, 2008, www.textjournal.com.au/oct08/hecq.htm.

Kristeva, J., *The Powers of Horror: An Essay on Abjection*, trans. L. S. Roudiez, Columbia University Press, New York, 1982.

McGirr, M., 'The room at the top', review of Tim Winton's *Eyrie*, *Sydney Morning Herald*, 2 November 2013, www.smh.com.au/entertainment/books/the-room-at-the-top-20131031-2wjpk.html.

Schürholz, H., '"Over the cliff and into the water": love, death and confession in Tim Winton's fiction', in L. McCredden and N. O'Reilly (eds), *Tim Winton: Critical Essays*, University of Western Australia Publishing, Perth, 2014, pp. 96–121.

Winton, T., *Eyrie*, Hamish Hamilton, Melbourne, 2013.

—— *Breath*, Hamish Hamilton, Melbourne, 2008.

—— *The Turning*, Picador, Sydney, 2004.

—— *Dirt Music*, Picador, Sydney, 2001.

—— *The Riders*, Macmillan, Sydney, 1994.

—— *Cloudstreet*, McPhee Gribble, Melbourne, 1991.

—— *Minimum of Two*, McPhee Gribble, Melbourne, 1987.

—— *That Eye, the Sky*, McPhee Gribble, Melbourne, 1986.

—— *Scission*, McPhee Gribble, Melbourne, 1985.

Appendix

THE WORKS OF TIM WINTON

The publication details given below are for the first Australian editions.

Novels
Eyrie (Hamish Hamilton, Melbourne, 2013)
Breath (Hamish Hamilton, Melbourne, 2008)
Dirt Music (Picador, Sydney, 2001)
The Riders (Macmillan, Sydney, 1994)
Cloudstreet (McPhee Gribble, Melbourne, 1991)
In the Winter Dark (McPhee Gribble, Melbourne, 1988)
That Eye, the Sky (McPhee Gribble, Melbourne, 1986)
Shallows (Allen & Unwin, Sydney, 1984)
An Open Swimmer (Allen & Unwin, Sydney, 1982)

Short stories
The Turning (Picador, Sydney, 2004)
Minimum of Two (McPhee Gribble, Melbourne, 1987)
Scission (McPhee Gribble, Melbourne, 1985)

For younger readers
The Deep (illustrated by Karen Louise, Sandcastle Books, Perth, 1998)

Blueback (Pan Macmillan, Sydney, 1997)

Lockie Leonard, Legend (Pan Macmillan, Sydney, 1997)

Lockie Leonard, Scumbuster (Piper, Sydney, 1993)

The Bugalugs Bum Thief (illustrated by Carol Pelham-Thorman, Puffin, Melbourne, 1991)

Lockie Leonard, Human Torpedo (McPhee Gribble, Melbourne, 1990)

Jesse (illustrated by Maureen Prichard, McPhee Gribble, Melbourne, 1988)

Non-fiction

Smalltown (with Martin Mischkulnig, Hamish Hamilton, Melbourne, 2009)

Down to Earth: Australian Landscapes (with Richard Woldendorp, Fremantle Arts Centre Press in association with Sandpiper Press, Fremantle, 1999)

Local Colour: Travels in the Other Australia (with Bill Bachman, The Guidebook Company, Hong Kong, 1994)

Land's Edge: A Coastal Memoir (photography by Trish Ainslie and Roger Garwood, Pan Macmillan in association with Plantagenet Press, Sydney, 1993)

Plays

Signs of Life (Penguin, Melbourne, 2013)

Rising Water (Currency Press, Sydney, 2012)

NOTES ON CONTRIBUTORS

Bill Ashcroft is an Australian professorial fellow at the University of New South Wales. A renowned critic and theorist, founding exponent of postcolonial theory, co-author of *The Empire Writes Back: Theory and Practice in Post-colonial Literatures* (the first text to examine systematically the field of postcolonial studies; 1989, with Gareth Griffiths and Helen Tiffin), he is author and co-author of fifteen other books (variously translated into six languages) and more than 160 chapters and papers, and he is on the editorial boards of ten international journals.

Nick Birns lives in New York, where he edits *Antipodes: A Global Journal of Australian/New Zealand Literature*. His latest book is *Barbarian Memory: The Legacy of Early Medieval History in Early Modern Literature* (2013). He is currently working on a book about contemporary Australian literature.

Tanya Dalziell works in the Department of English and Cultural Studies at The University of Western Australia. She recently co-edited *Telling Stories: Australian Life and Literature 1935–2012* (2013) with Paul Genoni.

Michael R. Griffiths is a lecturer in English Literatures at the University of Wollongong. He was previously a postdoctoral research fellow at the Institute for Comparative Literature and Society, Columbia University, New York. He has published essays in journals including *Postcolonial Studies, Postmodern Culture*; *Humanimalia*; *Antipodes*; and *Australian Literary Studies*; as well as in several edited collections.

Bridget Grogan lectures in the University of Johannesburg's Department of English. She researches literary depictions of affect and the body in colonial and postcolonial fiction, and has published articles on Patrick White, David Malouf, Doris Lessing and Julia Kristeva.

Sissy Helff is an anglicist with a broad range of interests in anglophone world literature, postcolonial and transcultural studies, visual culture, history and politics. She has published widely on migration, multiculturalism and transculturality. Her most recent monograph, *Unreliable Truths: Transcultural Homeworlds in Indian Women's Fiction of the Diaspora* (2013), is an overview of Indian women writing from around the world, including Australia.

Per Henningsgaard is an assistant professor of English and director of the master's program in publishing at Portland State University. He has also taught at the University of Wisconsin–Stevens Point, Curtin University of Technology and The University of Western Australia, from which he obtained his PhD in 2009. His research interests include editing and publishing, book history, Australian studies, postcolonial literature and regional literature.

Hou Fei is a doctoral candidate at Soochow University, China. Her research interests lie in Australian literary studies, and she is currently part of a research program on Tim Winton's works.

Lyn McCredden teaches and researches at Deakin University, Melbourne. She publishes on Australian literature, including poetry, fiction, Indigenous writing, and literature and the sacred. Her most recent critical volumes are *Intimate Horizons: The Post-colonial Sacred* (2009, with Bill Ashcroft and Frances Devlin-Glass) and *Luminous Moments: The Contemporary Sacred* (2010). She is now engaged in a three-year research project on Tim Winton's fiction and the sacred in literature.

Fiona Morrison is a lecturer in the English Program at the University of New South Wales, where she teaches Australian and postcolonial literature. Her most recent book is *The Selected Prose of Dorothy Hewett* (2011). Her current research is an Australian Research Council–funded project on Christina Stead in America.

Nathanael O'Reilly teaches Australian, British, Irish and postcolonial literature at Texas Christian University in Fort Worth. He is the author of *Exploring Suburbia: The Suburbs in the Contemporary Australian Novel* (2012), editor of *Postcolonial Issues in Australian Literature* (2010) and co-editor of special issues of *Antipodes* and the *Journal of Commonwealth and Postcolonial Studies*. He has published numerous journal articles and book chapters on writers including Tim Winton, Peter Carey, Murray Bail, Janette Turner Hospital, Melissa Lucashenko and Richard Flanagan, as well as interviews and reviews. He is the current president of the American Association of Australasian Literary Studies (AAALS).

Brigid Rooney teaches Australian literature at the University of Sydney. She has published a range of scholarly essays on contemporary Australian fiction and film, and is the author of *Literary Activists: Writer–Intellectuals and Australian Public Life* (2009).

Hannah Schürholz completed her PhD on self-harm and femininity in Tim Winton's novels at La Trobe University in 2012. In 2007, she was awarded her MA degree from the University of Bonn, Germany, focusing on the work of Irish playwright Brian Friel. She now works in Learning and Teaching for the Faculty of Humanities and Social Sciences at La Trobe. Her current research interests include representation of self-harm, depression and suicide in contemporary German and Australian fiction, architecture/ space/place in/as text, and happiness studies.

INDEX

Lightning Source UK Ltd.
Milton Keynes UK
UKHW010626270521
384470UK00002B/161